CARSTEN WIELAND

Syria at Bay

Secularism, Islamism and 'Pax Americana'

T0333220

HURST & COMPANY, LONDON

Published in the United Kingdom by
C. Hurst & Co. (Publishers) Ltd,
41 Great Russell Street, London WC1B 3PL
copyright © by Carsten Wieland, 2006
All rights reserved.
Printed in India

The right of Carsten Wieland to be identified
as the author of this volume has been asserted
by him in accordance with the Copyright, Patents
and Designs Act, 1988.

A catalogue record for this volume is available
from the British Library.

ISBN 1-85065-801-3

CONTENTS

FOREWORD

"Cooking stones" is what Syrians call it when someone stirs and stirs but nothing happens. Spices can be added for a nice aroma, but the stones remain stones. This is the political climate in Syria today, an analyst in Damascus complained to me. All appearance but no substance.

This is not generally true, however, for Syria has changed more in the past five years than it had in decades. The country, situated between the Euphrates and the Mediterranean, with its Roman ruins and Ottoman adobe houses, rocky deserts, and pine forests, has undergone more social change than Western societies can imagine. In a short span of time, Syrians have been catapulted from an age of ignorance, with two dusty state-run television stations, into the age of international satellite TV with hundreds of channels. The Internet has become accessible to a large part of the population and mobile phones have radically changed the lives of young people in particular. Above all, Syrians have entered a new century with their new, young president, Bashar al-Asad, who differs considerably in style and personality from Hafez al-Asad, his feared and revered father who governed Syria from 1971 to 2000.

In March 2003, Bashar—as Syrians simply call him—opposed the Anglo-American war in Iraq with more determination than any other Arab leader. For this reason the pan-Arab Baath regime attracted the admiration of many Arabs who furiously protested the war, and also often their own governments, in the streets of their capitals. But Bashar made a high stakes gamble. He deliberately took the risk of incurring increased displeasure from the US government led by George W. Bush. In the first few weeks after the Iraqi regime had been defeated in April 2003, it looked as if a US domino strategy was imminent: another military offensive, this time against Syria. Washington accused Damascus of supporting terrorism because it grants safe haven to Palestinian organizations, has been unable or unwilling to seal its border with Iraq, and fosters political ties to Hezbollah in Lebanon.

Washington turned up the heat on Syria again following the assassination of Lebanese ex-Prime Minister Rafiq Hariri in Beirut in February 2005. Fingers immediately pointed to Damascus, and Bashar faced the hardest test to date of his troubled presidency. Some even began counting down his days in office. Bashar's personal fallout with Hariri in the late summer of

2004 turned out to be a great mistake on Bashar's part. In the end, Bashar bowed to international pressure and, after twenty-nine years of occupation, withdrew Syrian troops from Lebanon, the last leaving in April 2005. The Hariri assassination damaged Bashar's image abroad. He also failed to pacify the United States since they never considered Syria's military withdrawal from Lebanon as a goal in itself, but only as the first step toward a US-led regime change in Damascus.

In the subsequent months after Hariri's murder, a political thriller developed in Damascus. The complicated plot involved an interior minister rumored to be planning a coup, and who finally committed suicide (or was he killed?), and Syria's former vice president who defected to Paris only to accuse the president of being involved in Hariri's assassination and to announce a government-in-exile. This continuing (and seemingly ever-expanding) drama has put Syria at a crossroads. No one knows how the drama will play out. An eerie feeling is creeping over Syrians as they stare into an uncertain future.

Syria at Bay looks at multiple possibilities for Syria's future. Will it be attacked or invaded like Iraq? Will Syria's Baath regime be undermined by "soft instruments" like economic sanctions, political intrigues, and political isolation? Will it make a more-or-less voluntary U-turn like Libya? Will the country enter the world of market economies and adopt the course of pluralization or even democratization? Or will it drown in the civil strife Syrians experienced so many times in the early second half of the twentieth century? Many options seemed open when this book was written, at the peak of international pressure against Syria.

Opinions are divided on whether growing US pressure will finally bring about the domestic changes in Syria that have long been hoped for, or if it will have a boomerang effect, preventing the country from opening up politically and economically. Signs point to the latter: the Syrian regime has taken a defensive position and has put national security before reforms. Sweeping political and economic changes have yet to be made. Both members of the opposition and progressive forces within the Syrian government are complaining about the cooking of stones. Patience is running out and disillusionment is growing. Changes in everyday life and access to information have not yet resulted in more political freedom or more participation in the political process despite initial hopes. Most Syrians are pressing for reforms, while at the same time calling for a gradual and well-ordered change under their own steam, rather than one dictated by the United States. Growing anti-Americanism, especially after the Iraq war, has brought the regime and parts of the opposition closer together, and narrowed the divide between the regime and the population. A wave of patriotism and solidarity for the president mixed with spite against the

United States swept the streets of Damascus after international—primarily US—pressure on Syria had been growing in the aftermath of the Hariri murder and the UN investigation that pointed its finger accusingly at Damascus.

Despite sluggish political reforms, Syria possesses several advantages that often go unnoticed by external observers. Because of its secular orientation, there is more freedom in Syria from a societal point of view than in many other Muslim countries, especially for women. Although Syria is located in the center of a battered region, a remarkable calm and order prevails in the country. The different religious groups live peacefully next to and even with each other, which should not be taken for granted given the tumultuous history of the Middle East. Despite all its defects, the Baath system has successfully repressed Islamism and sectarianism—factors that are causing strife in other parts of the region. In other words, there is much to lose if Syria drowns in chaos.

Political and economic contrasts appear harsher in Syria because of its long isolation. The question of whether Syria is a special case among the authoritarian Arab regimes in the Middle East often comes up in academic debates. However, few books have been written about Syria, and there is a tremendous lack of up-to-date, daily accounts of Syrian life and politics accessible to a broader, non-academic readership.

Obtaining such information remains a laborious undertaking in Syria. Most news circulates in a closed world of private residences and tearooms. The most important things are not talked about on the phone for fear of the octopus-like Mukhabarat, the Syrian secret service. It is essential in Syrian society to have a wide network of personal contacts in order to gain insight into the secrets of power and the heart of the society.

For almost two years, the Old City of Damascus was my second home. During this time, in 2003 and 2004, I worked as a journalist while conducting academic research and improving my Arabic. I had contact with many different individuals among the social strata—intellectuals, politicians, scholars, actors, journalists, students, greengrocers, and craftsmen.

This book is the result of long nights of discussion and countless interviews with political opposition figures, members of the government and their power circles, analysts, entrepreneurs, Islamic clerics, and many friends from different backgrounds. The book is a journalistic account of modern Syria, told for the benefit of a general readership, with the goal of providing a basic understanding of the country's social and political atmosphere. It is simultaneously meant as an academic contribution to Syria's most recent history. Despite chapters that illuminate the history of ideas, the heart of the book focuses on the current social and political situation in Syria. I hope that also those who do not necessarily agree with all of my conclusions will nevertheless gain new insights into the country.

Syria at Bay is not intended to put forward the "Syrian point of view"—a thing that does not exist as such, as the following chapters will show. Naturally, it offers a local perspective, since Syrians comprise the majority of those who speak and reflect about recent events in these pages. My hope is that this work may contribute to mutual understanding and dialogue, and because of the use of numerous primary sources and insider accounts may also offer new insights for policy analysis.

The German edition of the book was published in October 2004 by Klaus Schwarz Verlag in Berlin. The British edition has been revised and considerably updated in light of the most recent events. (The American edition is essentially the same as the British edition and is being released concurrently by Cune Press in Seattle under the title *Syria - Ballots or Bullets?*) I have incorporated new bibliographical sources. I also returned to Damascus in mid-2005, where I met many of those that I had previously interviewed, guaranteeing the topicality and authenticity of the accounts. Although I am sure that much will change in Syria during the coming months and years, the observations and conclusions drawn at this critical moment in the country's history can serve as a guideline for events to come.

I would like to thank the many Syrians who talked with me at great length, who showed patience and openness, and who offered their hospitality. I would particularly like to thank the Syrian historian Abdullah Hanna, who made himself available for many discussions that helped shape the book. I am also indebted to the German Press-Agency (DPA), whose management granted me a long sabbatical that made this project possible.

Finally, I thank those who made the British and American editions possible—Michael Dwyer from Hurst in London, Scott C. Davis from Cune Press in Seattle, as well as translators Hilary Teske in Berlin and Tina El-Azem in Bonn, the proofreaders Rania Jawat and Jennifer Kaplan in New York, and Dan Watkins of *verb*works in Sebastopal, California.

The book is a testament to all those individuals both inside and outside of the power structure (*as-sulta*) who are working for progressive change in Syria, despite the adverse circumstances, and who have not given up the hope that it is more than just stones that are being cooked.

Carsten Wieland
Washington DC, March 2006

TRANSLITERATION

There is no uniform system of transcribing Arabic characters into European languages, which often leads to confusion. There is usually a conflict between linguistic conventions, aesthetic aspects, and scientific rigor. Journalists usually adopt the spelling that seems to be most familiar to readers rather than what Arab linguists would suggest. In this book, I have thus decided against a strictly academic transcription for the sake of simplicity.

The article "al" before peoples' names is used in many different ways, even by the name-bearers themselves, as some omit it while others attach it to their names. A hyphenated version is used for names of people who normally use the article, but the article is omitted when the surname stands alone. We have used the assimilated article "al-" as "as-," "at-," etc. On the whole, all the proper names are in line with customary English spelling without special symbols. As an exception we have used "aa" in the name "Baath" for conventional reasons instead of the guttural 'a as in other expressions.

The above-mentioned spelling is used for any proper names referenced in the text. Arabic expressions or long Arabic phrases in italics, however, are in accord with the linguistical pronunciation, including the 'a or 'u spelling for the guttural vowel.

The "hamza" is represented as ' in all cases when it appears in the middle or at the end of a word. It has been omitted at the beginning of a word because it makes no difference in English pronunciation and may be confused with the apostrophe for a guttural vowel.

1

WRESTED FROM SLUMBER

A car with Saudi Arabian license plates is racing down the five-lane highway toward downtown Damascus, passing extravagant villas, office buildings, cafés, the white marble central office of the Baath Party, and the new building of the Ministry of Justice. The men seated in the car are sweating and nervous. They reach Mezzeh, the elegant uptown neighborhood of Damascus, seat of the Canadian and Iranian embassies. The driver of the car accelerates.

For the past twenty-five years, Syria has been considered by many to be one of the safest countries in the world. Its citizens are rigorously controlled by numerous secret services.[1] Syrians often state with a mixture of pride and fear that their country is a place where "law and order" prevails. The system of informers functions smoothly. Although people are no longer as fearful as they used to be, they still mistrust each other deeply. In this Arab country the word "prohibited" (*mamnu'a*) is ubiquitous. The time when policemen carried pistols in their belts is long past. Syria is now a safe and peaceful country. A truncheon is quite sufficient and even this is seldom put to use. Motorcycles are nowadays permitted, whereas they were once considered dangerous because of their potential use as vehicles in shoot-and-run attacks.

"The terrorists aren't interested in us," Syrians reason, reassuring themselves with a twinkle in their eyes. "In the Western countries' view we are all terrorists anyway." This is how it appears at least to many Syrians due to the fact that the United States and other Western countries have accused Syria of supporting terrorism in the wake of 9/11, and especially following the Iraq war. For Syria, the twenty-first century opened with a new president and great new challenges. It remains to be seen whether or not young Bashar al-Asad will pass his test. One thing is sure: things are changing in Syria. This realization evokes both fear and hope in Syrians.

On the evening of April 27, 2004, a further aspect of the Syrian myth is being destroyed. The car with the Saudi Arabian plates makes a sharp left turn at an intersection, its tires screeching. The driver attempts an illegal U-turn, catching the attention of a policeman. The cop tries to intercept the car. Its passengers open fire. The twenty-one-year-old police officer is shot in the chest and dies on the spot.

This is the outset of the first significant attack to take place in Syria in more than twenty-two years. Moments later the Mezzeh expressway is turned into a battlefield. Grenades are hurled and windowpanes shatter. Gunshots seem to come from every direction. A woman passing by is caught in the crossfire and falls dead to the ground. A building that was once used by the UN bursts into flames. The air is filled with smoke. Falling back on old and well-tried procedures, the authorities immediately cut all telephone lines, and even the new mobile phone network is shut down. Electricity in the neighborhood is cut off. At 8:40 PM, only seventy minutes after the attack, the authorities have control of the situation.

That same night groups of men gather, shouting slogans in support of the government. The following morning an enormous poster showing the president's portrait is hastily unrolled and hung upon the facade of the building next door to the former UN office, just in time to be filmed by the international media. The Ministry of Information issues a statement that two of the attackers have been killed and two arrested. The state-run press agency SANA proudly reports that a cache of arms have been found and confiscated in a village near Damascus shortly after the attack. Syria strongly emphasizes its commitment to fighting terrorism. Everything seems to be in order again. The next day, life in Damascus resumes its leisurely course, as if nothing had happened. No doubt exists as to who holds power in the country. But this is only part of the story.

The Mezzeh attack is particularly interesting because it is representative of many other recent developments in the country and tells quite a lot about contemporary Syria. The attack that took place on April 27 leads us directly into the heart of Syria's domestic politics, different aspects of which will be examined more closely in the following chapters.

In the first hours following the attack, the streets were completely empty on Hill 86, a part of town that lies directly above Mezzeh at the foot of the mountain, on which the bulky presidential palace, or "Palace of the People," stands watch over modern Damascus. Hill 86 is populated mainly by Alawite army officials and their families from the coastal city of Lathakia. "No one dared go into the streets," said the owner of a photo shop situated halfway between Hill 86 and the scene of the attack. "Everyone feared that it might be a coup. They knew that the government was weak and they also knew what they themselves were guilty of."

What had happened to Syria—the once strife-torn country that the Alawite Hafez al-Asad ruled with an iron hand, turning it into an important player in the region? What had happened to make those in power immediately suspect a coup in the poorly planned and amateur attack?

The insecurity that spread among the people directly after the attack of April 27 was telling. The usual mystery-mongering by the authorities and the fact that the house next to the torched building belonged to Hafez's younger brother, Rif'at al-Asad, fuelled peoples' fear and the always popular conspiracy theories. Rif'at had been considered persona non grata in Syria since 1984. He never made a secret of the fact that he saw himself as Hafez al-Asad's legitimate successor when the latter suddenly died in June 2000, shortly after disappointing US-brokered peace talks with Syria's archenemy Israel. Rif'at, who lives in exile in Spain, still has his supporters in Alawite opposition groups.

There was indeed something dubious about the attack. Many inconsistencies occurred in the course of events as well as in the official description of the incident. Information trickled down slowly and only when fresh doubts arose. The official version stated that there had been four victims. A doctor told me in confidence that more than four people had died. "I saw the bodies," he said. Besides, how was it possible for the authorities to locate a confiscated arms cache in a village near Damascus a mere twenty minutes after the shooting?

It was first supposed, as is usually the case, that al-Qaida had struck again. The fundamentalist terrorists did have reason to attack the officially secular Syria. Its regime has always dealt harshly with Islamic extremists, especially after 9/11, when it cracked down on Usama bin Laden's fanatical followers who had regarded Syria as a safe haven. Al-Qaida in fact issued a warning to its members, telling them to avoid Syria. Whatever the case may be, it is safe to assume that the organization that destroyed the World Trade Center in New York would have acted more professionally in the Mezzeh attack. Why did the terrorists seek trouble with a traffic policeman right before the attack? Why did a fleeing terrorist crash his car into a wall in panic? Why did the bomb detonate in front of an insignificant building instead of at the British ambassador's home just behind it?

We have to search for another possible explanation. The Syrian government initially blamed *Syrian* Islamic fundamentalists wishing to take advantage of the instability in the region and provoke the regime. A letter claiming responsibility for the attack, which seemed to corroborate this theory, had turned up in the media. It stated that "revenge for Hama" had been the motive for the attack. The authorities, however, did not regard the letter as conclusive evidence.

The city of Hama, situated in midwest Syria, is associated with the year 1982. Radical members of the Muslim Brotherhood (or Muslim Brothers) were the fiercest enemies of the Syrian regime in the late 1970s and early 1980s. Hafez al-Asad put a bloody end to the tug-of-war with the notorious massacre at Hama that left thousands of people dead. Islamic extremists have been successfully contained since then and never again gained a foothold in Syrian politics, unlike in other Arab countries. Nevertheless, they have noticeably gained ground in recent years on the societal level. The "secular" regime presents itself as a bulwark against the spread of Islamic fundamentalism in the region. It derives its legitimacy partly from the struggle against those radical forces that once hastened Syria into a bloody civil war. For most Syrians, this is still a convincing argument. Moderate Muslims and religious minorities especially pin their hopes on Baath secularism, even though critics maintain that Islamic fundamentalism is only being used as a pretext for not carrying out political liberalization.

The regime in Damascus has certainly not been able to play its role as a fighter against Islamic extremism as convincingly as Israel on the international level, when the latter promoted its line of action against the Palestinians after 9/11 as being part of the fight against international Islamic terrorism. On the contrary, Syria has been sharply criticized because of its pro-Palestinian rhetoric and its support of Palestinian organizations. But if the Mezzeh attackers were radical Islamists, why didn't they attack one of the government buildings nearby?

As a result of this logic, another theory—fueled by a media report—was widely discussed in Damascus teahouses: the terrorists might not have been Islamic extremists at all, but just the opposite, namely members of the Israeli intelligence service (Mossad) operating undercover. The new leader of the Palestinian Hamas movement, Khalid Mash'al (who usually resides in Damascus), was reported to have been in the Iranian embassy that day, which is only a stone's throw from the scene of the attack. However, the Mossad would certainly have planned and carried out the attack more professionally (although the idea is not so farfetched, as the Syrian intelligence service was said to have thwarted a Mossad plot to assassinate Mash'al in Yarmouk, the Palestinian quarter of Damascus, at the time of the attack). This information was dismissed by Mash'al as a rumor spread by the Syrian state-owned media, but the Mossad has also been blamed for subsequent attacks on members of Hamas in Syria.[2]

The US administration, on the other hand, claimed that the attack had been a "good show" staged by the Syrian government in order to present itself as a victim of international terrorism and divert attention from its alleged involvement. However, the attack in Mezzeh was not Bashar's nor his followers' style.

There is another version of the story that has become increasingly popular in Damascus. Dissolving the myth of a homogeneous regime, it would be possible that the attack was planned by rival factions that rank high in the hierarchy of power so as to weaken the government and thus Bashar. This would mean an internal enemy inside the power structure itself. According to this theory, the attack was to demonstrate to the Syrian people the young president's loss of control of the situation. One apparent validation of this theory is that the government first dealt with the attack as if it were a state secret, then as an "internal affair," and finally as the work of common criminals. In hindsight, this reading seems to foreshadow all that was to come over Bashar with the turbulent events in 2005.

A variation of this theory examines the political motives more closely, claiming that the attack was indeed planned by high-ranking members in power, that others may have planned the attack but sections of the Mukhabarat were informed and refrained from stopping the terrorists. Nevertheless, the situation was kept under some control so as to prevent any more serious damage from occurring. In any case, the message that came across was "Look! This is what happens when we loosen our grip on power. Liberalization will only bring chaos. We need an iron hand to rule us once again, otherwise the Islamic fundamentalists will plunge our country into chaos, as they did twenty-five years ago." This is the reasoning of the hardliners opposing the reformers in the country.

Others surmise that the terrorists were commissioned by Iraq. Supposedly they had been in Iraq to fight the Americans and had come into money on the side. According to this theory, their plan was to seize the Canadian embassy and take the staff hostage so as to exchange them for Iraqi prisoners. Their plan was thwarted, which is why the wrong building was attacked and why there was so little damage. A Lebanese newspaper wrote that Syria allows its citizens to cross the border into Iraq, who then come back as boomerang terrorists. But why did they single out the Canadians who are not even part of the occupying forces in Iraq? And why was the attack so late in the evening, when staff members would have already gone home?

The final version is the most harmless of them all and is the one that President Asad himself supported. It maintains that the attackers were nothing but ordinary criminals. At least one of them had been wanted by the security police for embezzling large sums of money. Allegedly he had also made a fortune smuggling weapons into Iraq. Some of the passengers did not even know that there were explosives in the car and thought they were just out on a crime spree. The weapons in the car were later identified as belonging to the Syrian army. After driving through a roadblock they were chased by the police, ending with the explosions in Mezzeh. According to this theory, the perpetrators are not terrorists, as they do not represent a foreign force, nor are they Islamic fundamentalists.

One attack and nine possible explanations! This is typical of quiet Damascus, where conspiracy theories spread like wildfire. Nevertheless, there is a rhyme and reason to each of these theories. At the very least, they tell us much about the situation in the country and its society. The regime in Syria continues to be one of the most unfathomable ruling systems in the world. Speculations are fed by the prevarications and machinations of those in power, the mystery-mongering of officials, and mysterious goings-on.

A leading political analyst in Syria interpreting the attack in Mezzeh said, "The poor planning, the perpetrators, and the timing of the attack indicate, in such a system, that we are dealing with an internal affair." Of the passengers in the car with the Saudi license plate, three were Syrians from the Golan Heights. "They and their families have connections to some of the centers of power [of the regime]," he added cautiously, lowering his voice.

We find a grain of truth in more than one of the theories. First, the above-mentioned analyst is correct that the attack was led by people who were involved in politics. One of the two brothers who led the attack and was sentenced to death in December 2004, Ahmed Shlash Hassan, had run for parliament the year before without success. Second, he and his henchmen may well be described as Islamists, although no link was established between them and any Islamist organization. Before the court, Hassan said that he launched the attack in order to protest the suppression of Muslims by Israel, the United States, and other "infidel countries." If he considered Syria an "infidel country," his reasoning makes some sense. Otherwise the question remains, why did he choose to attack Syria, whose regime is as anti-Israel and anti-United States as you can find in the region? The explanation he gave in court is one of the all-too-common, empty phrases that are meant to underline an "honorable" and "heroic" cause. Third, the perpetrators were in fact criminals, which supports the two previous elements because neither makes much sense alone. Hassan worked in the financial department of Quneitra where he was involved in the embezzlement of large sums of money, and whose building he had burned down to disguise his crime. In frustration against the authorities, the secular government, and the "global situation of Muslims," he and his brothers went over the edge.[3]

This is what is known so far. None of these findings exclude what the Syrian analyst said shortly after the attack. The incident has a lot to do with Syrian domestic politics today. Even if the culprits were just crazy, their families may still have "connections to some of the centers of power," or may have been used by them.

The plural "centers" is the keyword that describes the situation in Syria after the death of Hafez al-Asad. His westernized son, Bashar, who initially intended to become an ophthalmologist, lacks his father's charisma, craft, and experience. Beyond this, important funding sources that had been used to buy the loyalty of critical members of society have disappeared. A single and undisputed center of power is a thing of the past in Syria.

After the war and the ensuing chaos in Iraq, Syria is being put to a severe test. Those in the opposition, who had hoped for liberalization when Bashar took office, are exerting pressure, but they no longer face a homogeneous authority. This is causing confusion. Syrians are being ruled by different power centers that are blocking and even fighting one other. The challenges facing Syria, especially since the Iraq war, are a test for the young president in both domestic and foreign policy. Syria stands at a crossroads.

After the surprisingly rapid end to the war in the neighboring country of Iraq, and growing pressure from the United States and Israel, the Baath regime in Syria has found itself in a more and more precarious situation. Syria is surrounded by an archenemy (Israel), historically rather unfriendly neighbors (Jordan and, until 2004, Turkey), and an unstable one (Iraq). There remains small Lebanon to the west that has acted financially as the Syrian Hong Kong and, until the end of Syrian occupation, as the Damascene backyard for democratic experiments and critical debate. Most members of the Syrian opposition publish their writings predominantly in Lebanese newspapers. Even though these articles and commentaries often fall victim to censorship in Syria, the message nevertheless always reaches Damascus without fail.

Western countries have had little or no sympathy toward Syria since the coup by the pan-Arabic socialist Baath Party in 1963. Torture, despotism, oppression of political dissidents, and intimidation by the secret service machinery are part of the picture of the system. In addition, the country had formed an alliance with the Soviet Union, to which shabby army jeeps and trucks with smoking engines regularly seen in road-side ditches bear witness still today.

Although Hafez al-Asad surprisingly supported the US-led allies in the first Gulf War against Iraq in 1991, he never allowed his regime to be coerced into adopting a foreign policy that would have been convenient for Western countries. Israel especially sees Syria as a threat. Both countries are still officially at war with each other. The Anglo-American attack on Iraq in 2003 was absolutely in line with the Israeli political agenda. After the fall of Baghdad, Syria turned into Israel's "natural enemy" number one, along with Iran that is run by a religious fanatic who has vowed to destroy Israel and to develop nuclear weapons.

The main points at issue with Syria are the Israeli-occupied Golan Heights, Syria's presence in Lebanon, be it militarily or now by members of its secret service, and its support of Shiite Hezbollah, as well as its hospitality toward Palestinian resistance organizations, as Syria calls them, or terrorists as Israel describes them. At least until the end of 2005, a regime change in Damascus was openly on the to-do list of the United States and Israel as part of their effort to create a "new order" in the Middle East.

2

BASHAR AND BREACHES
IN THE LEADERSHIP

A slim young man in swimming trunks is sitting on the Blue Beach of Lathakia, Syria's Côte d'Azur. With its yachts, bungalows, and the luxurious Meridien Hotel, the seaside resort hardly differs from a coast in Greece or southern Spain. This is where the Syrian upper classes spend their vacations. Friends of the young man are sitting around him on towels and deck chairs. They are laughing because they are telling jokes about the Syrian government. Forbidden jokes. Even about the supreme father Hafez al-Asad, whose name is otherwise never spoken aloud without someone flinching or casting a frightened glance around. The young man is amused, pricks up his ears and cries, "More, more! Do you have another one?"

This was many years ago. The young man's name is Bashar al-Asad. At that time, he had not dreamt of one day acceding to his father's heritage. Friends from his youth describe him as frank, honest, and helpful. He never took advantage of his status as the president's son to show off his wealth or indulge in a wild life of pleasure. "After eating, he'd put his plate in the sink," recalls Asad's cousin, Rami Makhlouf. "At college, he parked his car outside campus like the other students. And he always scolds us for having chauffeurs."[1]

Bashar, the third child of the Asads and the second of four sons, is no fighter type and no braggart, as are so many sons of powerful fathers. He is more of an easy-going and reserved buddy. Instead of exploiting his privileges as the president's son, Bashar had already taken measures to improve law and order in the 1990s by enforcing discipline on the teenage ruffians from powerful Alawite circles who spread terror in the streets of Lathakia with their automatic weapons. In one case, he sent the bodyguard of one of his cousins to jail because he had screamed a litany of wild abuse at people. In 1996, Bashar fired thirteen of the nineteen Alawite professors at the Tishreen Medical School because they were involved in corruption. This was a sign that he rejected nepotism and would not spare members of his own religious group.[2]

A medical student, Bashar had prepared himself for a civilian's life. His father's political protégé was his elder son Basil, a passionate professional horseback rider who was very popular, especially among the ordinary soldiers. Today Syrians can still admire him on numerous murals, mostly in uniform with a severe expression and black sunglasses. The elder Asad created the same kind of leader cult around his son as he did around himself. Basil was systematically prepared to be his father's successor. It was therefore all the more painful for his father when the son on whom all hopes were pinned came to an early end. Basil died in a mysterious car accident in 1994. He was known for speeding. At any rate, this is the common story. Some people however speak in confidence of a rumor that he was murdered near the Beirut airport.

The story evokes memories of the Gandhi dynasty in India, though India enjoys a democratic system. Prime Minister Indira Gandhi, daughter of the father of Indian independence, Jawaharlal Nehru, prepared her son Sanjay to be her successor. He then was killed in a plane crash in 1980. Her (in this case older) son Rajiv had no political ambitions. His Italian wife Sonja had repeatedly begged him, "Please don't go into politics!"—but in vain. Rajiv became a weak prime minister who however began to open up the country economically. In the end, he paid for his efforts with his life. In 1991, Rajiv Gandhi was torn apart by a bomb in a Tamil attack in southern India.

Without dramatizing the parallels, like Rajiv Gandhi, Bashar al-Asad had never been interested in politics. He planned for a career in ophthalmology and went to England for training, where he kept his medical colleagues in the dark about his prominent background and drove a small car for the standards of a president's son, a BMW 3-Series. He got to know his future wife Asma during this time. After eighteen months he had to break off his training in order to submit himself to his father's strict schooling at home. Bashar was made the crown prince in the republic of Syria. Indeed, around the turn of this century, sons succeeded their fathers as heads of state in Morocco and Jordan. But these countries are ruled by royal and not by presidential families. Syria became the first case of a republican dynasty or dynastic republic in the Arab world. It is possible that Egypt or Libya will one day follow suit.

Bashar was the only person who would not upset the carefully balanced system of political power. Only thirty-four when his father died of leukemia, he was not strong enough to set his own mark immediately and defy adversaries. The fear of unrest between political, social, and religious groups was not unfounded at the time. Moreover, the somewhat sudden death of Hafez al-Asad left a tinge of uncertainty as to whether the way for Bashar had been paved sufficiently, although in the late 1990s the elder Asad had dismissed several leading figures in the army and the Mukhabarat who could have become dangerous when the overarching authority passed away. Those in charge in June 2000 staged a surprisingly gentle transition. This does not mean that it took place without internal friction. Minister of Defense Moustapha Tlass, for example, used strong threats to force Vice

President and acting President Abdul Halim Khaddam to sign the necessary documents. (This was the first visible sign of a power struggle between Bashar al-Asad and Khaddam as well as a prelude to Khaddam's spectacular defection to Paris at the end of 2005). In the parliamentary session that was broadcast live, a critical voice was raised asking why the constitution had to be adapted to Bashar's age.

But the parliament did change the constitution, lowering the minimum age required to hold the office of the president of Syria, and thus removing a formal hurdle. At the first Baath Congress held since 1985, the party elected Bashar secretary-general, while at the same time he became commander-in-chief of the armed forces, as his father had been.

At least formally, Bashar possessed the same amount of power his father had. However, the footprints which Hafez al-Asad had left behind were a few sizes too big, as would have been the case with any other successor. A friend from Bashar's youth said about Hafez al-Asad that "when you see a face on the front page of every newspaper and on every poster for thirty years, the person becomes like God for you. Bashar can't have this charisma now. But he'll have it in fifteen years if he's still in power then."[3]

Bashar, however, has made it clear that he does not want to be on the front pages of the newspapers every day. Neither his photo nor an article about him is to appear on the front page unless it is necessary from a professional journalistic point of view. This is what he told overzealous writers in the state media. The same applies for state television. Until recently, in the elder Asad tradition, the president's likeness would appear in a large format even when—as Syrians joke—His Excellency received a congratulatory telegram from the vice minister of infrastructure of Timbuktu. Bashar dislikes his father's cult of personality, although meanwhile his portrait does hang in the streets almost as often as his father's counterfeit used to before, frequently with his father's head in the background. However, Bashar has been able to reduce his presence in prominent squares like in the market in the Old City of Damascus. The traveler also still looks in vain for any statue of Bashar.

The vacuum left by the elder Asad's death is being filled slowly. In his fifth year in office, the young president is still consolidating his power. Or putting it another way: in contrast to the monolithic rule of his charismatic father, Syria is in a process of power pluralization, the outcome of which still remains in doubt. At any rate, courageous steps taken by Bashar or his government have been improbable, for nobody wanted to take great risks or embark on experiments.

The first years of Bashar's presidency have been marked by cautious measures, which have displeased even friends of the president. A member of the opposition reported that some have complained about his "weak character." "He holds the opinion of the person he last spoke to," said a journalist who prefers to remain anonymous. Even his sister Bushra reportedly called him "stupid and nervous" when he was among a circle of relatives after the turbulent events in Lebanon in early 2005, according to the same, well-informed source.

"People who know him very well from the time before he became president speak of him as a liberal, unideological person. He only became an opportunist after entering the machinery of power," said the journalist. Bashar is said to be overtaxed. Another person who is familiar with Bashar's surroundings complained that "the president is increasingly suffering from a loss of reality," that he sees everything through rose-colored spectacles. Others accuse him of already having wasted the authority that was his father's heritage, making it impossible for him to instigate reforms. Clearly, the above statements express disappointment at the very high expectations that even Bashar's critics had held for his regime.

A friend of Bashar's counters that "it's easy for intellectuals to express opinions when they don't have to make decisions. Besides, every decision depends on the information and data you get. When the information changes, so does the decision. Everybody changes when they're suddenly in a position of responsibility." [4]

The lack of a strong and predictable leadership, which for decades has been excessively provided to Syrians, creates uncertainty. Bashar's network of supporters in the state machinery may not be very stable. Back in early 2004, more and more ministers were said to be seeking backing from the conservative old guard instead of from the president. "Nobody would let himself down the well on the president's rope, for he would be afraid that it might be cut," an analyst explained.

On the other side of the spectrum, Michel Kilo, a leader of the oppositional Civil Society Movement, recently observed that increasing opportunism among those holding high positions in politics and the media convey the message that they in effect share the critical analysis of the opposition. "They want to keep a back door open in case of a regime change." The forces at the margins of power are drifting away from the center. "People are leaving the sinking ship," Kilo says, not without pleasure. [5] Especially after the Lebanon disaster (in Syria's eyes), several retired, high-ranking officials, including former members of the secret services, are reported to have tried to sell their real estate and emigrate. Some have bought land and houses in Jordan or have taken their money to Turkey. According to press reports, family members of ex-Prime Minister Moustapha Miro have transferred millions of US dollars abroad, and even ex-Mukhabarat chief Hassan Khalil tried to leave Syria. The authorities managed to thwart these escape attempts to a large extent by issuing travel bans. [6]

These dramatic developments may also be positively interpreted. It could mean that Bashar has pushed the reform process so far that it has reached a point of no return. Those who have much to lose are trying to escape before it is too late.

Hinnebusch sees only one possibility for Bashar's rule, namely that of a "consensual leader."[7] What is regarded as a weakness in the Arab political tradition can be seen in the Western view as conducive to the political culture of the country and the establishment of strong institutions—if this takes place hand-in-hand with the strengthening of civil society and political reforms. But it is here where the sore point lies.

For the time being, only a pluralization of authoritarian power has taken place, coupled with some economic reforms and a new and more open political atmosphere. "It isn't anymore the Syria of Hafez al-Asad," concludes Kilo. The deep-rooted fear people used to have during the elder Asad's time has disappeared, or at least diminished. Political discussions have become freer and criticism has become more open. Increasing numbers of people are professing to support the Civil Society Movement.

"The small Asad is a small step toward the great transition," hopes Kilo. "During the times of Hafez al-Asad the dynamics of the regime came out of the fact that there was a clearly determined and well-defined power center. It was Asad and a small group around him. He exported the problems of power into a society that was apolitical. This made the impression that the power was stable and unified." Inside the circle of power, there did not seem to be any contradictions, any differing interests. "With this power center, Hafez could play the regional and international game and maintain stability in the regime. This is not the case anymore. The power is no longer being reproduced from its head, rather the head is being reproduced by different power centers," Kilo explains.[8]

Another influential person in the Civil Society Movement, who prefers to remain anonymous, goes so far as to call Bashar a "junior partner" in the fabric of power. Strong personalities with their own power circles in the secret services, the military, and the intermarriages between the state economy and the machinery of government, have their own vested interests. The anonymous opposition figure compares Bashar's current position in politics with that of Anwar as-Sadat in Egypt after Jamal Abdul Nasser's death in 1970. "He only became a proper president after he had been able to get his own camp behind him." Bashar is largely keeping himself out of some areas of domestic policy because he is powerless against the vested interests that control these areas. "Since Hafez's death the Baath Party, the different branches of the Mukhabarat, and the army have become stronger," the opposition figure says.

Hakam al-Baba, the previous editor-in-chief of the banned weekly magazine *Ad-Domari* (founded by the political cartoonist Ali Farzat in 2001), made a similar observation. "Earlier it was one who ruled, now it is many who rule. This can be chaotic and dangerous," he says. People in the Damascus coffee houses remark with a wink, "Nowadays the power lies in the hands of phantoms." Of course, impressions can be extremely relative following the experience of three decades of authoritarian rule. The human rights lawyer Anwar al-Bounni speaks of "a number of power centers" that are paralyzing each other. "No more is there a coherent political concept. This has become even more obvious after the war in Iraq."

Various events point to breaches and inconsistencies in the political leadership. One example is the arrest of fourteen opposition figures in the northern Syrian city of Aleppo at the end of August 2003. The members of the Civil Society Movement were to attend a speech concerning the abolition of martial law that has been enforced since the first Baath coup in 1963. The lecture had been cancelled, but they were unaware of this. After their arrest, they were accused of being members of an anti-government organization. Oddly, the same speech had been permitted in Damascus and Sweda (in southern Syria, near the Jordan border) shortly before. Many people had attended those speeches, but nothing in particular had happened.

The trial in Aleppo quickly became a splinter in the eye of the authorities. Public interest assumed unforeseen dimensions and European diplomats were following the trial. The Civil Society Movement flexed its muscles. Its members organized protests and distributed leaflets. Nearly three hundred attorneys publicly volunteered their services to the accused. More than sixteen hundred people signed a petition for their release.[9]

The authorities attempted to turn a vice into a virtue. They demonstrated a new glasnost to observers from the European Union who had traveled to Aleppo to attend the proceedings. When the trial began at the end of October 2003, the red carpet was virtually rolled out before the astonished diplomats. Before, they had to be content if they were allowed admittance as spectators into the courtroom at all. This time they were received in person by the president of the tribunal and the chief prosecutor for three rounds of coffee and a round of tea. The military chiefs explained to them in detail, and in a friendly manner, upon which laws the charge was based and assured them in advance that only minor sentences were to be expected.

Pronouncement of the verdict was delayed for several months. It seemed that nobody really knew what should happen to the accused persons now that they had been arrested. It was not a time for severe punishments, as Syria was in the midst of negotiations over an association agreement with the European Union. Yet if the fourteen accused were simply allowed to go free, this would encourage the opposition just at a time when Syria was under so much pressure.

It was evident that several forces were pulling in different directions. "None of this is logical," said the attorney Bounni, shaking his head. But he sees things positively. "They would have long ago been awarded prison sentences of five or ten years and incarcerated. In this respect, the human rights situation has improved. Everything's relative."[10] The "fourteen from Aleppo," as they were soon called in the street, received light prison sentences between three months and one year. Significantly, it was an Alawite among the opposition figures who got the one-year sentence.

Another example of turbulence among the top leadership occurred in another arena when on May 22, 2003, the United Nations Security Council voted on Iraq Resolution 1483. The resolution was meant to lift the sanctions imposed on the now-defunct Saddam regime and define the role of the UN in postwar Iraq. In addition, the United States and Great Britain were given authority as the victorious powers to rebuild the country and set up an interim government. Syria happened to have a seat on the Security Council as a non-permanent member and was especially displeased with the second point, since in the Syrian view it amounted to legitimizing the war.

What happened? The Syrian UN ambassador was mysteriously absent when the vote was taken and his vote was thus counted as an abstention. The resolution was passed with a majority of fourteen out of fifteen votes. The Syrian representative was not able to submit his vote in time because he failed to receive clear instructions from Damascus. At home, politicians were racking their brains and the decision process dragged on. The opinions of Foreign Minister Faruq al-Shar'a, backed by the Baath Party, and President Asad cancelled each other out—an indication that the time of clear command decisions is over. Reacting to events rather than defining long-term strategies in advance is the order of the day. Shortly after the vote, the Syrian ambassador to the UN was replaced.[11]

Such disagreements are part of US and Israeli calculations. Although hardly anyone in Syria expects a broad attack from the southwest, or by the United States as against Iraq, the tactic of occasional preemptive attacks took effect on October 5, 2003, and has taken its toll on Syria. On that day, two Israeli F-16 jet fighters bombed an abandoned camp of the Popular Front for the Liberation of Palestine, only fifteen kilometers north of Damascus. "Threats mean a long-term erosion," says analyst Samir Altaqi from the Center for Strategic Studies and Research (CSSR), a think-tank at the University of Damascus. "The aim is to strangulate political options and to provoke internal contradictions within the regime."[12]

If this is meant to further complicate business for Bashar al-Asad, it has succeeded. But if the goal was to turn the majority of Syrians against their president and openly call for a regime change, this will hardly be achieved by external pressure. However much the Syrians' patience is running out because of the sluggish economic reforms, and however sharp the criticism against the government, the bureaucracy, and the power structure may be, Bashar has not yet lost his advantage as a young and unblemished successor. He enjoys sympathy, particularly among young people—more than half of Syrians are under the age of twenty—and among members of minorities.

Since mid-2004, some observers have concluded that Bashar has finally been able to consolidate his position within the regime machinery. In July of 2004, he got rid of long-serving military Chief of Staff Hikmat Shihabi and replaced four-hundred-and-fifty army officers. "We get the impression that the president is beginning to overcome his indecisiveness," said an analyst in Damascus. Over the years, Bashar has managed to place a considerable number of technocrats and personal trustees around himself, some of whom he has promoted to key positions at home and at embassies abroad, such as in Washington or London (more in the chapter "The Political Disillusionment").[13]

However, it seems that just at the time that Bashar began feeling more secure—maybe too secure—he committed his most grievous errors. At the end of August 2004, he pressed the Lebanese Parliament to change the constitution in order to keep the pro-Syrian President Emile Lahoud in office another three years. According to observers in Damascus, the decision was a very personal one against conservatives like former Vice President Abdul Halim Khaddam and the Baath Regional Command. Any other pro-Syrian figure could have done the job, as many critics pointed out, but Bashar insisted on Lahoud.

With this move, Bashar reaffirmed his strong grip on Beirut at a time of increasing international pressure to leave Lebanon. He also wanted to strike a blow against Prime Minister Rafiq Hariri. The multi-millionaire, pragmatic Sunni, and strongman of Lebanon had recently become more and more critical of Syrian influence, although he was known as a rather prudent and integrating figure compared to certain other Lebanese politicians. He was eager to point out, for instance, that an election victory by the opposition in May 2005 would not mean defeat for Syria.

It remains one of the riddles of political psychology why Bashar al-Asad and Rafiq Hariri clashed in such a personal way that no communication between them seemed possible thereafter. As reported by various observers, Bashar met Hariri in Damascus on August 26, 2004. During their meeting in the presidential palace, Bashar snubbed Hariri by not offering him a seat—a clear humiliation in the oriental context—and threatened him politically and, some claim, personally. The Lebanese strongman left the palace pale and shocked. Consequently, Hariri resigned as prime minister in October and aligned himself more closely with anti-Syrian opposition forces in Lebanon. This was the point when disaster struck and, if this story is true, Bashar has to take full responsibility. Nevertheless, Bashar denied that he threatened Hariri's life.[14]

A few days after the extension of Lahoud's term on September 2, the UN Security Council, led by the remarkable coalition of the United States and France, passed Resolution 1559. Although it did not name Syria directly, the resolution was a clear challenge to Damascus, calling for the withdrawal of foreign troops from Lebanon, for the disarmament of militias (which meant, above all, Hezbollah), and for free and fair elections the following May 2005. There is hardly any doubt that Hariri's close relationship with French President Jacques Chirac helped bring about this scenario and caused the loss of France as one of Syria's more benevolent partners abroad. The resolution was in the pipeline even before the situation escalated with the extension of Lahoud's term. Syria was isolated. Not a single Arab state moved a finger in support.

In the following months, the resolution became the main tool for pressuring Syria to withdraw its troops from Lebanon and for considerably narrowing Syria's room for political maneuvering. Hariri joined forces with Druze leader Walid Jumblatt and with the Christian leadership to issue a call for the implementation of the resolution. Bashar remained either steadfast or obstinate, according to one's interpretation. Two weeks prior to Hariri's assassination, Bashar affirmed to his confidants that he had not the slightest intention of leaving Lebanon. This drastically changed after a three hundred kilogram bomb tore apart Hariri and members of his entourage in the convoy of armored cars on the Beirut corniche on February 14, 2005. (More about the speculations of who was behind the attack can be found in the chapter "Syria the Rogue State?")

A wave of angry, anti-Syrian protests swept through the streets of Beirut. For the first time, posters of Bashar and Syrian flags were torn from buildings and burned. Syrian workers in Lebanon were attacked and some killed. Via Saudi Arabia, the United States sent a stern message that included threats of air strikes against Syria. Returning Bashar's snub of Hariri, the Saudi Crown Prince Abdullah played tough with Bashar when he saw him after the bombing. "Abdullah showed him a list of five hundred potential targets in Syria that the United States were ready to destroy," reports Michel Kilo. Abdullah was furious about Hariri's assassination because the tycoon held Saudi nationality and entertained profitable business connections with the country. "After this encounter, it became clear to Bashar that he had committed the mistake of his life," Kilo concludes.[15]

In the initial days after the assassination, the Syrian leadership did not speak with one voice. Bashar told Arab League President Amr Moussa that a withdrawal from Lebanon was imminent, only to have the Syrian Ministry of Information later state that Moussa had got it wrong and Syria was only redeploying its troops to the Beq'a Valley. The tap dance continued a few days longer until Bashar addressed the parliament in Damascus on March 5, when he scuttled back to his pre-Moussa position. He did not speak of an immediate and complete withdrawal, but rather of a re-deployment step by step, first to the Beq'a Valley and then to the Lebanese-Syrian border. Soon after his convoluted speech in parliament, events overtook Bashar once again and he ordered all Syrian troops home by April 26, even before the US deadline.

Observers in Damascus considered Bashar's speech a lost opportunity domestically and internationally. Although it should be recognized that he admitted that mistakes were made in Lebanon—probably alluding to the corruption and misbehavior of Syrian army and intelligence officers and maybe even to strategic errors—he did not offer an apology in order to win over the Lebanese people. He failed to deliver new insights, make bold announcements, and take initiative. Ayman Abdul Nour, a friend from Bashar's youth, said in frustration that "Bashar's speech was amateurish and full of mistakes. It was a golden opportunity to address the Lebanese people, especially the younger population. He should have played his age and said 'I'm young like you, I also want freedom, I can understand you, my country also needs freedom.' Instead, he threatened that problems will arise in Lebanon when Syria leaves."[16]

Apart from disappointing the reformers, the Lebanese disaster further damaged Bashar's standing among the conservative hardliners, most outstandingly with Vice President Abdul Halim Khaddam. It was more grist for the mills of those who claimed that Bashar was neither able to lead the country nor defend its interests against enemies during troubled times. For the first time, names of potential successors circulated among intellectuals and in the teahouses of Damascus in spring 2005, a development that would have been unimaginable during the reign of Hafez al-Asad.

All of this means that a big struggle lies ahead for Bashar to win back the confidence and advantage that he had gained by summer 2004. In one sense, leaving Lebanon may help him in the long run. He had already started a gradual redeployment in 2000, reducing troops from forty thousand to fourteen thousand, thus accepting additional pressure on the Syrian labor market in spite of the critical economic situation. Yet Syria still failed to implement the Ta'if Accord that ended the Lebanese civil war in 1989, which called for a withdrawal of foreign troops when the security situation permitted. As years passed and Lebanese institutions began to function without external assistance, Syrian troops all over Lebanon became more and more unnecessary. Even if Bashar had wanted them out, however, he would not have been able to push through a complete withdrawal against the will of nationalist hardliners. Only this unexpected turn of events made it possible and set free military and financial resources that were badly needed for the reform process at home. Trade and eventually the human bonds between people from both countries are likely to quickly normalize. Most Syrians and Lebanese have expressed their wish for good neighborly relations.

Indications that Bashar could again strengthen his hold on power arose during the Tenth Baath Congress on June 6-9, 2005, the second congress to take place after Bashar's inauguration. On the one hand, oppositional forces and some foreign observers were disappointed because they had expected more sweeping political reforms, the end of martial law, immediate permission for the creation of independent parties, reform of the judiciary, and the abolishment of the Baath monopoly, as well as the release of the key opposition figures of the Damascus Spring, the democratic movement that took place in late 2000 and early 2001. In an open letter to the Baath delegates titled "Let the Damascus Spring Bloom," 226 intellectuals— among them Michel Kilo, philosopher Sadiq al-Azm, human rights advocate Anwar al-Bounni, and journalist Hakam Baba—summarized their demands.

On the other hand, unlike the Iraqi Baath Party, the Syrian organization proved its willingness and ability to embark at least on piecemeal reforms from within. Most importantly, Bashar appeared able to strengthen his position of power. If this holds true, the "Lebanese disaster" would have produced a shake-up that could benefit Bashar in the long run despite the many temporary bruises. The most important outcomes of the Tenth Baath Congress were a thorough reshuffling of top positions in the National Command and the Central Committee of the party, the government, and the military, as well as a recommendation to allow independent political parties in the future, a separation of the party and government, further steps to combat corruption and open up the economy, and a relaxation of the emergency laws.

Although the influence of the Baath Party in government and society has been curbed, the Syrian protagonists are not ready to bow to US demands and entirely dismiss the party's purpose and ideology. During the congress, Buthaina Sh'aban, who had become a member of the Regional Command, made this clear. While accusing the United States of seeking to undermine Arab identity by fostering religious and ethnic divisions, she said, "If we are not Arabs what could we be? Do we want to be Sunnis and Shiites and Christians? Or do we want to be Arabs? I think I can speak in the name of millions of Arabs that we want to be Arabs. If the Baath Party were not here, I think we would have to invent it."[17] Sectarian politics in neighboring countries like Iraq and Lebanon gave weight to her arguments, although by referring to Arabs as an umbrella category, Sh'aban once again ignored the Kurdish problem.

Contrary to these official statements, critically minded Baath member Ayman Abdul Nour paints a different and bold scenario. In his eyes, the president has become tired of the old structures, despite the fact that he relies on them. "Bashar needs the Baathists for now. Otherwise, who will reelect him in 2007? But after that, he will try to get rid of the Party and found a party of his own. He is playing with time but feels the pressure because the US demands an immediate de-Baathification of Syria."[18]

Whether Bashar has this master plan in mind or not, during the congress the Baath Party experienced its greatest shake-up since 1970 when Hafez al-Asad took power. Out of the ninety-six members of the Central Committee—most of them nearly double Bashar's age—seventy were replaced, among them former Prime Minister Moustapha Miro, former Defense Minister Moustapha Tlass, and most importantly, Vice President Abdul Halim Khaddam, who also announced his resignation from his powerful government post. Khaddam's action was received with respect even by his critics because voluntary resignations are uncommon in the Arab world.

Only a few months later, however, this respect was to turn into dismay and rage. At that moment, the breaches in the crumbling Syrian leadership became visible for everyone. For shortly after the Baath Congress, the staunch Baathist Khaddam, the only senior official who had remained in office since the Baath revolution in 1963, took residence in Paris. Finally, in December 2005 the seventy-three-year-old hardliner set out to take revenge on Bashar and his family. In an interview, Khaddam accused Bashar of threatening Lebanese Prime Minister Rafiq Hariri in August 2004, and said that Hariri's murder could not have happened without Bashar's involvement. In addition, he listed many mistakes that the president made with regard to Lebanon (more on this issue, see chapter "Syria the Rogue State?"). This was a decisive blow to Bashar and represented the most eminent case of defection in Syrian politics since 1966. Moreover, the Sunni Khaddam announced his plan to organize a government-in-exile and invited defected military officers and other opposition groups abroad to join him (whereas the Syrian opposition at home swiftly rejected any form of cooperation because of Khaddam's anti-democratic and corrupt record). Consequently, the Baath Party stripped Khaddam of his membership and joined a unanimous vote in parliament calling on the government to try him for high treason.

Khaddam was a key player in Lebanese politics, helped to shape the Ta'if Peace Accord in 1989, was close to Rafiq Hariri, and backed his elections as Lebanese prime minister in 1992 and 2000. The former vice president, who used to be at the center of Syria's business mafia, shared economic interests with Hariri as his business partner in Syria, Lebanon, Saudi Arabia, and France. However, Khaddam and Hariri had an increasingly hard time fighting Bashar's family cronies over investment in the Syrian market. From the beginning, the experienced Khaddam was reluctant to accept the young Bashar as the ruler of the country after Hafez al-Asad died, and he was at odds with the president over many issues ranging from domestic to foreign politics. The recent developments in Lebanon had caused the final rift between him and Bashar.

The only old player left in the top ranks of the Syrian leadership is Foreign Minister Faruq as-Shar'a, a long time rival of Khaddam and one of the few clean hands in the Syrian regime when it comes to corruption and nepotism. But it seemed that his days are also numbered since speculations about his replacement have been circulating for over two years. But, on the other hand, with so many experienced politicians fired or in exile, Bashar counts on Shar'a more than ever, as a reliable link to the Baath Party and its establishment for instance. In early 2006, following another cabinet reshuffle, Bashar made Shar'a the new vice president of the country. This was the late but final victory of Shar'a over his rival Khaddam.

Another ideological hardliner is Muhammad Said Bukheitan who remains a member of the Baath Regional Command and head of the party's security committee. He and his supporters have already toppled several of the president's initiatives and will continue slamming on the breaks, especially since Bukheitan has been entrusted with the party office of economics and finance.

Another front for Bashar is the Mukhabarat. He must, above all, regain control of the different branches that monitor the ministries and at times neutralize political decisions. Parts of the secret service have taken power into their own hands and have operated against the president or have become infiltrated by Islamists. This is one of the greatest challenges for the president, and the restructuring of the security machinery is an initial step. Instead of being accountable to the Regional Command of the Baath Party as it had been since 1968, the political body of the Mukhabarat is now under direct control of the Ministry of Interior. The military part of the secret service remains accountable to the Syrian chief-of-staff and the secret service of the Air Force under control of the Air Force commanders.

The reform began in October 2004 after Ghazi Kan'an was appointed minister of interior. On a formal level, Bashar has undertaken several steps to curb the Mukhabarat's influence, and the Baath Congress in June 2005 backed his efforts. The Regional Command decided that the secret service no longer had to be consulted in sixty-seven different circumstances that include the celebration of weddings and the opening of new enterprises, shops, social and educational organizations, restaurants, etcetera. Embassies can now inquire after missing persons and visit them in the central Adra prison without permission from the Mukhabarat. Another far-reaching consequence of the congress is that security officers are no longer allowed to hold suspects in custody for longer than five days. After this period he or she has to be released or sent to court.

It remains to be seen if the reform will make the Mukhabarat toe the line. Bashar can at least rely on the army, which is largely under the command of Alawites who have much to lose.

Among the population there is widespread fear of an abrupt change or even a collapse of the political system. Bashar exploits this fear to mobilize the population, particularly with international sanctions looming after Syria had been accused by the UN fact-finding team of involvement in Hariri's murder. During the last months of 2005, public rallies by different groups supporting the president became part of everyday life in Damascus. People, if members of the Baath Party or not, shouldered up with Bashar's government, and even prisoners started a hunger strike for their president! A wave of patriotism swept the streets. Cities were plastered with huge posters and banners that concentrated on a message of support for Bashar and a "unified Syria". It is noteworthy that Baath flags and symbols did not appear.

The analyst Samir Altaqi points out that "any hope of a smooth landing of the reforms is through Bashar. This is why in the opposition gambling is going on." Regime critics are torn between their opposition to the Baathist system and their loyalty toward their endangered home country. Threats from Washington have boomeranged in many respects. Growing anti-Americanism, like in Iraq, has become the common denominator of rulers and ruled. Although disappointed and frustrated, the opposition has made it clear that they will not challenge the Syrian regime "on the back of an American tank."[19]

3

THE PILLARS OF
REGIME LEGITIMACY

On the whole Syria has remained stable despite contradictions within the regime since Hafez al-Asad's death, and despite US political pressure. The regime in Damascus cannot be compared with Saddam Hussein's brutal dictatorship. The calm in Syria is by no means the result of an oppressive government machinery only. Power in the country has several pillars of support that lend it legitimacy in the eyes of the public.

By contrast, the Iraqi leadership made no compromises. Saddam Hussein did not pursue a strategy of balance among different interests as did his more flexible alter ego, Hafez al-Asad. Neither did Saddam need to do this, for he was able to buy loyalty very easily with his country's plentiful oil resources and supplement this strategy with brute force if necessary. Asad played the balance of conflicting interests with clever tactics and alternating concessions. A report by the International Crisis Group came to the conclusion that "ironically, the Syrian regime has become far more embedded in the nation's social fabric than was its Iraqi counterpart *because of* its comparative limitations and weaknesses."[1]

The sources from which the Baath regime currently derives its legitimacy are partly nourished by Hafez al-Asad's political legacy and partly by the new developments under Bashar. Among these are the consequences of the Iraq war. The sources of legitimacy can be summarized by the following points.

Pro-Palestinian rhetoric

The two antagonized regimes in Syria and Iraq had distinguished themselves at home as advocates of the Palestinian cause and as hardliners against Israel. This is still true of Syria today. The Israeli occupation of Palestinian territory is the main topic covered by the Syrian state press each day. It is easy to gain the population's support for these matters, thus distracting them from economic and political problems at home. Syria never grows tired of proclaiming the Palestinian cause as its own, although its support is frequently no more than political rhetoric. Similar to other Arab states, many Syrians regard the some 410,000 Palestinians living in Syria only as tolerated guests, even if they enjoy equal rights with native Syrians.[2]

Rhetorical broadsides against Israel remain a welcome means of creating consensus. Bashar sometimes tries to outdo the hardliners in this effort and clearly goes over the top. In a speech at the Arab summit in Amman in March 2001, for example, he said that Israeli society is more racist than Nazism.[3] In his remarks welcoming Pope John Paul II to Syria two months later, he slipped into anti-Semitism when he referred to Jews as the killers of Jesus. "They try to kill all the principles of divine faiths with the same mentality of betraying Jesus Christ and torturing him, and in the same way that they tried to commit treachery against Prophet Muhammad (peace be upon him)."[4] Bashar, however, dismissed his speechwriter after this faux pas.

Despite all the rhetoric, solidarity with the Palestinians gives way to pragmatism in dangerous situations. The younger Asad has learned from his father, and his motto is "Give in as much as is necessary and persist as much as is possible." After the Iraq war, Bashar's position on the Palestinian issue oscillated between readiness to compromise and an ideological hard line.

Bashar gave in to American pressure and closed the contact offices of Palestinian organizations in Damascus. Washington however criticized this action as purely cosmetic as nobody really knows what "closure" means. Most of the offices were only private flats, from which public relations work was done.

Demonstrations by Palestinians were banned or more strongly kept in check than before the Iraq war, but Bashar made it clear that no Palestinian leaders would be expelled from Syria. He reaffirmed this position when on May 12, 2004, the United States stepped up its sanctions against Syria because of this stance among other things. The issue became more explosive after the Israeli government fired precision rockets at the Gaza Strip and liquidated the long-standing spiritual leader of Hamas, Sheikh Ahmed Yassin, at the end of March, and his successor Abdel Aziz Rantisi only two weeks later. This left Khalid Mash'al as the new leader of the Islamist organization. He had spent many years in Damascus and proclaimed from his new position that "it is undoubtedly safer in Syria than elsewhere."[5] At the same time, Mash'al publicly admitted to having close contacts with then PLO leader Yassir Arafat.

Encouraged by the severe problems the US troops were facing in Iraq, Bashar sharpened his tone toward Israel and the United States in early 2004. Making up for his low-profile strategy during the first months of the war, he regained sympathy in the streets at home. Yet, as Altaqi points out, "Syria is not able to make any further concessions (in the Palestinian issue) . . . This would harm the regime's identity."[6] Bashar had already stuck his neck out in May 2003 when he promised to accept any decision by the Palestinian leadership in peace negotiations with Israel. Until then, Syria had always officially insisted on co-representing the Palestinians, though in the peace negotiations with Israel in Shepherdstown, West Virginia, in January 2000, Hafez al-Asad had already secretly signaled that he would accept a peace settlement even if the Israeli-Palestinian conflict had not been satisfactorily resolved. In this regard, Bashar's strategy of pragmatism concerning the Palestinian issue did not constitute a breach of domestic policy.

Immediately after the Iraq war, Bashar signaled his readiness to hold talks with Israel and has repeated his offer several times since, especially at the end of 2003, despite the continuation of the Intifada. He is said to have sent his younger brother Maher to Amman for secret negotiations with Israeli representatives.[7] As tensions and hopes run high, every incident, no matter how minute, is subject to worldwide public scrutiny, as was the first handshake between a Syrian and an Israeli president, which took place at the funeral of Pope John Paul II on April 9, 2005, in Rome. When speculations arose, the Syrians hastened to clarify that this gesture between Bashar al-Asad and Iranian-born Moshe Katzav was nothing but "a formality."

In Israel there have been more voices calling for serious negotiations with Syria, though with no preconditions. Syria has always insisted on resuming negotiations at the point where the two sides had broken off in March 2000, shortly before Hafez al-Asad's death. Under these conditions, Syria would regain the entire Golan Heights in line with the borders of 1967. At the end of 2003, Bashar surprisingly dropped this condition—which was based on a promise from the assassinated Israeli Prime Minister Yitzhak Rabin—thus placing Israel in a temporary predicament. He directed his strategy toward Washington in order to demonstrate his good will and avert its pressure on Syria. Bashar has declared his readiness to negotiate without preconditions several times, as he did in the speech to parliament on March 5, 2005, when he announced the withdrawal of Syrian troops from Lebanon.

Minister Buthaina Sh'aban insists that "Syria would be prepared to resume peace negotiations today if only the United States would induce Israel to negotiate."[8] But Washington is not interested because it wants to hold on to arguments for putting pressure on Syria in the "war on terrorism." Israel has no interest in peace negotiations because it would rather wait and see how much Syria is being softened up, which would strengthen the Israeli position in negotiations over the Golan Heights. And Syria can easily disseminate such expressions of will in the media because it can be sure that Israel at this point would not accept any offer to negotiate. This Middle Eastern vicious cycle leaves Damascus a free hand to go on playing the Palestinian card that it needs as a pillar of its legitimacy.

Pan-Arab rhetoric

As the war raged in its neighboring country, as gigantic fireballs and bright flashes in Baghdad flickered on their TV screens, people in Damascus would meet each Thursday at the central Presidential Bridge. They marched through the streets with pictures and banners they had painted. Among them were many young people, mostly in jeans, some with baseball caps bearing the slogan, "We are all Iraqis." They gleefully carried placards mocking Jordan's King Abdullah II and Egypt's President Husni Mubarak in tight bras or black female clothing as George W. Bush's and the Zionists' whores. The American stars and stripes and the light blue Star of David against a white background regularly went up in flames. Yet beyond these common rituals, the strictly regulated marches (more reminiscent of theatrical performances with the Mukhabarat officials as directors) were more of a social event and an opportunity to meet old friends and get to know new people. Only on March 20, at the start of the war, were a number of people injured when some demonstrators tried to force their way to the American embassy, similar to what happened in Egypt. After that, everything remained peaceful.

Surprisingly, of all countries Syria was an oasis of calm and stability during those tense weeks. Between the rulers and the ruled existed a complete agreement on the question of Iraq. It was quite different in neighboring Arab countries where mass demonstrations occurred against the ruling governments. Many Arabs looked with admiration at the regime in Damascus that demonstrated unqualified opposition to the war in spite of its vulnerability and intimidation from the United States. Faruq as-Shar'a, Syria's long-serving foreign minister, publicly called the Bush administration the "most violent and stupid" government the United States had ever had.[9]

A paradoxical situation arose after the collapse of the Baath regime in Iraq. The role of representing the sole pan-Arab, and thus anti-imperialist, mouthpiece fell to the Syrian Baathists who were happy to receive it. The Iraqi and Syrian branches of the Baath Party had been bitter enemies since 1966. The Syrian Baathists wanted social revolution in their home country first and concentrated on a strong Syria. The Iraqi Baathists criticized this national agenda and adhered to the pan-Arab goal of uniting all Arabs in a single state. With the fall of Baghdad, however, Syria has obtained a monopoly on pan-Arab ideology, a source of legitimacy for the regime, with growth potential for the regime's popularity in the region that mirrors a rising anti-American sentiment. It depends upon the future policy of the United States whether Syrian Baathists can successfully maintain this status, whereas Jordan, Egypt, and Saudi Arabia are seen as traitors to the Arab cause among the Arab population.

The opposition figure Michel Kilo warns that "there is a risk that Arab nationalism will turn into a dangerous demagogy and a means toward achieving internal unity in Syria."[10] In the future, however, pan-Arab rhetoric will no longer suffice to conceal Syria's real problems. Anti-American pan-Arabism is also a danger for the Syrian regime because the United States sees pan-Arab rhetoric as equivalent to terrorism, which partly explains why the Syrian regime remained on the American and Israeli hit list.

Meanwhile, even in Bashar's entourage, criticism has been voiced concerning the hard line he took in the Iraq war. He is blamed for having provoked an unnecessary confrontation with the United States. His resolute anti-war stance was nonetheless very popular among the Syrian people, and the bloody scenes in post-war Iraq have only served to reinforce this mood.

Secularism

"We have a strong government that fights both radical Islamist and Christian fanatics alike and does not itself interfere with religion." This is how a young Christian from the Bab Touma quarter of the Old City in Damascus summed up Syrian secularism. It is not only the Christians who value this principle of the regime.

Fear of political Islamization after a violent revolution, possibly supported by petro-dollars from Saudi extremists, is a trump card of the ruling Alawites and their secular supporters. Whether the danger is exaggerated is a matter of opinion, but it continues to serve as a strong source of legitimacy for the regime. In view of the fact that radical Muslims have previously been funded and supported in many places by the United States to serve its own interests, the Syrian status quo appears quite acceptable. There is little confidence in any alternative that might be put in place by the United States. "Just look at Iraq!" said the Syrian philosopher Sadiq Jalal al-Azm. "If there is no higher civil national identity, people start to kill each other."[11]

Syria's secular experience is a distinct facet of its society that has to be considered by any person in power. The regime has so far shown no sign of making a Saddam-like U-turn from ideological secularism to populist Islamism in spite of the growing pressure from within and without Syria. This is something that the West should appreciate. (For more on this issue, see the chapters: "Che not Usama: Syrian Society and Western Ideals" and "Excursus: Secularism in Syria.")

Religious minorities

The thick walls of the Umayyad Mosque rise majestically in the heart of Damascus' Old City. For Sunnis this is the fourth most sacred place in the world after the K'aba in Mecca, the Prophet's Mosque in Medina, and the al-Aqsa Mosque in Jerusalem. It is also one of the most remarkable symbols of religious intertwinement in Syria's history. The main building behind the wide inner courtyard with its ornamented walls used to be a basilica, which can still be discerned today. Inside, Christians revere the alleged remains of John the Baptist and Muslims those of Prophet Yahia—both are one and the same person. When the Muslims took over Damascus in 636 AD, they allowed the Christians to continue praying in their church for seven more decades until it was converted into a mosque after the Christians had been paid compensation. Today there still remains a minaret dedicated to Jesus.

The Jewish community also has a place in Syrian society. Although their numbers have diminished to just a few hundred, they are not without influence, especially in economic life. For example, a Jewish meat entrepreneur supplies all the exclusive restaurants in the city from the Sheraton to the Cham Palace Hotel.[12] Hafez al-Asad lifted the ban on travel for Jews in the early 1990s. To his disappointment a large number—far more than he had expected—emigrated to the United States or to Israel. Now Palestinian refugees live next door to the remaining Jews and some Christians in the Ottoman adobe houses near the East Gate of Damascus, where the Jewish quarter once existed. An attentive visitor to the Old City can still see Stars of David on some walls. Nobody has chiseled them away in possible fury over their political archenemy Israel. The symbols have remained as a reminder of the long tradition of Jews, Christians, and Muslims living together. After all, modern anti-Semitism is no invention of Muslim Arabs, but was imported into the Middle East from Europe.

In conversations, the large majority of Syrians repeatedly stressed that in their opinion there was a significant difference between the Jews who have always lived in Syria and speak Arabic as their mother tongue and the Zionists who have come to Palestine from all over the world and have often brought with them ethno-nationalism and the notion of territorial expansion. Syrians make an equally clear distinction between US citizens and the US foreign policy. One repeatedly hears in the streets that Americans as people are as welcome as anyone else.

Syrians mention with pride that people of nearly two dozen different religions and confessions have lived in their country for centuries. Of these, eleven alone are of Christian denomination, as there was not a central church that played a unifying force after Islamization. These include Roman Orthodox, Armenian Orthodox, Roman Catholics, Syrian Orthodox,

Syrian Catholics, Armenian Catholics, Maronites, Protestants, Nestorians, Latiners, and Chaldeans. The government deliberately does not keep official statistics on religious groups and so estimates differ. According to one source, Sunnis account for 69 percent of the population, while Christians of various confessions represent 14.5 percent, Alawites 12 percent, Druze 3 percent, and Ismailites 1.5 percent.[13] Apart from this, there is also a small Shiite minority. Since Sunnis tend to have more children than Christians and Alawites, and because Christians tend to emigrate more often, the trend is shifting in favor of the Sunnis. The figure of 10 to 11 percent Christians and the same percentage of Alawites is often quoted. Many Christians have already emigrated but are still registered with the authorities as Syrian residents. Recently, however, the influx of Christian refugees from Iraq may counteract these numbers.

Religious affiliation is crosscut with ethnic identity. Some 90 percent of Syrians are Arabs living alongside Kurds and Turks (mostly Sunnis), Christian Armenians, Circassians (whom the Ottomans removed from the Caucasus and resettled in Syria), and Assyrians of various old Christian confessions who still speak Aramaic, the language of Jesus.

As a consequence of this mosaic, everyday life in Syria is regulated with flexibility around religious traditions. Muslims close their shops on Fridays, Christians on Sundays, and Jews on Saturdays. One religious group patronizes the open bazaars of the others on their free days. Thus an especially large number of Muslim women crowd into the modern clothing stores in Qasa' near the Christian quarter in Bab Touma on Friday evenings, some in tight jeans and with styled hair and others in long garments and headscarves. The accommodating system of holidays applies also to private schools. For example, the muezzins of mosques in any one quarter are prohibited by law from simultaneously broadcasting the call to prayer over loudspeakers. They must take turns so as not to strain the tolerance of believers of other religions.

Minorities enjoy equal rights under the law except for the clause in the constitution that stipulates that only a Muslim can be president. Christian churches can develop freely in Syria and are often very well endowed financially. The government subsidizes them by building asphalt roads to remote monasteries and other projects. Like mosques, churches are exempt from taxes on their purchases. Many Christians are traders, craftsmen, and merchants and have achieved a relative degree of prosperity. They are in a similar social and economic position as the class of Sunni traders.

That Syria is attractive for minorities in the region has become more evident since the Iraq war. Christians living between the Euphrates and Tigris streamed west in the thousands to escape the daily violence in Iraq, and settled in Damascus or on the coast of the Mediterranean. The migration swelled more and more after a series of attacks on churches in Iraq. The contrast between Iraq and its calm and socially tolerant neighbor could not be more distinct. The former Mufti of Damascus, Ahmed Kuftaro, was quick to condemn the church attacks.

In the summer of 2004 alone, 250,000 Christians were reported to have come to Syria from war-torn Iraq either for recreation or permanent residence. In the beginning of 2005, the number of refugees, whether Christians or other groups, rose to 700,000. UN officials say many are doctors, professors, business owners, and recent college graduates—the intellectual core that officials in Washington hoped would rebuild Iraq.[14]

As a result, rents have risen considerably, particularly in the Damascus district of Jaramana, east of Bab Touma. Because not all the refugees are poor, hotels are fully booked. Iraqi license plates on old and new American cars are now part of the street scene in the Syrian capital. Damascene natives worry that the new arrivals will bring about a change in the city's relaxed and trusting atmosphere. An elderly Christian mosaic manufacturer in Bab Touma said that Iraqis had brought with them their "tough business methods" and "reckless attitudes" after decades of suppression under Saddam Hussein and the trauma of having to save one's skin after the Iraq war. Asked whether he wasn't happy that the refugees increased the number of Christians in Syria, he replied, "I don't care if they are Christians or not. Here, we Damascene people trust each other, Christian, Muslim, Jew, or whoever. We know each other and each other's families, we live together, and we do fair business with each other. The Iraqis are different. I don't trust them." In contrast, Anwar al-Bounni stressed that "Syrians have always proven hospitable to all kinds of refugees whether Palestinians, Lebanese, or Iraqis." However, he did not dismiss the current problems. "In Iraq, religious groups are used to living in separate areas and communities. Here, we are used to living as neighbors."[15]

In Syria, open conflicts are rarely shaped along religious cleavages. On the whole, the various religious groups live peacefully next to one another or even together, whereas in other countries in the region such as Jordan, Egypt, Iraq, and even in the politically more open Lebanon, religious communities withdraw into separate shells, cut themselves off, and become encrusted. They have entered into a competition of identity whose own dialectic momentum has created the compulsion for people to assign themselves more and more clearly along religious or ethnic cleavages. Also in Syria, the philosopher Sadiq Jalal al-Azm has observed an increasing unrest among the minorities because of the rise of Islamic fundamentalism. "There is a kind of competition to demonstrate more clearly one's religious identity. The Muslims are building more mosques; the Christians organize more lavish processions and hang bigger crosses round their necks."[16]

Naturally, prejudices have also arisen among the religious groups in Syria as has happened elsewhere. Every now and then people refer to the Christian pogroms in the Old City of Damascus in 1860. To this day, the exact reason and chain of events behind the murdering and looting suffered by the Catholic population in Bab Touma remains unclear, though academics are certain that it had political and perhaps socio-economic causes, but no religious ones.

The Catholics in the ailing Ottoman Empire had increasingly become protégés of French missionaries and French colonial policy that saw a bridgehead for French interests in the Lebanon Mountains. On the other hand, Russia made a show of being the protector of the Orthodox Christians, who in the Maydan quarter of Damascus mostly remained unscathed in the terrible summer of 1860. The English, in turn—for want of Protestants— concentrated on the Druze as protégés or accomplices for their interests.

Some Muslims and Druze were reminded of the Crusades. Bloody battles between the religious groups in Mount Lebanon and on the coast had been the order of the day for a long time until the unrest finally spilled over into Damascus on July 9, 1860. On that day, Muslims and Druze in Bab Touma slaughtered a great number of Christians and set fire to the quarter along the northern wall of the city. The reported number of victims varies between six hundred and ten thousand, depending on the source. People in Damascus generally speak of three thousand dead.[17]

Syrians today still speak of how many local Muslims ran the risk of hiding Christians in their houses, thus saving them from certain death. Sheikh Abdul Qadir al-Jaza'iri, the leader of the Algerian resistance movement living in exile in Damascus, also marched into the old quarter of Damascus with his men to help the Christians. The Ottoman administration had not been able to prevent the pogroms (most of their local police troops even took part in the persecution), but their headquarters in Istanbul organized a thorough investigation afterward and severely punished those who had perpetrated and planned the pogroms. They were strongly supported by Damascene Muslims. At least one-hundred-and-seventy men were executed, including the governor of Damascus and the Ottoman ruler Ahmed Pasha. After this strict intervention by the Ottomans, the French no longer had a pretext for invading Damascus. Six thousand French troops had already landed in Lebanon and were waiting for their marching orders. The events of 1860 show that it was mainly Muslims who helped in time of need, investigated the massacre, and brought the culprits to justice. It always depends on which view of events prevails in a certain situation.

The present Baath government has made efforts to present itself as a mediator between the religions and guarantor of the religious tolerance that has evolved over the course of Syria's history. Bashar likes to be filmed by

Syrian television when he receives Christian patriarchs. Pope John Paul II's visit to Syria with his much-publicized prayer in the Umayyad Mosque in May 2001 was a welcome highlight meant to underline the regime's political interest in propagating religious tolerance. During the Iraq war, Bashar praised the pope for his anti-war stance. He said that the religions again have a common position after a disruption of Christian-Muslim relations following 9/11. To reinforce the welcoming attitude toward Christians in Syria, the government opened the world's first center for the Aramaic language in M'alula, north of Damascus, in July 2004. The remaining Christians who still have a command of Aramaic live in this monastery town.

The ruling Baathists are dependent on religious peace for they are, after all, also members of a minority. Opinions differ, though, as to whether the rule of the Asads has had a positive influence on relations between the religions.

Nihad Nahas is a communist in the political opposition who spent fifteen years in prison. A Sunni by birth and married to a Christian, he said that "Syrian society used to be much more liberal and more secular. It was not until after the Alawites strong-armed Asad to power that tribes and religious groups gained importance. The ideological rift between them has deepened." His wife Leila Nahal, who was also in prison for being a communist, said in fluent French, "We never used to know what a person's religion was. Today young girls ask about a man's religion on their first date to know if there is any question of marriage." Mixed marriages are more difficult and less common than they used to be.[18] "In the 50s," as Volker Perthes quotes an intellectual, "we were communists, Baathists, Nasserists, or Syrian nationalists. Today we are Sunnis, Alawites, Druze, or Christians again." Perthes attributes this development to the lack of an open political discourse.[19]

On the other side, the philosopher Sadiq al-Azm has a different experience. He focuses on the consequences of a modernizing economy. "If you compare modern Syria with the Syria of thirty years ago, society has become more coherent," he points out. The industrialization carried out under Hafez al-Asad made society more mobile. Towns grew and people began to travel and intermingle more. "When I was a small boy," the seventy-year-old reminisced, "you only heard about some minorities and religions from other people. The Druze all lived at the Druze Hill in Sweda and the Alawites in the mountains of Lathakia. Society may not be so coherent as in developed countries but there are no longer any closed communities. Our feeling for Syrianness has grown."[20]

This is exactly what the Baathists are counting on—Syrian nationalism. But the paradox remains. They rule with a pan-Arab and nationalist ideology encompassing all religions. "Even the Christians hold up the flag of Arab nationalism and not the American one," said the historian Abdullah Hanna.[21] At the same time, the Baathists are dependent on clans and religious connections in order to support their rule, not exclusively but as an important pillar.

The relationship between religious groups still resembles a fragile mosaic, though overall the degree of social interaction and tolerance remains a model for the battered region. It at least gives the regime a significant plus in the minorities' view, with no sign either that the Sunni majority deems the regime's minority policy a deficiency.

Domestic security

Brandishing pistols with silencers and automatic machine guns, a four-member gang is storming a money-transfer agency in downtown Damascus on February 7, 2005. In broad daylight, the unmasked robbers force the customers to the walls. The bandits then fire two shots into the air and escape in a Mercedes with forty-three million lira (approximately $800,000).[22]

The ten-minute scene could have happened anywhere in the world, and is among the most familiar scenarios of Hollywood films set in modern urban landscapes. In Damascus, however, the crime was so unheard-of that Minister of Interior Ghazi Kan'an personally hurried to the site and, together with the chief of Damascus police, interrogated some of the customers and employees in an attempt to identify the robbers. The unusual personal involvement of a minister in this minor incident puts the robbery into perspective.

Syria is a police state (*daula al-'amniyya*), and according to one estimate there is one secret service member for every 153 Syrians over the age of fifteen.[23] Law and order in the country is proverbial for both the native population and its tourists. Of course, drug-trafficking and gang crime exists, especially in the commercial metropolis of Aleppo, but the overall crime rate remains extremely low, though it is difficult to obtain concrete figures. Crimes are not reported in the media and relevant statistics are kept secret. Not only is the strong state machinery the reason for this peace, but also the still largely intact traditions and a strict code of values (despite the growing challenge through social change).

It is safe for anyone, including women, to stroll through the streets at night. The narrow doors of the Ottoman houses in the old parts of cities stand open as a rule, allowing glimpses of shady inner courtyards and family life. Windows of parked cars are left ajar in the heat of summer without worry of car radios being stolen. "You don't need police on the streets when there is a hidden policeman in each of us," jokes a Syrian, alluding to the ubiquitous Mukhabarat.

However, recently, worrying developments have taken place that could undermine this pillar of regime legitimacy. Militia-like groups have taken to the streets in order to beat up opposition figures and human rights activists during demonstrations, sometimes with more brutality than the police or the Mukhabarat. These gangs of thugs are sent in buses by family clans of the ruling elite surrounding the president who have much to lose if political change occurred. Such incidents create growing fear among the population and threaten one of the most important remnants of Hafez al-Asad's legacy.

Nevertheless, across the board, safety is a factor that all Syrians, including members of the opposition, still speak of positively when they describe their country. The looting and excesses of violence in post-war Iraq have made even more evident its contrast to the tranquility in Syria. The situation is likewise worse in Lebanon due to its greater social and sectarian divisions.

Social balance

The gap between rich and poor has remained tolerable in Syria to this day, especially in comparison to Egypt where slums are part of daily life. The residual socialism in Syria has not failed to have a social impact.

Many prices are fixed by the government and marked on products, including some restaurant menus. The fact that Syria doesn't recognize international copyright laws enables poor families to buy these books, cassettes, music, and computer CDs produced cheaply in Syria or China. Numerous products are imitations of foreign brands, costing only a fraction of the originals. Affordable and acceptable medical care, cheap medicine, subsidized gasoline, free public schools and nursery schools, and universities, as well as free school uniforms and holiday youth camps, are made available by the government.

In order to secure peasants as traditional clientele, the government buys farmers' crops at twice the market price ("strategic crop"). In May 2004, the government abruptly increased the salaries and pensions of government employees by 20 percent. This was to counter inevitable price increases, especially for imports (because of the strong euro), and for certain basic foodstuffs. It was, at the same time, an act of political defiance against the United States' economic sanctions.

Although the closed economic system has become increasingly unstable and cannot be maintained in the long-term, it serves as an argument for maintaining the status quo, especially among the poorer classes. In Alan George's words, the situation can be caustically described as "a certain equality of misery."[24]

There are, however, two risks which will be described in more detail later. First, the Syrian government is finding it increasingly difficult to procure resources for redistribution, not least because of the new international political constellations. Second, Syria's relative social balance is tipping. The nouveaux riches are flouting their accumulated wealth more and more blithely, with expensive cars, high-tech TV sets, and exclusive restaurants. Access to modern equipment such as mobile phones, computers, and satellite dishes creates desires that can no longer be satisfied by an ordinary civil service salary.

Bashar

My car mechanic (who incidentally is also named Bashar) has hidden a banned opposition magazine with biting caricatures of those in power in the glove compartment of his Skoda pickup. He also has set a beaming president as the screensaver for his mobile phone. This is not a contradiction in today's Syria. Many taxi drivers display the president's portrait on the rear window of their cars—which is by no means prescribed!—often in the style of a pop star with abstract black and silver features and sunglasses, though sometimes in uniform, and occasionally in a family photo with his wife and two children. The leader cult that used to be dictated from above has become popularized.

After the thirty-year rule of the untouchable and inscrutable sphinx in the presidential palace, people like to hear that Bashar occasionally goes out alone to buy vegetables or dines with his family in a restaurant without visible bodyguards. After all, the president had commended modestly in his inaugural speech. "I feel that the man you have known [...] will not change at all once he assumes his post. He came out of the people and lived with them and shall remain one of them. You may expect to see him everywhere whether in the work place or in the streets or at your picnics in order to learn from you [...]. The man who has become a president is the same man who was a doctor and an officer and first and foremost is a citizen."[25]

Although his nimbus is fading, the young president possesses an image that, from the point of view of most Syrians, is neither stained with blood nor corrupted by radicalism or incompetence (though some would say rather the latter than the former). He has successfully been able to distance himself from his father's political Stone Age. Most Syrians tend to look for faults in Bashar's surroundings rather than in Bashar himself, which may be a result of the leader cult and traditional taboo against directly criticizing the president. Yet even with these restrictions, Bashar still represents stability for many Syrians, as well as the hope for modernization.

A factor in Bashar's favor is his socially committed, politically active, and cosmopolitan wife Asma Akhras. Born in 1976 into an affluent Sunni family with origins in Homs, she grew up in Great Britain, graduated with a degree in computer science, and enjoyed excellent training and professional experience in business, finance, and investment banking, among other things in Wall Street in New York with the renowned investment banking firm J.P. Morgan. For Syrian standards, she at times holds provokingly modern views. However, she has also made enemies within the power structure. Conservatives criticize her for exerting too much influence on the president and interfering in personnel matters.

Through the widespread introduction of the Internet, mobile phones, and the legalization of satellite TV, Bashar, the then-chairman of the Syrian Computer Society, was received positively by many Syrians at the start of his presidency. He is not only associated with the new technologies, but knows how to use them effectively to serve his own purposes. A brilliant example is the largest ever pro-Bashar demonstration in Damascus that followed increasing international pressure after the Hariri assassination in February 2005. Half a million people, many of them youngsters dressed in jeans and T-shirts, or teenage girls waving pom poms, festively marched through the streets for their president after the mobile phone company Syriatel (which belongs to Bashar's cousin Rami Makhlouf) had sent an SMS calling for the event. This marks a new style of Syrian politics. A call from the Baath Party would never have gotten as many people into the streets as did a few text lines on a mobile phone!

Part of the attraction lies in his youth, though the president frequently appears stiff during public appearances and in front of TV cameras. A grotesque similarity to George W. Bush exists in terms of Bashar's dependency on dynastic appeal and continuing policies of his father's old guard. For want of alternatives, and due to the lack of democratic experience in the country, Bashar remains a projection of personal authority and popularity for many Syrians with traditional roots as well. His first period of office ends in 2007. The greatest threat to him politically—and personally—is lurking in the immediate surroundings of his power circle and not among the Syrian people.

Chaos in Iraq

The failure of the US occupying forces to gain the Iraqi peoples' confidence, the moral catastrophe due to the pictures of torture that came out of Abu Ghraib prison managed by the Americans, and the growing uncertainty about the future of Iraq has had positive repercussions for Syria. True, the relatively easy victory of the Anglo-American troops was initially a slap in the face for Syrian strategists. But now that it is clear that the reconstruction of Iraq will be an extremely arduous process, Syria can again capitalize on the situation.

During the war, Sadiq al-Azm said that "it would strengthen the position of the regime here [in Syria] if Iraq were to sink into chaos, resistance, and civil war. The argument would be that we don't want to end up like Algeria, Lebanon, or Iraq."[26] In this respect, the regime has the majority of Syrians on its side.

4

THE NEGATIVE BALANCE

In spite of conditions in its favor, the Baath regime is facing a growing crisis of legitimacy. The reasons are structural in nature and concern the economy and domestic politics far preceding the Iraq war. It was not international pressure that first revealed them.

Political disillusionment

In his inaugural speech in June 2000, Bashar made his position clear. "We cannot apply the democracy of others to ourselves. Western democracy, for example, is the outcome of a long history that resulted in customs and traditions, which distinguish the current culture of Western societies. [...] We have to have our democratic experience which is special to us, which stems from our history, culture, civilization, and which is a response to the needs of our society and the requirements of our reality."[1] Simply, this means that the Baath Party is to retain political leadership. In reply to questions about political reform, the president later answered with stilted formulations such as: "We need an intellectual basis. There should be a connection between the political proposal and the social structure in society."[2] And the latter, he implied, is not yet mature enough for the population to participate in politics as in a Western-style democracy.

This means that Syria is trying to follow the Chinese example: economic liberalization without, or with only minor, political reforms at home—or bread before freedom, as expressed by the entrepreneur, ex-member of parliament, and regime critic Riad Seif.[3] Many opposition figures are wondering if Bashar still wants political reforms at all or if he is aiming for bread *instead of* freedom.

Michel Kilo of the Civil Society Movement complains that "Bashar has allied himself with the corrupt forces. Thus he has basically renounced reform. [...] Bashar is not only unable to act, he does not want to act either." The president, he laments, wants to circumvent the issue of democracy. "He only wants a reform of power, not of the system." The regime cannot be reformed in Kilo's view. Another leading member of the Civil Society Movement, who prefers to remain anonymous, comes to a

37

similar conclusion. "Bashar is aware of his weaknesses." For this reason he is largely keeping out of domestic politics and has abandoned his originally ambitious reform program. "He has capitulated to the hardliners and opted for stability instead of progress."

This is true for all authoritarian regimes in the Arab world, says Kilo. "They are not in a situation of stability but in a stable crisis." The Syrian government has lost the connection to its own ideology. "It does not have the same flexibility or the same unity anymore." The authorities know that they have to change, but they do not have the means to do it. "This is part of the drama of these regimes," says Kilo. "When the regime in the Soviet Union wanted to reform itself, the regime was gone. It will happen the same way with the regimes in the Arab world."[4]

Bashar, in contrast, defends his different viewpoint concerning Western-style democracy with cultural, societal, and developmental arguments. As the former president of the Syrian Computer Society, he likes to explain hard realities with software analogies: "If they want to understand me as a president, they have to understand whom I represent, and this is related to the culture of my people," he addressed Western leaders in an interview with the American TV station PBS in March 2006. "So, this is the problem with the West: If I want to make an analogy to two computers with different systems—if we talk about Windows—we notice that they do the same job but they have different systems. So, you have sometimes some software to make the translation between the two systems. We do not have to talk about the events; we have to explain and analyze these events and translate them from our culture to another culture. That is what we want from the media in your country and from the politicians. That is how they can understand, and then they will understand that we need peace, we need prosperity and we need reform."[5]

Probably, Bashar has tried out various scenarios in order to get out of this predicament of reforming the country without destroying his rule or even plunging the whole country into disaster. "If there were free elections controlled by the UN, the president would be sure to win," says Baath member Ayman Abdul Nour in a quite realistic assessment. "But if he did this, he would admit that the past thirty years were illegitimate." This is an ideological dead-end. Nour concedes that if there were free parliamentary elections with new parties, the percentage of Baath Party members in parliament would be certain to slide to below 50 percent. He adds cautiously, "I don't know how much below 50 percent." The engineer considers the hardliners within the Baath Party as the greatest obstacle to progress in Syria and still remains impatient and critical even after the significant reshuffling of the Party Congress in June 2005.

Nour is playing out his personal confrontation with the hardliners on an Internet portal that he created—www.all4syria.com—which quickly became the most popular forum for the exchange of political opinions both inside and outside of Syria. Nour also posts critical texts from the Civil Society Movement on the web and sends them as electronic circulars. "The country must become pluralistic," he insists. His closeness to the president suggests that Bashar somehow sympathizes with his demand, although the two men seem to have drifted apart in recent years. The new ideas posted on the website, as well as the open criticism of the political leadership, corruption, and mismanagement can be considered an indirect weapon for the president in his fight against obstructionists. Therefore, Nour cannot understand why his website was suddenly disabled in March 2004. "Everyone puts the blame on someone else. Nobody will own up to it," he says with a shrug of the shoulders. He suspects that the National Command of the Baath Party was behind it.[6]

Observers who believe in Bashar's good intentions see a desperate fight taking place. After becoming president, Bashar first tried to ally himself with the people against the machinery of power. He thus conjured up a new Damascus Spring that soon got out of hand in the view of the regime and was put down. After that he made an attempt to reform the institutions and bring new people and concepts into the administration. As this proved much harder than he had expected, he then concentrated on reforming the party. "This is the last step he can take," one analyst holds. "If this doesn't work, he will be overtaken by the crisis. He may remain in power but he will no longer be part of the solution."

Bashar's minister for expatriates does not mince matters. "When the whole institution is rotten, you can't do anything about it. You have to rebuild the institution." Even though the reforms have proven harder to carry out than everyone had hoped, Buthaina Sh'aban gives the assurance that "the reforms are supported by the president and many others in the government. We need people who believe in reforms and carry them out. The president can't go into each institute and reform it. We must do this ourselves, and we have political backing and the political mandate."[7]

A reform of the administration does not suffice in the view of many people. The opposition's frustration stems above all from the crushing of the Damascus Spring in 2001. It had been a kind of glasnost when, in his inaugural speech, the young Bashar had spoken out in favor of "accepting others' opinions." The opposition took him at his word and political debating clubs mushroomed. Criticism of the state of affairs was voiced more and more loudly. Initially, the president went along and dismissed the heads of the state radio and television companies as well as of the three major state daily newspapers, *al-Thawra*, *al-Baath*, and *Tishreen*. The new editor-in-chief of *al-Thawra* was not even a party member. The paper became a courageous forum against corruption and mismanagement.

In September 2000, Syrian opposition members wrote the "Manifesto of the 99" under Michel Kilo's lead, followed in December by the "Manifesto of the 1000." It was the heyday of the young Civil Society Movement, composed mainly of intellectuals and academics. Their aim was both bread *and* freedom. Riad Seif, a member of parliament and an entrepreneur, went the furthest. In his companies, he held up social standards and put forward social-democratic ideas. Politically, he called for a constitutional state, a fair market economy, an independent parliament, independent courts, and a free media. He established the Independent Parliamentary Block and called for the break-up of economic and political monopolies. This was a direct broadside against one-party rule. He had crossed the red line.

The conservative forces around Bashar called a halt. The first warnings came in February 2001. Soon the sharpest critics of the regime were arrested one by one, among them Seif in September. Member of Parliament M'amoun al-Homsi was also jailed, as were other activists of the Civil Society Movement, such as the economics professor Aref Dalila and Riad Turk, leader of the banned former Syrian Communist Party Politburo.[8]

The Publishing Law of September 2001 was also a giant step backward. True, it permitted the operation of private newspapers for the first time, and many specialist magazines appeared alongside the caustic weekly magazine *Ad-Domari* (that was banned once again in July 2003). However, the strict conditions limiting freedom of the press gave rise to angry criticism and disillusionment amongst the Syrian people.

The regime fought the Damascus Spring with arrests and bans. Although the president had for a long time defied the conservatives, backing the Civil Society Movement and courageously supporting their aims, he was finally trumped by the hardliners, led by Vice President Abdul Halim Khaddam.[9] This corroborates the theory that Syria is experiencing a pluralization of power centers, and explains as well why critics of the regime—such as Hakam al-Baba, the last editor-in-chief of *Ad-Domari*, and even leading human rights activists like Haitham Maleh and others—continue to stand up for the president personally.

In the meantime, many members of the opposition have started to reflect critically on the events of the Damascus Spring, conceding that they wanted too much too quickly. Tayyeb Tizini, a liberal philosophy professor at the University of Damascus who studied in East Germany, recalls the wild months of the Spring. "First, I was with the Civil Society Movement, but then I distanced myself from it. They wanted all or nothing, and they would have destroyed everything. They wanted to storm the Bastille."[10] Today, the movement's supporters stress that a too abrupt swing to democratization could lead to chaos and to a reinforcement of sectarian and radical forces.

This is similar to what the government is saying. Opinions differ as to the timing and the manner in which the country should be opened.

After the Iraq war, there were initial signs that the government was taking a step toward the secular opposition. Opposition supporters pricked up their ears in surprise when in May 2003, just after the war's proclaimed end, a central regime figure expressed commendatory words for the opposition's prudence and even for its goals. Of all people, Bahjat Suleiman, the powerful head of the Syrian intelligence service, wrote in the Lebanese newspaper *As-Safir* that "in Syria, the regime does not have enemies but 'opponents' whose demands do not go beyond certain political and economic reforms such as the end of the state of emergency and of martial law, the adoption of a law on political parties, and the equitable redistribution of national wealth."[11]

At any rate, the first parliamentary elections under Bashar two months earlier had not brought any progress as far as the opposition was concerned. Competition was limited to eighty-three independent candidates. The results for two-thirds of the seats were predetermined as in previous years. Opposition candidates had not put their names forward for election in the first place or had withdrawn their candidatures in protest. Only a small percentage of the population went to the polling booths.[12]

Furthermore, Syrians witnessed a bitter setback in June 2004, three months after the Kurdish riots, when the government instituted a ban on political parties outside the National Front. Those parties had not been official anyway, but they had at least been permitted to be active. The regime threatened the party leaders with serious consequences if they did not observe the ban. This affected Kurdish organizations in particular. It remained unclear if the ban also extended to Nasserist, nationalist, and other left-wing parties united in the so-called National Democratic Block, which had so far enjoyed a relative degree of freedom under Bashar. The contradictory and unclear instructions about the party ban again suggested that there was a power struggle going on behind the scenes. The challenge becomes more and more urgent with new (illegal) parties popping up, like the Movement of Free Patriots, founded in Aleppo in June 2005 by members of the mercantile, professional, and landowning communities.

According to the opposition, a law permitting new parties has been lying in a drawer for years, blocked by the hardliners. However, a first step in this direction was made when the Tenth Baath Congress in June 2005 recommended allowing new parties to exist independent of the leftist National Front. The measures aim at creating a safety valve for opposition groups, although an important restriction states that no parties will be allowed that follow an ethnic or religious agenda. This leaves Islamists and Kurds out of the political system unless they ally with other political forces—a wise step with regard to the rise of sectarian politics in the region. There might be another reason as well, for behind the scenes in Alawite circles there is talk of possible Alawite opposition parties if new forces are allowed. This would be a sensation in Syrian politics.

Despite the recommendations of the Baath Congress, Ayman Abdúl Nour and others remain pessimistic in the short run. He estimates that a new party law will not take effect before 2007. Opposition figures were disappointed, too. In his opening speech at the congress, Bashar avoided any allusion to political reforms. Instead, in a remarkable admission of government failure, he mentioned "numerous difficulties because of the weakness of the administrative structure, the lack of qualified people, and because of the chronic accumulation of these problems." Thus he continues to focus on administrative reform instead of political changes. Nevertheless, if allowing independent parties is really the direction Syria is headed, one key demand of Western countries would be met: political pluralism, if not democratic elections one day. But this is still a future scenario and many obstacles lie ahead.

During his years in office, Bashar has managed to introduce some small but significant changes. For example, he cut down the military service by six months, from thirty months to two years, and since the fall of 2003, children wear new school uniforms. Instead of military green, the boys' uniforms are now dark blue/light blue and the girls' dark blue/pink. At the same time, corporal punishment in classrooms was abolished, and some military elements were deleted from the school curricula. Schools are now also allowed to accept help with English lessons from the US embassy in Damascus, breaking with the state monopoly in higher education. Eight private universities have been granted licenses and more are waiting in the pipeline.[13] The Ministry for Higher Education even invited the American University in Beirut to set up a campus in Syria. Non-governmental organizations in the fields of environmental protection and women's rights have been given the go-ahead to start their work.

Another step is that the next local elections are planned to be completely free. This reminds one of the early 1970s, when Hafez al-Asad held free elections and awakened democratic hopes that were later crushed in the civil war with the Muslim Brothers.

Despite these important changes, it is questionable how long Bashar can continue to present himself as the "good guy among bad guys." The long-awaited formation of a new government in September 2003 was at any rate not very encouraging. First of all, he had promised to limit the power of the Baath Party in everyday politics and to confine it to its leading ideological role. Besides this, he announced that technocrats would become more influential in politics. But in the end there were eighteen Baath members serving under new Prime Minister Muhammad Naji al-Utri rather than the previous fifteen. Nearly half of the new ministers had already belonged to the old government. Neither has fifty-nine-year-old Utri himself, an easy-going but rather colorless Baath cadre from Aleppo, and an uncle of Bashar's wife Asma, put up a very convincing performance so far. The president set the agenda for the new cabinet to reform the economy, the tax system, and the administration in order to create a better investment climate.

The cases of the key reform-oriented ministers, Issam az-Zaim (Industry) and Muhammad al-Atrash (Finance), were a painful setback. Zaim, who had fought resolutely against corruption and the parasitical caste of entrepreneurs in Aleppo, paid the highest price. He himself was charged with corruption on specious grounds and imprisoned. A court rehabilitated him in August 2004. These incidents show, however, that in serious situations Bashar has been either unable or unwilling to support the people he himself selected. In a similar turn of events, Hussein Amash, a staunch reformer and once Bashar's confidant, was fired from head of the Agency for Combating Unemployment (ACU) in January 2005 quite suddenly by the prime minister. Amash had to pay for an interview he had given to the state newspaper *Tishreen* in which he criticized the sluggish reform process. Shortly before, the prime minister had cut the ACU's budget and subsumed it under the Ministry of Labor. Founded in late 2001, the organization that was once a showpiece of reform has since been reduced to an idle facade. Amash did not even get an appointment with Bashar after the incident.

On the other hand, in the third cabinet reshuffle of his presidency in October 2004, Bashar managed to increase the number of reformers, if only slightly. The most prominent figures were undoubtedly Minister of Information Mahdi Dakhlalah and Minister of Interior Ghazi Kan'an, who (reportedly) committed suicide on October 12, 2005.

The appointment of Dakhlalah came as a surprise to many. After he publicly questioned the leading role of the Baath Party in politics and society, many thought that he had committed professional suicide as editor-in-chief of the *al-Baath* newspaper. But instead of falling into disgrace, he became minister. Dakhlalah immediately introduced what were revolutionary changes for Syria; state television now broadcasts the cabinet's weekly meetings, and journalists are allowed to interview all of the ministers, including the minister of defense. A television reporter, who has been placed in the Supreme State Security Court, also films trials of Kurds and protests in front of the court building. The SANA news agency was given instructions to quote UN resolutions in full, even when they are directed against Syria. The minister has replaced the old TV and radio presenters with younger ones. Observers are expecting Dakhlalah to reform the strict press laws and to permit private political media.[14] This, however, has not kept Prime Minister Utri from continuing to ban private magazines on occasion, as he did once again in March 2005.

Michel Kilo remains pessimistic all the same. Dakhlalah was very bold, he concedes. But after encouraging the journalists to write freely, he soon called them traitors, criticizing their bluntness and saying that they should write in the *Washington Post*, but not at home. "I don't believe that Dakhlalah's words mean real reforms. They [those in power] utter such diverging statements in order to confuse the opposition. I think Dakhlalah tries to wrap the existing reality in different catchphrases."[15] Moreover, his ministry is a hotspot where the Mukhabarat chiefs reign alongside the conservative Foreign Minister Faruq as-Shar'a and, until his resignation, Vice President Abdul Halim Khaddam.

In the fourth cabinet reshuffle beginning in February 2006, Bashar launched two major coups. As mentioned earlier, he appointed Farouq as-Shar'a as vice president. But then, one month later, he pulled off an even bigger surprise: adding a second vice president, Najah al-Attar, a veteran woman of letters, who became the first female vice president of Syria. Attar is the first non-Baathist in this job since the party came to power in 1963. More strikingly, her brother, Issam al-Attar, is a former leader of the Muslim Brotherhood and currently in exile in Europe. But Najah has never agreed with her brother's opinions. She has been with the government since the 1970s and, among other things, occupied the post of minister of culture. In 2002, Attar became director of the Syrian Center for the Dialogue of Civilizations. Her appointment as vice president sends an important message with regard to the role of women in Syrian society.

This is a continuation of various replacements undertaken by Bashar since the year 2000. Only two years into his presidency, he had already managed to replace three quarters of the approximately sixty leading officials in politics, the military, and the administration.[16] Technocrats who had distinguished themselves by good performance rather than party connections were also appointed to a large number of positions in the middle levels of administration. The top officials and ministers have a relatively clean record and have so far not been known, at least not publicly, for being involved in corruption.

But new brains do not necessarily come with new ideas. A confidant of the president conceded that Bashar failed to create his own power base during his first months in office. "He ought to have placed advisors with their own staff in the government palace so that their offices could support him institutionally. But he failed to do so because he was afraid of conflicts with the government. He has lost a lot as a result." Hafez al-Asad, by contrast, had his advisors, at least at the beginning. However, he closed their offices when they took up other positions. "He thought he came from

Allah, and who could be an advisor to Allah?" my source jokes.

The mortal Bashar realized too late that he is dependent on a new power base. It was not until 2003 that he appointed close, well-educated friends as economic advisors—Haitham Saytahi and Nabras al-Fadil—but neither of them with staff of their own. Fadil, who was in charge of administrative reform, left in frustration in early 2005. "This is bad news for Western actors," a European diplomat in Damascus said in regret. Alluding to the events in Lebanon, Michel Kilo quotes Fadil as having said that "Bashar is a man who does not need advisors, who takes the most dangerous decisions within five minutes, who leads a presidency in which nobody really knows what his responsibilities are."[17]

The president has to struggle with the reputation that his decrees tend to gather dust and not be implemented. The fact that he is knocking his head against the wall of the government machinery dents his credibility. "Bashar is akin to the traffic signs in this country. It is in principle forbidden to use your horn and yet the noise is overwhelming," a parliamentarian remarked.[18] The effects of the Party Congress in June 2005 and the far-reaching reshuffle in the party, government, and military increase the pressure on Bashar to deliver, as it makes any pretext of being hampered by obstructing hardliners more flimsy.

Another problem neglected by the regime is the Kurdish issue. This became clear most recently on March 12, 2004, when once more the government paid a price for having shelved urgent problems.

It started quite harmlessly with a soccer match. The local al-Jihad team in Qamishli, the center of the northern province inhabited by Kurds, was scheduled to play against the al-Futwa team from the east Syrian town of Deir az-Zour that is strongly marked by Arab tribal ties. The Arab fans suddenly started waving posters of Saddam Hussein instead of their team's banners, while the Kurds responded by waving US stars and stripes. Before the match could begin, the two sides went for each other with stones and knives. Shots were heard instead of the kicking of a football. The security forces fired into the crowd and the unrest soon spread throughout the town. Kurdish rioters attacked the station and set fire to other official buildings such as schools and a grain factory. Some twenty people were killed and dozens were injured.

In the days that followed, the danger seemed high that the entire country would erupt in violence. Troops of Kurdish demonstrators rioted in several cities, including Aleppo and Damascus, setting fire to cars and fighting battles with the security police. The Syrians held their breath, for they had not seen anything like this since the civil war with the Muslim Brothers. How could it happen? Did Bashar still have the situation under control? He did, for the whole scare was over in a week. More than a thousand Kurds were arrested, with some people even speaking of six thousand. Hundreds were sent to prison for several months.[19] A total of thirty-one people were killed in the riots.

However, the danger continues to smolder. It was the first time that collapsing post-war Iraq had a direct impact on its neighbor Syria. The new federalism in the recently created Iraqi constitution that grants a large degree of autonomy to the three Kurdish provinces in the north brought the Syrian Kurds back to the forefront. The Iraqi Kurdish leader Masoud Barazani provoked discussion more so by using the expression "Syrian Kurdistan."[20] The Baath Party has always viewed the northeast of Syria as an intractable spot. Bedouin life, tribal loyalties, and conservative Islam, together with a neglected infrastructure, combine to make it difficult terrain to control from the center of Damascus. When Syrian journalists a few years ago (before the advent of satellite TV) interviewed some inhabitants in the far north-east and asked them who their president was, they answered with all seriousness Saddam Hussein.

During the riots in March 2004, even Kurdish party leaders in Syria admitted that they had lost control over their own people. Young Kurds, mostly teenagers, had taken things into their own hands and carelessly defied the government. Moreover, the Communist Party of Kurdistan (PKK), that operates in southeastern Turkey and was led by the now imprisoned leader Ocalan, is now also active in northern Syria. In addition, the Israeli intelligence service Mossad operates increasingly in the Iraqi, Iranian, and Syrian Kurdish areas and inflames feelings against the central administrations in order to weaken the nation-states (which has contributed to the impairment of the once good relationship between Turkey and Israel). At the same time, suspicion circulated that the Arab hooligans had received support from groups within the Syrian machinery of power. The Arabs were supposed to provoke the Kurds in order to destabilize the regime.

It appears that both sides, Kurds and Arabs, may have received backing from third parties. Without this aid, many felt it would have been difficult to organize countrywide uprisings over such a long period of time.[21] If true, this would mean that it is not an ethnic problem, but a current political one through and through. But regardless of the events in Iraq, the Syrian Kurds have a score to settle with the Syrian regime. A Syrian population census in 1962 simply ignored about ninety thousand Kurds in order to stop the demographic balance in the north tilting to the Arabs' disadvantage. Incidentally, even the Syrian army's then-general chief of staff and his family were among the Kurds who were deprived of Syrian citizenship! As a countermeasure, the Baath regime tried to settle Arabs in a belt along the Turkish border.

An estimated two to three hundred thousand Kurds are without citizenship, including descendants, and subsequently illegal, Kurdish immigrants from Turkey and Iraq. Syria has never registered them as refugees on an international level. They are not allowed to travel or to own land, among other things. Today a total of one-and-a-half to two million Kurds live in Syria, some of whom have been there for centuries. During the time of the Ottoman Empire, Kurdish tribes started to migrate back and forth in the present borderland between Syria and Turkey. Even after the fall of the empire, the Kurds were still allowed to cross the border between the two new states from 1919 to 1958. Some of them fled from ethno-national Kemalism to the more tolerant Syria in the south, where they also found better economic conditions because of the land reform and comparatively advanced agricultural techniques. Thus, Syria was a refuge for Kurds from the north until not so long ago.

Many Kurds have become assimilated and today consider themselves Syrians more than Kurds. The Kurdish language is forbidden in schools and public life under the Baathists. By contrast, on the other side of the border, the first Kurds are just starting to get their school education in their own language following Turkish reforms. Kurdish activists in Syria have long been calling for more cultural autonomy and an ethnically neutral state. According to them, the state's name should be changed from "Arab Republic of Syria" to simply "Republic of Syria."[22]

However, there can be no talk of political unity among the Kurds. They continue to be so strongly entrenched in their tribal structures that there are twelve (illegal) Kurdish parties in Syria, each one associated with a different tribe. Up to now the majority of Syrian Kurds have neither been ethno-nationalists as in Iraq nor have they showed themselves particularly receptive to Islamic fundamentalism that could be propagated as a unifying bond between Arabs and Kurds. Many Kurds used to sympathize with communism, but this influence is declining.

The majority of Syrian Kurds have not yet been radicalized in any direction. But time is running out for the regime in Damascus to address their concerns about citizenship. Unlike the issue of religious minorities, the pan-Arab Baath ideology cannot provide a solution in this case but is rather part of the problem. The balancing act between ethno-national pan-Arabism and Syrian nationalism appears increasingly paradoxical against the background of a growing ethnicization of the region following the Iraq war.

Ironically, the riots in Qamishli almost brought about historic cooperation between government and opposition. It was an extraordinary event when representatives of the Civil Society Movement and leading figures of the Syrian human rights movement met in the office of the head of the National Security Service. The opposition offered help in finding a peaceful solution to the Kurdish problem, for none of them were interested in a violent revolution. The opposition fears that such unrest will set the reform efforts back for years, giving the government a pretext for tightening the reins. An old supporter of the Civil Society Movement said in frustration after the Kurds' revolt that "during the last fifty years they have ruled us under the pretext of liberating Palestine, and during the next hundred years they will rule us under on the grounds of preserving Syrian unity."

The meeting between the representatives of the government and the opposition turned out to be disappointing. "The government refused to talk about politics," reports Anwar al-Bounni, "although the problem is a political one and not one of law and order." Only a small Kurdish minority is calling for a Kurdish state. "Most of them would be satisfied if they were given normal citizens' rights. Otherwise they will only get more radical." Most of the leaders of the Kurdish groups exercised a moderating influence after the riots. The Civil Society Movement, for their part, spontaneously set up committees. Their representatives traveled to Qamishli and Deir az-Zour to pacify those involved in the riots. It is quite rare that a country can enjoy an opposition with such a sense of responsibility!

Bounni spoke to the Kurds in the Damascus suburb of Dummar and tried to appease them. "Not all Arabs are in favor of the regime and want to oppress you. There are many who are on your side!" Although the government refused to cooperate in these efforts with the Civil Society Movement, the latter helped to restore peace. "We won't allow the regime to drive a wedge between segments of the population," Bounni explained. "We aren't helping the government, we are helping our country."[23]

The Kurdish problem is an example of the regime's obstinacy. It prefers to wait out problems, but what is supposed to be strength proves to be weakness in the end. In July 2002, Bashar had visited the Kurdish region and promised to tackle the citizenship problem, though nothing happened thereafter. Insiders say that Bashar long ago drew up a plan to grant some of the Kurds Syrian citizenship, but that hard-line pan-Arab chauvinists in the Baath Party have blocked his initiative. The primary individuals obstructing the plan in the machinery of government have been Vice President Khaddam and the Baath cadre Muhammad Bukheitan.

In his distinct manner, Bashar worked around Baath obstacles and notched a small success in March 2005, at a time when external pressures on Syria were mounting. In a gentlemen's agreement with Kurdish leaders, and in the name of "national unity," he had a large Kurdish pro-government rally staged in Qamishli of all places. In return, he released 312 Kurdish prisoners and promised to found an association dedicated to the promotion of Kurdish culture and interests.[24]

Whether the riots in March 2004 sped up or slowed down a more profound solution to the problem is a matter of dispute among members of the opposition. Bashar and some progressive members of the government continue to pledge that they will tackle the matter "very soon." Insiders anticipate that fewer than one hundred thousand Kurds will be granted Syrian citizenship. The government will continue to regard the rest as illegal immigrants who have trickled in over the years.[25] At the beginning of 2006, after Khaddam's defection, word of solving the Kurdish problem "soon" spread once again throughout the teahouses of Damascus.

It is the regime's tactic to play the role of rescuer and pull a solution out of its quiver at the last moment. "On his desk Bashar has several files of matters to be resubmitted for discussion," one of the president's confidants explains. "One is labeled 'Kurdish issue' and others 'Release of Riad Seif' and 'Release of M'amoun al-Homsi.' There was also a file labeled 'Pay Raise' for civil servants that Bashar took out just when Washington imposed the sanctions. He always waits for a suitable opportunity." Interpreted in a less strategic manner, it could be said that the obstructionists keep their feet on the brakes until events make it unavoidable to react. To what extent Bashar himself can get these files resubmitted is a secret that remains hidden behind the palace walls.

Actions lose their political value when they are accomplished in the last minute or under strong pressure. This is how many see the sudden reopening of the files of Riad Seif and M'amoun al-Homsi. Surprisingly, both were released in January 2006, along with three other opposition figures from the Damascus Spring, Walid Bounni, Habib Issa, and Fawaz Tello. Each had been sentenced to five years in prison for violating the constitution and inciting sectarian strife. They became free men seven months before their terms ended. This early release of some of the most charismatic figures of Syria's opposition gave hope to many of a revival of the Damascus Spring.

The economic time bomb

On the door of the Syrian Chamber of Commerce in Damascus is pinned a saying that merits thought: *Minuka al-'ata wa minna al-wala'*. You give us [prosperity], and we will give you loyalty.

This may sound like cynical opportunism in the environment of a Baath regime that demands an ideological following, but the slogan is by no means new. The idea can be found in a similar form in Western state theories. Jürgen Habermas, for example, is convinced that in modern, democratic societies, commitment to the nation is linked to the efficiency of the welfare state.[26] But this saying is to be taken much more literally in Syria: if the regime distributes enough goodies to vital persons and posts, it can be sure that criticism of the leadership will remain low. If the economy is ailing and the predatory state is no longer able to hand out the same benefits, this lack will very soon have an impact on the stability of the regime.

The oppositional journalist Michel Kilo accuses the government of buying entrepreneurs and sectors of the middle class as an "alternative to reform." Without this strategy, Kilo says, there would be a risk that young members of the bourgeoisie in particular would dissociate themselves from the regime. "This is exactly the reason why the rulers need Iraq and Lebanon as sources of money," Kilo adds.[27]

The elder Asad ran a clever foreign policy as far as securing sources of money, and his son is attempting to follow in his footsteps. Analyst Samir Altaqi describes the method as follows: Syria received money from Arab states in 1967 because it was engaged in a war with Israel, again in 1973, and once more in 1976 when Syrian troops intervened in the civil war in Lebanon. Then, in 1982, Syria was given support when Israel invaded Lebanon and occupied the southern part of the country. At the same time, Asad secured extensive debt relief from the Soviet Union in exchange for approving the Russian invasion of Afghanistan. In the Gulf War in 1991, Asad did a U-turn and accepted financial aid from the Gulf States, primarily Kuwait, as thanks for supporting the coalition troops against Iraq. Finally, in another U-turn, money flowed from Baghdad after an unexpected honeymoon with the Saddam regime after 1997, and especially after Hafez al-Asad's death. Altaqi concludes that "the best export product Syria has is its foreign policy."

"This explains why a Syrian employee only has to work thirty-seven minutes a day on average, and can still enjoy free health care and a free educational system," says the analyst with a grin. "The political welfare system is the main instrument of social appeasement. Redistribution, not production, is the priority of the Syrian government. The system of corruption is a political system of loyalty."

But what has been happening since the Iraq war began? "This system is in the process of collapsing," says Altaqi dryly as he takes a sip from his cup of strong Arabic coffee, sitting of all places in the Café Havana in the colonial center of Damascus.

Nevertheless, another opportunity for procuring money in like fashion has arisen. In a message in March 2004, Prince Abdullah of Saudi Arabia promised Bashar financial aid. "They're begging the Syrians not to abandon their hard line against Israel and the American policy in Iraq," reports Altaqi. "Syria is a reassurance for them against an American aggression." The closing of ranks between George W. Bush and Israeli Prime Minister Ariel Sharon on the Israeli settlement policy turned into a financial blessing for Bashar.[28]

By means of these tactics, Syria, a country poor in raw materials, has been able to amass the third largest foreign currency reserves in the Arab world, between $12 and $17 billion. Compared to the size of the Syrian economy, these reserves equal between six and eight months of imports. The debt ratio is close to ten percent of the GDP, which is also a very sound figure compared to other countries. In late 2004 and early 2005, Syria achieved advantageous debt deals with a number of former Soviet Union countries, including Russia, Poland, Slovakia, and the Czech Republic. With Russia, for example, Damascus achieved a debt reduction of 73 percent and will pay back only $3.6 billion instead of $14.5 billion. Up to now the country has been able to maintain a trade surplus although, according to experts, such a surplus will no longer be sustainable in the next few years.[29]

The backdoor strategy in foreign policy has diminished the need for economic pressure to carry out painful reforms. After a relaxation of economic policy, a new class of entrepreneurs has developed a know-how to make use of their modest room for maneuver, but they still cannot be considered a true bourgeoisie like the one that was both the engine and the champion of political reforms in nineteenth-century Europe.

The political scientist Raymond Hinnebusch classifies Syria under the Middle East model of populist authoritarian regimes that came into being after the colonial powers withdrew. The national elites of these regimes saw themselves exposed to external threat and internal instability. At first, they looked to the military and the administrative machinery for support. At the same time, they tried to extend their social base to the lower middle class and thus increase their legitimacy. Authoritarian regimes attempt to guard their independence with "defensive modernization." Although they enter the circle of the worldwide capitalist system, they try to build up an industry for imitating and producing cheap consumer goods in order to avoid becoming dependent on imports. It is the state that takes charge in these matters while the industrial bourgeoisie remains weak.[30]

In Syria's state patronage system, big orders go to large families loyal to the regime or to members of the president's clan. Prominent examples are licenses for the mobile phone network or for foreign car agents. One of the richest beneficiaries of the corrupt patronage economy is the Makhlouf clan, from Bashar's mother's family branch. The empire of Rami Makhlouf, a cousin of Bashar, is estimated at $3 billion.[31] Syrian analysts say he makes a million dollars a day. Besides the two mobile phone companies, he also owns the port of Lathakia, numerous key factories, hotels, duty-free shops, and even private schools—or "half of the country," as Syrians lament, shaking their heads in resignation. The fact that Bashar allegedly kicked Makhlouf out of the country as part of an anti-corruption campaign in early 2005 diminishes neither his wealth nor his political influence.[32]

The so-called entrepreneurs are completely dependent on the regime.

The money tends to flow into their pockets and not into the economic cycle as new investments. This tendency is reinforced by the monopoly of licenses. Entrepreneurship thus remains politically conservative and seeks the regime's protection, including protection from foreign competition. An economic divide-and-rule situation develops instead of an economically and socially vibrant entrepreneurship. A European diplomat in Damascus describes it as a "segmentation of the bourgeoisie." The caste loyal to the regime, the oligarchic bourgeoisie, is especially strong in Damascus. In addition, there are those who work as top bureaucrats in the state machinery and obtain juicy commissions. As a rule, they are also close to the president's family. Sometimes they are referred to as the "state bourgeoisie."[33]

Apart from this "parasitic caste"—or the "Mafiosi," as Syrians call them—there are two other groups of businessmen. One group consists of long-established merchants whose traditions go back hundreds of years as landowners and traders. Among them are merchants in the old souqs (markets), whose shops may be less than three square meters in size, but who enjoy a surplus of profitable business connections. The other group is the new entrepreneurs or the business society. Their members have often been educated abroad or bring in foreign capital. These two groups are the "true entrepreneurs" who are pressing especially strongly for the abolition of Mafiosi privileges and for liberalization of the economic system.[34]

Increasing friction is developing among these groups. Their dispute has reached violent proportions in the business metropolis of Aleppo near the Turkish border, where rival gangs flourish. Segments of the Mukhabarat are also said to be involved in the gang fighting. In this respect, the Syrian law and order state seems to be losing control. This gives a boost to gangs and private security troops while frustrating the general population. One reason for the dispute is that the above-mentioned slogan at the Chamber of Commerce no longer applies across the board. The government is unable to hand out such large sums of money to the parasitic caste of entrepreneurs, who in addition are experiencing increasingly keen competition from the new business class. This confrontation extends into government circles, where those wishing to curb the reform process represent the interests of the parasitic bourgeoisie and oppose the liberals.

Meanwhile, the Syrian people are getting increasingly impatient for economic reform. When he first took office, Bashar aroused expectations that for the most part he has yet to fulfill. Initially, hopes were high. Whereas his father had placed foreign policy in the foreground, subordinating economic policy to "the requirements of the battle" and making reforms dependent on peace with Israel, Bashar turned the agenda upside-down and recognized that a modernization of the country was overdue. Previously, reforms had only been doled out piecemeal to avert worse situations, without any logical overall concept. Bashar wanted to change this. A number of draft laws had been gathering dust in drawers for years and were put on the agenda again after he took office. In spite of this, the few reforms that have materialized continue to resemble his father's patchwork approach.

The sudden introduction of modern means of communication exposed the country to the influences of globalization, while the opening up of an economy that has been isolated for decades is still lagging far behind. The government has no plans for privatization. Instead, the model followed is public-private partnerships. Syria cannot meet the challenges of the world market, or even the requirements of regional cooperation that might result from a peace agreement with Israel one day.

The regime has in the meantime recognized that economic stimulation can only come from outside, and it has granted relief for investments and foreign trade. Investors are now allowed to buy land and have easier access to foreign currency, a stock exchange is planned, and private banks have been able to operate in Syria since 2004, although with many bureaucratic restraints still in place. For the average consumer, the most obvious signs of change are the automatic teller machines that are mushrooming in the cities. Sometimes they are clad in white marble, as if to underline optically this precious achievement: the exit from the financial Stone Age. I can still remember, only a few years ago, when foreign students had to reserve a weekend to travel to Lebanon in order to withdraw US dollars to then exchange in Damascus.

Despite undeniable progress, many important measures are still waiting to be implemented. Syria cannot compete with countries like Jordan or Lebanon when it comes to the investment climate, taking into account the regime, legal security, training, and worker qualification. Syria's advantages are low production costs on the one hand and its geography on the other. Its proximity to the EU market is an asset, as is its increasingly permeable border with Turkey. Syria could make more use of its central position as a trade hub. The recent rapprochement with Turkey and the booming consumer demand in Iraq are encouraging.

Bashar has repeatedly admitted that economic reforms are not proceeding as fast as he would have liked. "It is true that there is tardiness," he conceded in an interview in May 2003. "We have somebody who is pushing the process in the right direction; there is somebody who is pushing it in the wrong direction, and somebody who is pulling it back." Thus he alluded to the old guard who shy away from economic reforms as much as from a political opening. "But this does not mean that I have changed," the president added, "and it does not mean that I'm not working to achieve what I have said."[35] This was a reference to his inaugural speech on July 17, 2000, when he underlined the need for change and gave the opposition reason for hope.

The president knows that Syria cannot meet the challenges of globalization in its present economic state. There is a foreseeable disaster if stagnation continues. Only in a few places in the world is the population growing as fast as it is in Syria. Although the present annual growth rate has fallen to 2.4 percent, it reaches nearly 3 percent if one takes a longer time period into account. Syria currently has some eighteen million inhabitants. During Bashar's period of government alone the population has increased by nearly four million.[36]

At the same time, there is not much more to distribute. Particularly since the inception of the Iraq war, the economy has grown at a slower or around the same pace as the population. Nevertheless, the Syrian economy has performed better than estimates have forecast. In 2004, the GDP grew at 3 percent, compared to 2.6 percent in 2003, and 3.6 percent in 2002.[37] Despite international pressure and domestic political crises, the GDP rose to a stunning 4.5 percent in 2005, according to official figures.[38] The government is striving to increase the growth rate to 6 to 7 percent by 2010 with its reforms. However, studies estimate that Syria needs investments of $50 billion if it is to counteract falling growth, declining productivity, and rising unemployment during the next ten years.[39] (The need for direct foreign investment per year is greater if compared to actual figures, such as $150 million in 2003 or $115 million in 2002. This is a meager 10 percent of the country's GDP.)[40]

In addition, every year two to three hundred thousand young people crowd the labor market, and more and more of them are women. The public sector, which employs about a quarter of the working population, has not created more than twenty thousand jobs annually since the mid-1990s.[41] The sudden withdrawal from Lebanon in 2005 could aggravate the problem, as tens of thousands of poorly educated and jobless Syrian workers could return home and become a burden on the labor market. The total number of workers now in Lebanon is estimated between three hundred thousand and half a million. Even before the pullout, independent estimates put the Syrian unemployment rate as high as 30 percent, while the government Agency for Combating Unemployment (ACU) put it at 17 percent, and the official government figure is 9.5 percent.[42] One should bear in mind, however, that these figures incorporate several elements of uncertainty. It is difficult to establish who can be counted as part of the labor force and who not in a setting where family businesses, irregular working conditions, and child labor play a role.

Although it is still better than in neighboring countries, the gap between poor and rich has steadily grown in recent years. It is estimated that 5 percent of the population own 50 percent of the nation's wealth. Child labor, cuts in education funding, and growing poverty are having a negative impact on the population's level of education.[43] Between 11 and 30 percent of Syrians are said to live below the poverty line, mostly in the less developed rural areas close to the Turkish and Iraqi borders.[44] The system of traditional, extended families still helps to prevent social need, but these issues will become increasingly pressing in the future without a social security system. This is a crucial factor that threatens to undermine the legitimacy of the regime. However, the government is also using this argument for its own purposes in refusing to carry out reforms more quickly. "How do we achieve real economic reform without harming the social make-up of the country?" Bashar asked in an interview soon after the beginning of the Iraq war.[45]

According to European diplomats, the reformers aim to replace the costly and ineffective system of across-the-board subsidies with a social security system targeted at the needy. However, for this purpose they need more statistics and data, and unfortunately few of the necessary preparations are taking place. Instead, the cutting of subsidies has already started, which will ultimately hurt the poor much more than the rich. In October 2004, the government increased the price of industrial diesel oil by 450 percent. Fuel rose by 25 percent in January 2006 and electricity is next on the list.

On the other side of the balance sheet, the 20 percent pay raise for state employees in May 2004 was meant to signal that the government still holds the economic reins and acts in a socially responsible manner. A staggered increase in private sector salaries also occurred at between 5 and 15 percent. Moreover, at the end of Ramadan in November 2004, Bashar granted 50 percent bonuses based on one month's salary for civil servants. But even these measures and the fact that Bashar has doubled the wages since he came to power in 2000 cannot mitigate the impatience of most Syrians for greater reform in the long run.[46]

For despite these developments, Syrians are experiencing an inflation that is unprecedented for most of the young population. The semi-socialist coziness is giving way to harsher capitalist winds and is creating fears. In mid-2005, visitors could already bear witness that taxi drivers, shopkeepers, and traders were showing less of their characteristic *shami* relaxedness, instead becoming more insistent on making a living. Used to an inflation of less than one percent over the years, Syrians are now confronted with price hikes such as 4.8 percent in 2003 and an estimated 20 percent in 2004![47] This is a consequence of rising consumer prices, the pay raise, the new Consumption Tax law (as a temporary measure preparing the way for a more sophisticated value added tax (VAT)), and of the strong euro that puts the lira under pressure, further raising the costs of imports. Moreover, real estate prices have risen dramatically, even doubling in some areas of the capital. Among other causes is the influx of Iraqi refugees settling in Damascus. In an attempt to alleviate the pressure on the lira, the government has reduced interest rates for business loans and eased businessmens' access to loans in foreign currencies.[48] This measure seemed like a drop in the ocean compared to the many factors spurring inflation, but Western analysts are optimistic that the price hike can be stabilized in the medium term. At any rate, plans to make the lira convertible have been postponed for the time being. Much will depend on the political developments, too. After the assassination of Lebanese Prime Minister Rafiq Hariri, the lira has lost considerable ground again and reports of capital flight emerged in late 2005.

The economic modernization in the growing private sector is in stark contrast to the encrusted state structures and the old-fashioned setup in the public sector. Up to 1991, Hafez al-Asad had inflated the public sector to 1.215 million employees. Currently there are 1.6 million.[49] Thus, in spite of the generally low state salaries of $145 dollars per month (plus benefits such as cheap housing and holiday chalets), a large number of families depend on the survival of the regime. When all economic sectors are taken into account, a Syrian only earns between $1,000 and $1,300 a year on average.[50]

Since the collapse of the Baath regime in Iraq, the economic thumbscrews have tightened. Bashar has admitted that Syria's economy has suffered due to the Iraq war and the ensuing chaos. He conceded that foreign investments declined, as not only foreigners but also Arab investors have kept their distance.[51] Syria received a paltry $1.7 million in Arab direct investment in 2003, or 1.12 percent of all inter-Arab investments. This is less than a twentieth of what much smaller Lebanon received. In the same year, trade slumped by 22 percent from its previous level.[52] However, in 2005 the Syrian economy picked up and managed to attract considerable investment again.

Nevertheless, Iraq's cheap oil is especially missed in Syria. Before the war, Syria imported oil at dumping prices behind the back of the UN-controlled Oil for Food Program, with the United States turning a blind eye. From 2000 until the Iraq war, 200,000 barrels per day went to Syria, amounting to a sum of $1.3 billion a year. Syria was able to sell the surplus from its own production at a profit abroad in return for foreign exchange. At the same time, the country exported goods from its own production, worth an estimated $2 billion, to Iraq in the year before the war. This resulted in a 40 percent growth of official Syrian exports. Once the US troops gained control of oil production in Iraq, they turned off the tap for the pipeline to Syria. Perthes and Schwitzke rate the loss from the drying up of cheap oil from Iraq and falling oil prices at 20 percent of the official state budget.[53]

Most of those in charge in Damascus play down the damage from the Iraq war. But it is also clear to them that Syrian oil resources will probably be exhausted in the next decade.[54] The economic helmsmen in Syria do not appear to have made any preparations for this structural shock. The entire Syrian economic system is sitting on a time bomb, for the oil business has accounted for 40 to 50 percent of the state budget and 60 to 70 percent of exports in the last few years.[55] Some unexpected good news came in January 2006 when a new oil structure was found in the Tigris area, boosting Syria's overall reserves significantly. However, more long-term hopes reside above all in the large natural gas resources. The government is considering an international call for tenders for the production of cars driven by natural gas, which would be a step in the right direction.

The second silver lining is tourism. After 9/11, because of stricter visa policies, many Arab travelers shifted from US and European destinations to closer resorts. In 2004, after the turbulence of the Iraq war had settled down, some two-and-a-half million tourists crossed the border to Syria, pouring $2 billion into the Syrian economy and creating approximately one hundred thousand new jobs. Nevertheless, the tourism sector is still a stepchild and in urgent need of reform compared to the performance of neighbors like Jordan or Lebanon.[56]

In spite of this critical appraisal, it is hard to estimate what damage the country has really suffered from the Iraq war. Since the end of 2003, trade with Iraq has revived sooner than expected. Iraq represents the main trading partner for Syria in the Arab world, with a share of 16 percent of Syrian exports. The chaos in the neighboring country seems to be more of a help than a hindrance. The coalition troops cannot afford to block goods coming from Syria, even if they were in a military position to do so. They need any kind of help to stabilize the country, even from Syria. Such contradictions are part of life in post-war Iraq. At least one US commander in a region bordering on Syria made a deal with Syrian authorities. He supplied oil and the Syrians sent badly needed consumer goods in return—despite the US sanctions against Syria. This is reminiscent of the Oil for Food Program, only at a local level and with pragmatic individuals taking the initiative.[57] Even more ironically, media reports indicate that, of all people, Bashar's cousin, the business tycoon Rami Makhlouf, meanwhile exports Syrian premium gas to Iraq that is needed to fill US military vehicles. So one of the worst figures of the regime circle and a symbol of the corrupt Baathist power structure is supplying the American enemy across the border.[58]

In July 2004, when the situation had eased somewhat and the US administration had withdrawn from Baghdad and turned over control of Iraq to the interim government, the regime in Damascus had officially signed an oil agreement with the new Iraqi government. As an affront to the United States, however, the Syrians simultaneously made plans to carry out all their future oil business in euros instead of dollars. Saddam Hussein had also done this to the annoyance of the US administration.

Most of the trade between Syria and Iraq takes place in the private sector through century-old connections between merchant families. "Every day some seven hundred trucks drive between Aleppo and Mosul alone," reported Samir Altaqi already in late 2003, barely after the dust had settled in the Iraq war. The analyst is himself of merchant stock. "This trade is a grassroots trade grown over a long time," he explains. Altaqi has credible reports from his relatives that US soldiers accepted bribes from Syrian traders in order to let them pass.[59]

Nevertheless, the Iraqi market is not a sufficient alternative for Syria, which has been subject to a more stringent American embargo under the Syrian Accountability and Lebanese Sovereignty Restoration Act (SALSA) since May 2004. US President Bush hesitated for a long time before signing the sanctions into effect under great pressure from Congress. The consequences are more political than economic in nature and have increased anti-American sentiments in Syria's streets.[60] The sanctions are controversial from an economic point of view. Even before their introduction, there had been no civilian airline flights to the United States, and the mutual trade in goods had been relatively small, accounting for only 5 percent of Syrian exports. Of course, there is one exception: American firms are still allowed to drill for oil in Syria and earn money in other sectors. Neither has there been any restriction in diplomatic relations.[61] Another thing sanctions cannot stop is investments in Syria's oil business by other countries. Trade with Syria's Hong Kong—Lebanon—continues to flourish, allowing all kinds of goods to enter Syria, including merchandise from the United States. However, Syrian Trade Minister Rassan Rifai was one of the few to admit publicly that the sanctions were also harmful. They are deterring investors at a time when Syria needs them most. It also became known that Syrian entrepreneurs lost contracts worth $30 million after the sanctions had become law. An agreement between the American corporation General Electric and the Syrian state railway company worth $300 million was put on ice.[62]

The economic damage from Syria's military withdrawal from Lebanon still remains difficult to assess. Much of the trade has always taken place through obscure channels and does not appear in official statistics. It is likely that much will continue as it is, as the economic side of a story is often more of a political drama. Whereas some point to the problematic return of Syrian guest workers from Lebanon, as mentioned above, others argue that they will soon go west again, and that the draining of Syrian deposits from Lebanese banks could benefit the newly established Syrian private banking system—in light of recent events, this turns out to have been a reform just at the right time.[63]

Suffocating in its isolation, Syria is looking for new partners. Future alliances might have more of a functional than an ethno-national (i. e. pan-Arab) character. Pragmatism instead of ideology would be the alternative.[64]

Syria's recent rapprochement with Turkey, for instance, indicates a move in this direction. It was only in 1998 that the two countries were on the brink of war. Ankara accused Damascus of supporting Kurdish rebels in Turkey, and Syria reproached its neighbor for withholding precious water from the Euphrates River. Syria gave in at the last minute and expelled Abdullah Ocalan, former leader of the separatist Kurdish Communist Party (PKK). Since then, Syria has concluded an anti-terror agreement with its neighbor and regularly extradites PKK activists to Turkey.

After Bashar's historic visit to Turkey in January 2004, bilateral relations between the two nations gained breathtaking momentum. At the end of the same year both countries signed a free-trade agreement. The mines at the border were cleared and Syria reduced its area of maritime sovereignty. The neighbors intend to use the new free spaces for joint marine and agricultural projects. The former enemies are even cooperating on a military level. Against this background, it almost seems forgotten that Syrian maps still portray today's Turkish province of Alexandretta with the cities of Antakya/Hatay and Iskanderun as Syrian territory. However, a sensational exception occurred in the state-run newspaper *Tishreen* in September 2005 that, for the first time, printed a map without the disputed areas. The new realities no longer leave room for nationalist revisionism.

In contrast, the military alliance that Turkey concluded with Israel in 1996 no longer seems to fit into the picture, as Ankara has drastically sharpened its tone against Israeli actions in the Occupied Palestinian Territories. The Turkish government has also turned a cold shoulder to harsh American criticism against its rapprochement with Syria. In April 2005, Turkish President Ahmet Necdet Sezer returned Bashar's visit to Ankara. Despite pressure from Washington to cancel the trip, Sezer went and emphasized that "Turkey is willing to further improve its relations with Syria." Nearly at the same time, however, Turkish Prime Minister Erdogan attempted to appease the other side with a visit to Israel, and also offered his services as a mediator between Damascus and Tel Aviv.

In a quieter undertaking, Syria has proven ready to fix relations with its southern neighbor Jordan. At the beginning of 2005, the two countries solved a border dispute that had been smoldering for decades, ever since the French and the British had drawn the line in 1931. Syria agreed to hand over 125 square kilometers of land to Jordan, while it recovered 2.5 square kilometers from its neighbor.

In its effort to find new partners, Syria is putting out its feelers even farther abroad. The Asian countries have strengthened their position as first providers for the Syrian market with a considerable increase in import shares compared to 2003 (increases of 80 percent in China, 56 percent in South Korea, and 50 percent in Malaysia). They represent 28 percent of total Syrian imports and thus double the share of the EU in 2004.

Bashar visited China in June 2004, the first time a Syrian president had been there since the beginning of diplomatic relations between the two countries in the late 1950s. China, however, has not yet shown any interest in an extensive and strategic political alliance. Instead, the Chinese are pressing the Syrians to fight red tape and facilitate trade. Pragmatism prevails even if the two socialist states have taken a similar path: a cautious economic opening without political reforms. China's interest is in trade with the capitalist West. The time for ideological alliances is past: a hard lesson for hardliners in Damascus.

A new rapprochement with Moscow may prove more important strategically. Bashar freshened up relations with Russia during his state visit there in January 2005, the first by a Syrian head of state since 1999. Besides boosting economic ties, he was interested in purchasing missiles and seemed to have found in Russia one of the few remaining states that would sell weapons to Syria.

Bashar did not get everything he wanted, for on the same day that he began his visit, Ariel Sharon made a phone call to Vladimir Putin and convinced him to drop an arms deal that involved SA-18 surface-to-air missiles. However, the Russian president stuck to his promise to sell the Syrians mobile short-range air defense systems. During his first visit to Israel in April of the same year, the Russian president justified his arms sale to Syria and stressed that it would not tip the balance of power in the Middle East. In a somewhat snide comment he added that "this will, of course, complicate low-flying flights over the residence of the Syrian president, but I'm not sure that such flights would be a good idea if we all, including in the interest of the Israeli people, want to create an atmosphere favorable to the pursuit of the peace process."[65] This must have filled Bashar with glee, for he had been furious when Israeli warplanes flew over his presidential palace in Damascus in August 2003.

With this stand, Putin suggested that he saw a new possibility of increasing Russia's curtailed influence in the Middle East through Syria, just like in old times. Both sides also agreed to intensify their commercial relations, which had fizzled out. In December 2005, Russian parliamentarians who visited Damascus underlined Russia's support for Syria in the aftermath of the Hariri killing. If Russia had to choose between defending US or Syrian interests in the region, it would definitely opt for Syria, they said.[66]

On another front, closer ties with the European Union have emerged as a central interest of progressive forces in the Syrian government. Many Syrians see Europe as a counterweight to the United States and as a moderate force that could lend them support. Syria exports about half of its products to the EU and 15 percent of its imports came from the EU in 2004. (This is a drop of 15 percent compared to 2000/2001.)[67] Products from US firms are often cheaper, but even before the Iraq war the United States had stopped supplying certain goods because the White House had refused to grant American firms licenses to export to Syria, including providers of urgently needed Internet equipment.

As a result, Syria brought renewed energy to discussions of an economic association agreement with the European Union, after such talks had come to a standstill in 1998. Syria was one of the few missing links among the states bordering the Mediterranean in the brokering of the so-called Barcelona Process. Both sides had hoped to have the agreement settled by the end of 2003. The reformers also see the agreement as an important step toward membership in the World Trade Organization (WTO).

Yet negotiations suddenly turned highly explosive when Great Britain and Germany wanted Syria to sign a more sharply worded memorandum against weapons of mass destruction. Damascus protested that the EU displayed a double standard in this matter, as it had long before signed an association agreement with the nuclear power Israel. The EU states were split down the middle: supporters of the agreement accused their opponents of pursuing an American policy and of attacking Syria too one-sidedly. The decision did not become easier with East European countries entering the EU. Interestingly, after the enlargement, when new quotas had to be fixed for the member states, there was the chance to conclude the association agreement in principle by making the signing of a memorandum against weapons of mass destruction obligatory for all Mediterranean partners— but nothing happened.

Syria has to take a share of the blame as well. True, the complications were bad luck from a Syrian point of view, but those in charge in Damascus were asleep at the wheel or had blocked any progress throughout the years, at the very least by not promoting the agreement. The conservatives within the regime had slammed on the brakes, warning that Syria was in danger of losing its independence, but in reality they feared that the opening of the market would endanger their privileges. Apart from this, the majority of "ignorant apparatchiks" did not recognize the benefits of the agreement, as the former member of the Syrian negotiating team and today's ambassador to London, Sami Khiyami, concedes. "It was Bashar who spurred on the Syrian negotiating team to reach an agreement," Khiyami says.[68] But at the same time, it was Bashar who, in the first months of 2004, rarely passed up an opportunity to make a provocative statement involving the issue of weapons of mass destruction. Such weapons were easy to get and could be justifiably stockpiled as long as Israel possessed them, he blustered. In addition, media reports speculated that Syria had tinkered with a nuclear program and also had chemical weapons.[69]

The ball undoubtedly lay in Syria's court. Those in charge had to consider whether it was worth sacrificing political rhetoric for the sake of economic opportunities, especially since they had already gone such a long and arduous way in their negotiations. During the negotiations, the Syrians were willing to make several concessions that they had refused to make for a long time. One point was the human rights clause, which was a normal part of the agreement, and the formulation concerning the fight against terrorism. It seems that American pressure had an indirect impact here.

Something else held up the negotiations: the Syrian side insisted on more generous aid from the Europeans. "This has nothing to do with begging," a person involved in the negotiations said, justifying the strategy. "We want the Europeans to make a stronger commitment to the stability of our country in the long-term. When the Europeans had paid millions of Euros to the Palestinians in reconstruction aid and the Israelis then destroyed the facilities again, the Europeans almost flipped out. Such support creates ties." But, without a doubt, Syria was in the weaker position. "They just think we will sign anything," said the negotiator in frustration.

Other concessions made by Damascus were of a more technical nature, such as a linear reduction of the high import tariffs within the next twelve years. (The highest rate, until recently, was 250 percent for certain imported cars and engines.) In this way, Syrian industry must adjust gradually to growing competition from abroad. But EU observers doubt whether the agreement will really benefit Syrian industry so much in the end. Apart from oil, most of its exported goods are agricultural products (especially cotton, textiles, olive oil, fruits, and vegetables), for which the EU has set up protective barriers in any case. Nevertheless, the Syrian side is pleased about "good quotas" for fruit and potatoes, for example.

Many of the benefits are more of a political value in the long run. The Syrian negotiators hope that the agreement will bring Syria and the EU closer together (on the issue of the Israeli-Palestinian conflict as well), attract European investors, and above all trigger domestic economic reforms. The initial signatures were finally set under the agreement in Brussels in October 2004. But the Council of the EU, i.e. each member state, still has to give its green light before the agreement can become law. The developments in Lebanon have further delayed the process.

The second set of thumbscrews being applied to the Syrian economy is the accession to the Greater Arab Free Trade Agreement (GAFTA). Following this, Syria reduced its tariffs to zero for its Arab neighbors in 2005. Against this background, government resources are drying up and new sources of income have to be found in order to replace the dubious advantage of high tariffs. One challenge will be the effective collection of taxes. The private sector that makes up 87 percent of the GDP and employs 60 percent of the workforce pays only one ninth of the taxes. The rest is borne by public employees who have taxes directly taken from their income.

All these developments show that the president and his ministers are heading for hard times unless decisive reforms are soon realized and growth rates rise further. While most analysts hold that Syria's external vulnerability remains limited in the medium term because of its high stock of foreign currency and low debt rate, others do not exclude the possibility of a balance of payments crisis. "Syria must finally stop whitewashing its economic failure with oil sales," says an economic advisor to the president quite openly. There is good reason why figures that have to do with Syria's oil production are treated like a state secret, locked away in the presidential palace.

One of the greatest challenges is to cushion the economic reforms socially. Otherwise an important pillar of legitimacy will collapse. This is a delicate tightrope walk for the regime. Social imbalance could foster the revival of Islamist forces that attract supporters by offering social benefits in order to close the welfare gap, as is the case in other Muslim states.

An Arab proverb says, "Those who eat from the sultan's table wield his sword (*men ya'kul min sufra as-sultan, yadrub bisaifihi*)." If there is no longer enough food for everyone at the table, those left out may well take up someone else's sword.

Human rights violations

"It's a good thing that I became an attorney," jokes Anwar al-Bounni with his distinctive mischievous humor. "I'm never without work." The human rights activist takes a long draw on his cigarette stump. We are sitting in his modest apartment in the Damascus suburb of Masaken Berze, just next to the high walls of the military academy and, of all places, the Mukhabarat's bugging service. Bounni calculates that members of his family have served sixty years in prison altogether. Things are also getting tight for him, as the Mukhabarat's threatening warnings not to pass on any information about human rights violations to foreigners become sharper. He has loads of work, but most of it he does for free, serving as a messenger and mediator in conflicts between individuals and the government, lending a voice to people who need help against the regime. Paying clients stay away, and he is struggling for a living. When I visited him again in April 2005, he had sold his antique Opel Kadett and was just about to move to a smaller and cheaper office. In October, he spent ten days in hiding after he was framed for a fake crime meant to intimidate him into silence. After he came out of hiding, he was dragged from a car and beaten up in the street by unknown assailants.

His journalist brother Akram, who was released in 2001 after seventeen years in prison, can remember only too well the notorious—although meanwhile closed—jail in the Tadmor desert in the heart of Syria. Tourists are more familiar with the place under the name of Palmyra and associate it with one of the world's most impressive Roman archeological sites. While busloads of tourists were taking their vacation snapshots, the journalist was stewing in the ghastly prison nearby for five years. "There were no beds. We only had blankets on the concrete floor," remembers the forty-eight-year-old in a calm voice. "The prison is a round building with a space in the middle surrounded by cells. There are gaping holes in the ceilings of the cells so that the guards can look inside. In winter rain and bitter cold comes in, and in summer the sun beats down. We were tortured every day."

Arbitrary arrests, confiscations, torture, solitary confinement underground, ill-treatment, and dismal conditions in the crowded prisons make up the dark side of everyday life in a Syria that otherwise appears peaceful. Earlier group arrests were notorious, as the Mukhabarat would simply seize anyone who was sitting in a suspicious dwelling, even members of a family who had nothing to do with politics, and lock them up for years. Islamists and communists were most affected. The judiciary is corrupt today, whereas it had still been considered exemplary in the Syria of the 1940s and 1950s.

In the spring of 2005, Bounni stated that the number of long-held political prisoners had gone down to about three hundred, according to information derived from reports by prison doctors. Taking the more recent arrests into account—illegal fighters and Islamists who returned from Iraq, new radical Islamists in Syria—the number rises again to some fifteen hundred. In addition, according to Bounni, there are more than a hundred Kurds still behind bars since the upheaval in March 2004, although the government claims it released all of those involved exactly one year later. In the past four years, Bashar has released some twelve hundred political prisoners, Bounni said in an interview in April 2005.[70] More than 230 were set free in March alone.[71] In November, another amnesty granted freedom to 190 political detainees. For comparison: in the early 1990s there were still 7,500 dissenters behind bars, including many Muslim Brothers.[72] However, there remain seven thousand "missing persons" since the 1980s, according to the Bounnis. Today only three large prisons remain in service, in Sednaya near Damascus, Adra, and Aleppo. The others have closed. Nevertheless, more cells can be found in the barracks of the police and secret service.

The Islamic human rights activist Haitham Maleh, who has been active for decades, takes particular offense at Act Number 14 of 1969. Section 16 of this secret service law says that a supervisor can object to a criminal charge being raised against a member of his staff. "This makes employees even more dependent on their bosses, who can force them to commit an increasing number of crimes and exert pressure on them," says Maleh. "There has not been a single court case involving Mukhabarat staff." Furthermore, any law can be suspended under the existing emergency law. Military tribunals instead of civil courts conduct the trials, if any. According to Maleh, the situation has not improved very much under Bashar al-Asad. "We don't notice any real change. The atmosphere is just a bit more relaxed," says the seventy-one-year-old lawyer, who also keeps contact with the Muslim Brothers. "But young Bashar is a prisoner of his power clique." Maleh is now counting on the EU and urges them to take more decisive legal action against violations of human rights. "This would help us a lot."[73]

The changes in the atmosphere under Bashar manifest themselves, for example, in the fact that the secret service no longer necessarily enter homes and arrest people on the spot. Now persons are sent a written summons to present themselves to the Mukhabarat. Some even report lively discussions with Mukhabarat staff about the country's problems. "They listen more now," members of the opposition agree.

One sign of change is the Human Rights Association of Syria that Maleh founded in July 2001. The government did not lodge an appeal against the establishment of the organization. Under Syrian law, an association is automatically legal after a period of sixty days if there is no objection, says Maleh. The minister of home affairs had even replied to his letters, thus indirectly recognizing the organization. In February 2005, new Justice Minister Muhammad al-Ghofari even received Maleh for an unprecedented visit. This was interpreted as the final recognition of the Human Rights Association. Maleh, who is still barred from traveling abroad, handed over to Ghofari a forbidden copy of the organization's newspaper and letters that he had once sent to the president.

Diplomats report that the government now at least gives reliable information on arrests and institutes court proceedings that are sometimes open to observers. The Bounni brothers see progress as well. "Prison conditions have improved since Hafez al-Asad's death but they are not yet as they should be," says Akram. "There used to be perhaps fifty people penned up in one cell whereas today there are only ten." During the last two years, the prisoners have even been allowed books, televisions, radios, and telephones. Political prisoners are now also permitted to receive visitors.

During 2004 alone, hundreds of political prisoners were released, especially Islamists and members of their families. According to Muhammad al-Habash, a member of parliament, there are now no longer any members of the former Muslim Brothers in Syrian prisons, although Bounni disputes this.[74] Members of the Iraqi Baath Party and communists were also released under the amnesties. In August 2004, fifty-one-year-old Imad Shiha, who held the unfortunate record for time in a Syrian prison—and even the world record at that time, according to Bounni—was set free after thirty years. He was jailed for belonging to the Arab Communist Organization. In comparison, Nelson Mandela spent twenty-seven years in prison in South Africa before being freed in 1990.

The Syrian Fariz Murad also spent a longer time in prison than Mandela—twenty-nine years, sixteen of them in solitary confinement in Tadmor. As a young man, he had demonstrated with friends against the American policy in the Middle East and had detonated a homemade sound bomb at four o'clock in the morning. Nothing much happened and nobody was injured. At the beginning of 2004, the fifty-four-year-old communist resembled a living corpse. His hunchback forces him to look down at the ground. "Tadmor is a coffin," he said after his release, pale in the face. "We were buried alive without being alive. The food is awful, nobody cares about you, you are tortured day and night, you can't imagine how they beat you. It is like a miracle to leave Tadmor."[75] Some of those released with him had spent several years longer in prison than their actual sentences. Many of them were physically wrecked or terminally ill.

"Those [releases] are all measures with a placebo effect," says a Western diplomat in Damascus. "There is a temporizing policy in the human rights issue. The so-called concessions are only for things that were illegal and excessive anyway under international law."[76]

The regime seems to have adopted a dual-track procedure since the Iraq war. "The big names are spared because Syria now can't afford to have a bad image abroad," says the medical doctor Maya al-Rahabi from the Civil Society Movement. Those in power are making compromises, especially when Syria was in the final stage of negotiations with the EU on the association agreement. "But work has become harder for most of us," complains Rahabi.[77] News of fresh arrests or attempts at intimidation is constantly circulating in the opposition backrooms. According to Maleh, the regime has arrested more political opponents on average since the Iraq war than before.

After the Kurdish unrest in March 2004, young people between the ages of fourteen and seventeen, among others, suffered torture in prisons for months. According to reports from human rights organizations, they were tortured with electric shocks and whipped with cables, their toe nails were torn out, their heads knocked together, and they were forced to strip naked. Some suffered constant nose bleeding, pierced eardrums, or infected wounds.[78] The fact that Syria signed the International Anti-Torture Convention in July 2004 sounds like mockery against this background. Not even the "big names" seem to be safe altogether. Aktham Nu'ayssa, the fifty-four-year-old chairman of the Committee for the Defense of Democratic Liberties and Human Rights in Syria (CDDLHR), was arrested in April 2004. In spite of a heart disorder and other health problems, he was kept in solitary confinement in Sednaya with no contact with his family. The charge against him was worded in the old and familiar style: "activities against the socialist system of the state" and "rejection of revolutionary goals." Nu'ayssa had especially stood up for the abolition of martial law, for Kurdish rights, and for information about the fate of "missing persons." He was released on a symbolic bail in the late summer of 2004 and was even allowed to receive a human rights award in Brussels in October. The activist had already spent the years between 1991 and 1998 in prison where he was tortured.[79]

In May 2005, the regime decided to send a particularly strong signal and infuriated civil society activists when all eight board members of the last remaining political dissident forum were arrested. This happened just before the Tenth Baath Congress and sent a worrisome message that brought back memories of the clampdown on the Damascus Spring in 2001. It turned out to be merely an act of intimidation because all eight men were set free after five days. Although the Jamal Atasi forum is a secular debating club, the writer Ali Abdullah had read a message by the exiled head of the Muslim Brotherhood, Sheikh al-Bayanuni. Abdullah was arrested one week before the Atasi board members. In a separate incident also in May, Muhammad R'adoun was put behind bars. The lawyer and chief of the Arab Organization of Human Rights in Syria (AOHRS) had warned Muslim Brothers in exile not to return to Syria, even though the government had promised them amnesty (often without keeping their word). Both Abdullah and R'adoun were set free again in the November amnesty.

That May, before the Baath Congress, was a particularly dark month for all kinds of opposition figures, as a wave of arrests swept the country. The arrests hit many radical Islamists but also others, like the Kurdish sheikh Muhammad Mashouk al-Khaznawi. He disappeared and was later found murdered. His family blamed the secret service, but officials pointed to a criminal incident. The forty-seven-year-old was an advocate of Kurdish rights. Several other Kurdish activists were also arrested in May.

In a nutshell, the human rights situation in Syria is closely linked to the international setting. On the one hand, the negotiations with the EU on the association agreement had a positive effect. On the other hand, the overall scenario of growing international pressure after the Iraq war, above all from the United States, as well as from Syria's self-inflicted humiliation in Lebanon, affected the opposition in a negative way. The rulers of Syria have become more nervous and react accordingly, since the whole world is watching.

Corruption

Corruption pervades all areas of public life. The Baathist system of patronage acts as a broad framework in which corruption flourishes. The low pay of public service employees is another reason. Students can buy their degrees at universities, especially in the law faculty. This frustrates a lot of young people and deprives bright students of possibilities for promotion. The recruitment of the elite is so distorted that a lot of young Syrians only see a future abroad.

Corruption in the administration, judiciary, police, and customs, and the awarding of public contracts is one of the main reasons for the paralysis in the Syrian economy. The military is also affected. Officers and their soldiers have built up a parallel economy with little "military fiefdoms."[80]

Bashar had a Mr. Clean image when he took office and put the fight against corruption on his agenda. But the resistance inherent in the system proved too strong. After the Iraq war, a group of French experts was invited to Syria to inspect the system and make suggestions for improvements. There was little hope that this new attempt would bear fruit. According to Michel Kilo, the chairman of the new institute for administrative reform is himself "one of the most corrupt officials of the Syrian state," with a counterfeit degree and a record of embezzlement.[81]

5

CHE NOT USAMA: SYRIAN
SOCIETY AND WESTERN IDEALS

The bearded warrior is leading the fight against a superior colonial and occupying power on behalf of those deprived of their rights. He is hiding in the mountains, conducting his guerilla warfare from there. His followers are motivated by his charisma and unshakeable ideological convictions to such an extent that they are ready to die for him. Almost everywhere in the world he is revered as a saint. This figure symbolizing resistance to oppression and Western capitalism also looks down from posters in Damascus. Young demonstrators carry his picture as a protest against the American occupation of Iraq, against the oppression of the Palestinians, against the perceived threat of globalization, and against a "new Western imperialism."

The man who stands for all these goals is not Usama bin Laden—not in Syria, at least. You will not find bin Laden's likeness here. The hero who frequently appears at public demonstrations is Che Guevara! T-shirts, banners, and stickers with the socialist revolutionary's portrait are just as common in Damascus, Aleppo, and Homs as in Havana, Berlin, or Boston. Red flags, some still bearing the Soviet hammer and sickle, fluttered in the streets of the Syrian capital when people demonstrated against the war in Iraq in 2003. Time seemed to stand still. Of course, Islamic demonstrators also walked next to communists with their own slogans, but without foaming at the mouth and calling for a worldwide jihad. After all, the protest marches were controlled by members of the civilian branch of the Mukhabarat and staged for the TV cameras.

Che Guevara is also seen on posters hanging in student hostels, not only during political demonstrations. Syrian society is a colorful cocktail of lifestyles and convictions. It is a melting pot of Islamists, humanists, atheists, pan-Islamists, pan-Arabists, nationalists, liberals, communists, and traditionalists. Not all of them are able to act openly, let alone engage in politics. But because of its isolation, Syria has remained a bizarre biotope. Some things appear dusty, dreamy, and old-fashioned. But Syria is certainly not a hotbed of Islamic fanaticism whose members want to carry the Prophet's ensign to the West and proclaim international terrorism as a legitimate means to this end. American propaganda is out of place here, especially as it exclusively targets the regime as a thorn in the side of the

American administration because it is dictatorial, played for the wrong side in the Cold War, and is opposed to Israel. US rhetoric completely disregards the social reality in Syria. If it was a matter of social values instead of oil, the Syrian people say in frustration, the United States would align itself with secular Syria instead of with the totalitarian Saudi regime from the "Islamic Stone Age." The negative image that Syria has in the West can be explained in many ways, reasons which have to do with Damascus itself and with the political system. Syria would be assessed differently, however, with regard to social aspects if the criteria of Western ideals were truly applied.

Some people in the Syrian government have used this argument as well, presenting themselves as a partner of the West in view of growing international pressure. "If the United States seriously wanted the Middle East to be peaceful, safe, and prosperous, Syria would be the most obvious partner in the region," says energetic Minister for Expatriates Buthaina Sh'aban. "It's the only secular regime in the region. We have a multi-ethnic, multi-religious society like in the United States. For forty years, we have had the best policy in the Arab world for promoting women's rights. I can't see why the United States would have any problem with us. If you take Israel out of the equation, I can't see any collisions of interests."[1]

Particularly in comparison with its neighbors in the region, Syria has retained a qualified but remarkable social secularism. This is an important realization at a time when Western decision-makers are concerned about the rise of a radical political Islam in the Arab world. After all, this kind of Islam is regarded as a hotbed of international terrorism, such as the world has experienced, especially since September 11, 2001. Societies in the Arab world have become more Islamic in recent years. A central reason for this is the unending conflict between Israel and the Palestinians that distorts the realities. The influence of conservative Islamic scholars and the numbers of women in head scarves have visibly increased in recent times. Nevertheless, a relative variety of lifestyles and customs have endured in Syria that are not based on religion.

For example, in Jordan, eating in public places during the day is forbidden during Ramadan. In Syria, on the other hand, many restaurants stay open, and not only in the Christian quarters. Although an old Syrian law from 1971 does forbid eating and smoking in the street during the Muslim fasting period, it is hardly ever enforced.[2] The cones of golden, grilled chicken and juicy kebab meat sizzle openly on spits along the boulevards in downtown Damascus with hardly anybody taking offence.

Many restaurants and bars sell alcohol, again not only in the Christian areas. There is Syrian wine, Syrian beer, and of course the national drink *araq*, a high-proof aniseed schnapps. A topless pin-up girl hangs on the wall of a tiny den near the East Gate in the Old City of Damascus, where mostly old men sit in the evenings at three small tables with their heads close together. This is another part of the Syrian mosaic.

Nightclubs and cabaret shows, usually with Russian or Iraqi girls, are part of the street scene in Damascus and are mainly patronized by Saudi men during the summer months. Here they can gratify their sexual desires, for which there is no outlet in the radically puritanical society of Saudi Arabia. If they are married, their wives, who may number up to four, remain in the hotel suite. Syrian TV shows nowadays caricature the Saudis' behavior during their summer holidays in Syria. For many Arabs in the Middle East, Syria is a place of social liberty compared to their home countries, which increasingly displeases conservative circles. Only in Lebanon, a special case because of its large Christian population, does everyday life appear more liberal.

It is not uncommon to see long manes of hair, skintight T-shirts and leggings, audaciously low necklines, and provocative make-up on university campuses in Damascus, Homs, Aleppo, or Lathakia, as well as in the streets and shopping quarters. The university also plays a part in the marriage market. Girls with and without *hijab* (headscarves) mingle with one another in groups. Guys wear jeans, T-shirts, sunglasses, baseball caps, and have gel in their hair.

In spite of certain restrictions, everyday life for women is better in Syria than in many other Muslim Arab countries. The Civil Code of 1949, which to a large extent still applies today, was modeled on the secular French code. Women are allowed to file for divorce, which is far from the customary convention, as debates in Egypt have shown. They enjoy equality with men in the eyes of the law and receive equal pay for equal work, which is not always the case even in some Western countries. There is a large number of Syrian women in middle-management positions, and women account for more than half of the students in the universities. Since 1980, the military is no longer an exclusively male domain, and since 1983, boys and girls have been taught in common classrooms.[3]

Despite all of this, religion, and traditions influenced by religion, play a significant role in the everyday life of all Syrians—Sunnis, Christians of all stripes, Alawites, Druze, Shiites, and Jews. Some communists, for example, regularly go to the mosque or church. Religion and tradition are most noticeable in the case of marriage. The Sharia, the Islamic law, governs matters relating to the family and inheritances. In 1970, Hafez al-Asad, startled by widespread protests, yielded to the demands of the Muslim Brothers and had the Sharia anchored in the constitution as "*the* main source" of legislation, rather than "*a* main source," as the constitution of 1950 had stated. It is not possible to marry at a registry office. People who want to marry must profess to a religious faith. In case they are registered without any faith, they are automatically considered Muslims. Islamic marriage law states that Muslim men may marry Christian women, but the latter will not be allowed to inherit wealth or property. Christian men who marry Muslim women have to convert to Islam. In these respects, Syria is hardly different from any other Muslim country.

The Islamic command for tolerance was, in fact, far superior to the intolerant Christian practice until the early twentieth century. However, in comparison with today's legislation in the Western world influenced by the Enlightenment of the eighteenth century, the Islamic command looks more like toleration than real tolerance. Although it technically accepts members of other scriptural religions, it does not meet them eye-to-eye, but looks down on them morally. Why else—as the final argument in a chain of reasons—must a man who marries a Muslim woman convert to her religion, or only a Muslim is allowed to be head of state in most Muslim countries? Even in secular Syria there is no social or legal room for atheists or members of other than the traditional scriptural religions.

The free spaces in private and social life untouched by Islam have decreased in the past few years. Islam has become a stronger base of orientation for many Syrians, not in spite of but because of the new openness, the erosion of traditions, and Western influences through the media and the Internet. This is less a "return to Islam" than an entirely new development, as headscarves testify. According to a Syrian political scientist, meanwhile 85 percent of the women in conservative Aleppo wear the *hijab* and the number is increasing.

The black veils of the radical Wahhabites from Saudi Arabia, who for a long time were unable to get a foothold in Syrian society, are today part of the street scene, even if they only play a marginal role. The origin of the new Wahhabite influence in Syria dates back to horse-trading between Hafez al-Asad and Saudi Arabia in 1980. Asad managed to dissuade the Saudis from supporting the militant Muslim Brothers in Syria, an important step that assured his political survival. In return, the secular Asad allowed Saudi Arabia to set up Quranic schools, welfare organizations, and mosques in Syria. According to estimates from Islamic sources, within the past fifteen years $1.5 billion was poured into Syria, Jordan, and Lebanon to promote Wahhabism. "The petro-dollars have destroyed the remarkably tolerant Islam over time," says analyst Samir Altaqi. Sufism and tolerant, popular Islam in Syria are the greatest victims of this trend. Altaqi recalls his childhood, when even Jews sometimes went to sheikhs because they were more open-minded and tolerant than their own rabbis. What seems incredible today was quite common fifty years ago. "If an unmarried girl got pregnant, she went to the sheikh in her predicament. He then protected her in order to prevent a scandal."[4]

Traditions shared by Muslims, Christians, and others are increasingly losing their bonding power. But the West, whose values are often only perceived in a distorted manner through cheap Hollywood movies, does not offer a convincing alternative. The West's inconsistent Middle East policy also leads people to discount Western values.

A Syrian photographer, aged around fifty and an experienced world traveler, describes the paradoxical change of values in Syria. "When I was small, it was almost impossible to speak to strange girls. I had a crush on a girl and we always made a date for four o'clock every afternoon to wave to each other at the windows of our apartments. After many months we even dared to start writing to each other. Those were the traditions. Today you can approach any girl in the street and give her your mobile phone number or she will even give you hers. When you go to a university campus, you see naked belly buttons and you don't know where to look. This is why so many people are escaping to Islam and headscarves, because they have lost their orientation."

The contrasts have become more extreme. "Either you cover yourself up or you run around half-naked," a student of economics pointedly remarks. "Either you say, 'Long live Islam!' or you demonstrate that you are against Islam. There is hardly a middle way," says twenty-five-year-old Shuruq, who attends lectures in ordinary blue jeans and without make-up.

Older secular Syrians reminisce fondly of the 1960s and 1970s, when women sat in tearooms with men long into the night, instead of the men who generally sit alone drinking tea these days. Looking at old family photos, you can often see mothers in mini-skirts, which would be quite daring today. An Alawite friend told me that her family used to have a holiday house at the beach north of Lathakia, but they sold it because they did not feel comfortable living there any longer. "In the end, we were almost the only women still bathing in bikinis," she reported. "More and more women were coming from the countryside, bathing with all their clothes and veils on, and the large number of Saudi tourists reinforced this trend. Today when you're the only person who wants to swim in a bikini, people stare at you and consider you a slut."

The wife of Sadiq al-, Iyman Shaker, a vivid lady with short, uncovered hair, recounted how recently—and for the first time—she had been asked by an Islamic zealot to wear a veil at the market in the Old City of Damascus. He pressed a sheet of paper into her hand that described in detail how "the sister" should put on a *hijab*. It had to be gray, without any lively colors, and without perfume. Mosques in Mohajereen, the district where she lives, she continued, used spies in the neighborhood to check up on the lifestyle of the faithful. Taxis had at times passed her by only to stop a few yards farther on to pick up a veiled woman. A secular, Muslim intellectual from Aleppo recounted that a taxi driver had thrown him out of his taxi merely because he had a bottle of *araq* with him. "This wouldn't have happened fifteen years ago. They learn all that from the hate-preachers in the mosques," he said in frustration.

Another well-known intellectual from Aleppo, Abdel Razaq Eid, added: "There are conservative sheikhs who preach all kinds of things. For example against the woman—we have to kill her if she does this and that. But the Mukhabarat doesn't have a problem with that. Radical positions in questions of belief and society are ok. The main thing is that they don't talk against the regime. Syria is fighting Islamism on a security level but not ideologically and culturally."[5]

Attempts by the secret service to put an end to radical tirades by Islamists are leading to more and more open conflicts. There is a risk that the balance of power between radical preachers of hate and the government will be tipped. The murder of a member of the political secret service in Homs at the end of 2004 brought things to a head. The man was in charge of observing the Ghufari Mosque in Homs. In this capacity, he had forbidden radical religious instruction to children under the age of eighteen. The mosque supervisor had assisted in his murder. This incident was of course not reported in the Syrian press because the case was explosive for another reason—the murderers were radical Sunnis and the victim was an Alawite.

The frequency of these incidents demonstrates a new trend in Syria. Social pressure on secular Syrians is increasing. Conservative Muslim forces are now daring to come out of cover more and more, especially after the death of the elder Asad. Mukhabarat members can no longer be seen as often in some Islamic districts such as Bab Srija in Damascus. Passers-by can witness today what was once impossible: the name and symbols of the president scratched away from walls and plaques. What a contrast to the time when the female elite troops of Hafez's brother Rif'at tore veils off womens' heads in the streets twenty years ago with an excessive zeal similar to what took place at the beginning of Kemalism in Turkey.

6

EXCURSUS: SECULARISM IN SYRIA

The term secularism must be explained in more detail, especially in the context of the Middle East, as Europeans and Muslim Arabs often have different experiences and ideas about their understanding of the term.[1]

Secularism in Europe is embedded in a long process of philosophical, social, and political developments. It largely stems from the ideas of the Enlightenment, when people questioned religious dogmas and interpretations and courageously defied the powerful Christian clergy. Among the things that developed from these acts of liberation was the possibility to publicly confess to being an atheist or a deist, someone who believes in a private God without adopting the interpretations and rituals of the church. Faith increasingly became an individual decision, even though it was not until recent decades that this freedom became a social reality. Only after the social revolutions in Western societies in 1968 did individual and free self-determination win its decisive victory over tradition.

Secularism in the West is thus less a political ideology than part of social development and personal experience, with the separation of church and state only one possible result. Secularism in the European sense can also include the privatization of religion and the disappearance of personal faith and religious practices among the population.[2] These three aspects of Western secularization, however, do not have to occur everywhere at the same time.

For example, eastern Germany has become one of the most irreligious regions in Europe with 69 percent of the population professing no faith in 2000.[3] Religious practice is disappearing to a great extent in western Germany as well. Nevertheless, church and state are not entirely separated, as the German government collects a special tax on behalf of the church. In Scandinavia, where a Protestant state church exists, although only a small number of people declares itself religious. In France, on the other hand, the separation of church and state is strict and consistent, while large parts of the population are profoundly Catholic.

In the United States, one can observe an increasing role for religion and the public display of personal faith in everyday life during the past years, particularly with rising activities of the so-called Christian Right whose members often display a missionary zeal, and social and political ambitions similar to Islamic fundamentalists elsewhere. However, rhetorical reference to "God" has always been omnipresent in political and public life in the US and is a normal ingredient of public culture. No speech of the president ends without the religious-nationalist phrase "God bless America!" But at the same time, prayer in public schools, for example, is forbidden by law and religious organizations exist independently of the government. There is no general church tax like in Germany, although the religious organizations may get financial support for clearly defined purposes. The relationship between religion and state in the United States is a very complex one that is partly in flux and also controversial within the US with some legal rulings contested in various states. Although religious forces have gained influence under the administration of George W. Bush, US society and politics are also known for their strong ability of self-correction, and thus current trends are likely to be reversed again in time.

But in a nutshell, the principle difference between the United States and Europe stems, above all, from the history of the seventeenth and eighteenth centuries. For the early settlers and founders of the United States, the free practice of religion played the role of a liberation ideology during the new nation-building. It was thus conceived as a progressive force. In contrast, the "old" Europeans increasingly saw religion as part of the oppressive political establishment, from which they freed themselves not by emigration (with religion) but by emancipation (from religion).

These examples show how the practical impact of secularism in the Western world has varied greatly. It is difficult to say which country is more and which less secular. Secularism in the western world is a flexible concept that also leaves room for religion. However, a common denominator exists in spite of these differences. Secularism is a cultural experience, an intellectual and social movement with simultaneous and intertwined developments of liberal democracy, constitutionalism, individual liberties, and human rights, independent of personal faith or religious conviction.

Secularism is something quite different in the Arab world. The idea of a state education system, modern forms of administration, and the separation of religion and state came to the Arab region from Europe. It was Egypt that first came into contact with the ideas of the French Revolution when Napoleon landed there for an expedition in 1798. Radical reforms were initiated in 1801 by Muhammad Ali, an Albanian officer, who initially went to Egypt on behalf of the Ottoman Empire to get rid of the Mamlukes. Afterward he proclaimed himself regent of the Nile. The country soon became the first modern, secular nation-state in the region.[4]

With the rise of pan-Arab nationalism, shortly before the collapse of the Ottoman Empire in World War I, secular elements increasingly entered the rhetoric and finally the politics of the Arab Middle East (see the chapter "Is

Baathism Bankrupt?"). The concept, however, suffered a major defect: it came along with European colonization. Apart from many other negative experiences, the Western powers in the colonized territories scarcely applied the values that they praised and implemented at home, which explains the defiant attitude of many Muslims who reject ideas simply because they come from the West. (This attitude also exists the other way round, of course.)

Secularism as many Arabs experience it means the replacement of one tyranny by another. It was an imported ideology grafted in a distorted form onto societies that had entirely different backgrounds of experience. Secularism was associated with imperialism and later with Western-backed authoritarian regimes, with etatism, cultural disorientation, and often with the violation of human rights and personal liberties. Secularism became a platform for Western-educated elites to legitimatize their rule without themselves adhering to the intellectual and social pillars of Western secularism.[5]

Secularism was thus degraded to a political instrument and an ideological facade. This explains why secularism was so easily exchangeable with Islamic populism in Iraq. As soon as Saddam Hussein felt that he needed more support from the Sunni religious scholars and believers after the disaster of the Gulf War in 1991, he switched in a flash from Baathist secularism to Islam. He had *"Allahu Akbar"* (God is Great) written on the Iraqi flag in green lettering. He banned alcohol and nightclubs and restricted women's rights. It is scarcely conceivable that such a U-turn could have taken place in a secular Western environment. The danger in Iraq lies in the fact that the former was not real secularism or the latter real Islam.

To summarize, in the West an *embedded secularism* has grown in harmony with philosophical, social, and moral aspirations. In contrast, we can speak of an *imposed secularism* in the Arab world.

In Syria, there is no secularism in the European sense. The spiritual fathers of secular pan-Arabism and later of the Baath ideology considered Arab nationalism and Islam (at least as a cultural factor) as inseparable components.[6] Syrian secularism is part of the state ideology, yet tolerance and religious pluralism have a long tradition in the country that goes far beyond the seizure of power by members of the socialist Baath Party and the liberal Shiite sect of the Alawites. Secular views were widespread in society and politics after Syria gained its independence from France in 1946. There was even a Christian prime minister in the mid-1940s and 1950s. "To a large extent Islam had lost its political and partly also its social function a long time before March 8, 1963 when the Baath Party came to power," concluded Hans Günter Lobmeyer.[7]

True, socialist ideas prevailed that impacted economic policy, especially between 1966 and 1970 when the left wing of the party (the Neo-Baathists) was in power. But sweeping secular social reforms—an inevitable consequence of atheist Marxist-Leninist ideology—did not take place. The traditional forces were too strong. Instead, socialism had become more of a signpost of foreign policy pointing toward Moscow.

The Baath Party had thus been in command for eight years when Hafez al-Asad became president in 1971. Along with him, many Alawites strengthened their positions of power. Most of them were poor peasants in the mountains around Lathakia who experienced social advancement due to the French colonial policy. (Quite in contrast to their understanding of the state as a citizens' democracy in their own country, the French took advantage of the existence of different sects in their colonies and played religious groups against one another in a "divide-and-rule" strategy.)[8] It was no "Alawite Revolution," but rather a coincidence that an Alawite proved to be hard and unscrupulous enough to play the intrigues and power struggles of the time in his favor. Nevertheless, the fact that Asad had a personal secular background played a role. So it was not primarily a (Western) ideology—socialism—but a very traditional player—a religious group—that favored social liberalism on account of their religious teachings, implemented it, and has maintained it up to today in spite of opposition.

It was not the socialist Baath Party itself but Asad the Alawite who began to introduce secular reforms and grant more rights to women. In 1973, he even wanted to delete the requirement from the constitution that the president be a Muslim, in an attempt to gain more support from minority groups.[9] He provoked intense opposition from the Islamists.

Startled, Asad backed down, shelved his proposal, and made a number of far-reaching concessions. To appease conservative Muslims he started demonstratively going to mosques and set up Quranic schools in the name of the regime, bearing the contradictory and grotesque name: "Asad Institute for Quranic Studies" (*m'ahad al-Asad li tahfith al-quran*). Secular critics in Damascus maintain that the Mamlukes, who ruled in the thirteenth and fourteenth centuries, and the Alawites under Asad had more mosques built than any other rulers in Syrian history. Both had the same goal: as former political and religious outsiders, they wanted to prove their faith to the Sunni majority and thus avoid public unrest. Islamic trust properties (*auqaf*), that arrange for the construction of mosques funded by private and public money, were nationalized under the Baathists and put under the control of a government ministry. This is a clear example of how institutional formal laicism—the separation of church and state—does not necessarily entail social secularism.

Paradoxes can be found at all levels. Shortly after becoming president in 1971, Asad re-introduced the religious oath for taking office that the

Baathists had abolished two years before. He established a ban on eating in public during the fasting period of Ramadan and was not averse to including religious expressions in his speeches.

Deep inside, however, the pragmatist Asad detested religious conservatism and the politicizing of religion. He demanded that Islam be free of "the ugly face of fanaticism" and maintained that moral values, not religion, should be the crucial component for the development of a society.[10] In his polemics against the Muslim Brothers, Asad stressed that "No party has the right to monopolize Islam or any other religion." He also said, "The Arab Ba'th Socialist Party is a nationalist socialist party that does not differentiate between religions [...]. If Syria had not always been above sectarianism, it would not now exist."[11]

The Muslim Brothers of the 1970s and 1980s, however, no longer used religious arguments but anti-Alawite ones, thereby trying to take advantage of the fact that Alawites were the backbone of the regime. During that time, many Alawites were assassinated. The Muslim Brothers presented them as a sect of non-believers who abused the country and oppressed the faithful Sunnis. The Islamists discredited Baath secularism as an Alawite heresy.[12]

The Alawite card is still played in the Syrian system of loyalty. Membership in a particular religion has increasingly become part of the political poker game. However, as already mentioned, it is not justified to speak about an "Alawite rule." There is no exclusive clientelism by and for Alawites in Syria. The Baath Party is not an Alawite party and its base is formed out of various social, not religious, groups. Alawites do not dominate society, let alone business. Neither are they supported by special infrastructure measures. Most Alawites do not fare any better than the other groups in Syria.[13] Some of Asad's most faithful supporters were Sunnis, including Moustapha Tlass who retired in May 2004 after a record thirty-two years as minister of defense. Bashar al-Asad, in a politically astute move, married a Sunni woman and is anxious to achieve a balance in the machinery of power. There is also enmity and distrust between the Alawite tribes and a large number of Alawites are in prison for opposing the government. They often get harsher sentences from the regime than members of other religions.

The Muslim Brothers pursued concrete *political* interests, namely the fall of Hafez al-Asad and the "Alawite clique." Islam served as a mobilizing ideology to this end. Nevertheless, both sides used Islamic rhetoric, claiming that the other side was not truly religious and accusing them of misusing Islam for political purposes. The conflict escalated and Asad was no longer able to pacify the Islamists with cosmetic and symbolic religious action. The mistrust between the two sides was too profound.

The public trial of strength between the regime and the Sunni Islamists continued over several turbulent years. It was not a religious conflict. Asad was supported by large segments of the Syrian population—the peasantry, a liberal-minded class of Sunni traders especially in Damascus, Kurds, Sunni Bedouin tribes, and religious minorities were largely on his side. "These combined forces were just able to prevent the country from Islamization," says the historian Abdullah Hanna. "The odds were fifty to fifty."[14] The tactician Asad made large concessions to Sunni businessmen in Aleppo, after which they handed over more and more Muslim Brothers from their street quarters to the authorities. In addition, Asad managed to pull off the already-mentioned deal with Saudi Arabia that stopped Saudi support for the militant wing of the Muslim Brothers.

The decisive turn of events though was finally brought about by the military. In 1982, Asad put a bloody end to the civil war by the notorious Hama massacre. It is likely that tens of thousands of people died during the bombardment and storming of the Old City, where the Muslim Brothers had barricaded themselves in among the population. Since then, radical Islamists have no longer been able to gain a foothold in public life in Syria.

A high price is to be paid for maintaining the status quo. Yet even critics of the Syrian regime do not dare risk the current stability in view of the social and political Islamization that is encircling Syria.

7

IS BAATHISM BANKRUPT?

One of the Baathists' political symbols is a map uniting all the Arab countries around the Mediterranean in a dark green semicircle. A pennant in the pan-Arab colors of black, white, red, and green is stuck in the heart of Syria. Usually a portrait of Hafez or Bashar Asad is pictured next to it—the leader of the Syrian Baath Party as the guarantor of and fighter for pan-Arab unity. The map was also part of a gigantic mural in the Baghdad National Museum until it was looted after the American invasion in 2003. In the mural Iraqis were carrying the map as an ensign, only this time the masses were following Saddam Hussein who was riding toward Jerusalem on a proud white horse with a sword in his hand.

For outsiders it is hard to grasp why two countries that had committed themselves to the same ideology were bitter enemies for decades. Branches of the Baath Party were ruling in both Syria and Iraq, but they seemed to hate each other more than their archenemy Israel or the United States. What were the reasons for this brotherly feud? And what are the roots of pan-Arabism anyway as a political force?

The development of Arab nationalism coincided with numerous social and economic upheavals in the Middle East that were strongly marked by European influence. A better infrastructure came into being and with it arose greater social mobility. More and more people moved to the fast-growing cities. As a result, traditional ties and identities dissolved. A middle class started to develop, as did new possibilities for mass communication with the use of printing presses. A modern educational system resulted in more uniform curricula, and along with it came higher literacy rates. These are factors that have fostered a homogenization of cultural units (or what were then perceived as such), as well as nationalist movements in other parts of the world.[1]

The history of ideas also plays a role. Nationalist ideologies that spread to the rest of the world from Europe in the nineteenth century exerted a great influence on the Orient. The ethno-national ideas of the German Romanticists occupy an important position in the Arab case. Pan-Arab nationalism sharpened its political profile on this spiritual foundation at the end of World War I in order to demarcate itself from the ethno-national ideology of the Young Turks, whose revolution had shattered the traditional foundations of the Ottoman Empire. European imperialism and colonialism were other sources of friction for the young Arab ideology. In addition, political pan-Arabism was fed by its resistance to Zionism, the growing Jewish nationalism in Palestine.

The phenomenon has many facets, political causes, and social circumstances. The framework after the collapse of the Ottoman Empire was a fragmented political landscape—newly formed states whose frontiers were artificially drawn by the European colonial powers. The nation-state identity created a counterforce to pan-Arabism and developed surprisingly rapidly into a significant and distinctive social and political framework for action. "One of the most extraordinary features of the modern Middle East is indeed this strength of the states and their ability to resist pressures either to disintegrate into their local components or to coalesce into some larger union," Bernard Lewis writes.[2]

More recent historiography focuses on the socio-economic factors of nationalism in the Arab region and tries to embed Arab nationalism in its political, institutional, and social context, with less emphasis on the aspects of the history of ideas. Recent approaches do not consider Arab nationalism to be a purely mechanical reaction to the weakness of the Ottoman Empire, the Young Turks, or European colonialism. They nevertheless recognize that there is a close connection between the phenomena. Here the focus is on the players, the functions that nationalism has in various contexts, and its different forms in the various regions.[3]

Thus Philip S. Khoury, for example, states that during the inter-war period, Arab nationalism was strongest where large religious and ethnic minorities existed and where nation-building and gaining independence from colonial powers was a particularly difficult process. This applies to Syria and Iraq.[4] Syria had to struggle with comparatively greater problems during its state-building. While the monarchy had an integrating effect in Iraq until 1958 and oil revenues helped to assure a certain degree of stability, the political landscape in Syria was hopelessly fragmented.[5]

By the 1970s, Arab nationalism had passed its zenith as a political force. Recent historiography deals with Arab nationalism more as a tool of the rulers than a deep-rooted ideology. As Malik Mufti has pointed out, seventeen attempts to permanently merge the individual Arab states into various combinations have so far failed. He sees scarcely a more profound purpose to Arab nationalism than as a political diversionary tactic on the part of the Arab heads of state. "Lacking the dynastic claims to leadership of their royal predecessors and too preoccupied with the struggle for survival to worry about economic and social issues, most rulers who managed to claw their way to the top sought support and legitimacy through pan-Arab unity schemes."[6] Under these circumstances, nationalism was an important instrument to stabilize the young state structure. On the one hand, the new states were too narrowly focused for pan-Arab ideas to take off and, on the other hand, too large for clear, traditional, primordial ties to hold people together.[7] "State building in Syria, unable to fall back on distinctively Syrian historic loyalties or myths, could, paradoxically, only succeed by the exploitation of both pre-existing sub-state loyalties, such as sect, and the dominant pan-Arabic ideology," writes Raymond Hinnebusch.[8] Both become even more important as pillars of legitimacy and stability when authoritarian regimes fail to create strong institutions.

Arab nationalism in its beginning phase, during World Wars I and II, had already been a mosaic of different persuasions and intentions that were partly working against each another. Behind the ideological façade, bizarre alliances emerged. As an example, in spite of juxtaposed, ethno-national ideologies, the Young Turks were able to win over high-ranking Arabs as their supporters. They came from the local administrative dynasties of the Ottoman Empire, such as Rafiq al-Azm from Damascus or the Arab general Mahmoud Shawkat. Both were members of the Young Turkish Committee of Union and Progress (CUP) based in Saloniki. One of their common denominators was secularism.[9] In contrast to this, in 1913-14 some Arab nationalists were ready to conclude an anti-Ottoman agreement with the Zionists.[10] Others, in turn, allied with France against the British and the Zionists, hoping to obtain self-determination and to maintain their own positions of power.[11] On the other side, there were Egyptian nationalists who thought in terms of nation-states and rejected any form of pan-Arabism as reactionary and a form of foreign control. Finally, after the dream of Greater Syria had collapsed in 1918, Palestinian nationals sometimes fought quite solitarily—abandoned by all the Arab states—against both the British and the Zionists for a political identity of their own.[12]

Despite the many contradictions in everyday politics, a glance at the ideological origins should not be omitted. This is necessary for a better understanding of the ideology of the later Baath parties in Syria and Iraq.

Since nationalism in Europe arose as a mass movement with the French Revolution in 1789, two ideological variants have been competing with each other. One is the so-called French concept of nation and the other one is the German variant.[13] The French concept of a citizens' democracy leaves the choice to the individual if he wants to belong to the nation or not (subjectivity). The nation is an open society, a community of choice. First the state is created and then the nation grows within its borders. Its members share common values and legal opinions (Immanuel Kant). What counts is what people think and profess, not where they come from. The protagonists of the Enlightenment advocated this variant.

On the other side, the German or ethno-national concept divides people into various categories from the beginning. They have no choice (objectivity). What counts is origin and lineage, not convictions—*origio* is more important than *ratio*. People "of the same blood" are automatically members of the nation. According to this idea, a nation comes into being before the state, which then ideally embraces the whole nation within its borders. The nation is an organic structure, a cultural nation (*Kulturnation*), a closed community with a common origin, language, history, etcetera. This variant gained popularity in the nineteenth century, particularly on account of the German Romanticists Johann Gottfried von Herder (1744-1803) and Johann Gottlieb Fichte (1762-1814).

Today the ethno-national concept has undoubtedly prevailed over the democratic citizens' concept of nation. Wherever in the world someone speaks of a nation, he mostly means the German variant with all its negative consequences. When the two concepts overlap, a particularly explosive blend results, as happened in the Balkans in the 1990s.

Herder and Fichte's ideas were also received in the colonies. The later ideologues of ethno-nationalism largely went to schools in Europe or enjoyed a Western education in their homelands. Thus, Hindu nationalism in India is based on the German thinkers. The pan-Arab ideologues of the Baath Party likewise drew their ideas from this body of thought.[14] As with the German Romanticists, language played an eminent role in the idea of the nation. In this case, all who speak Arabic are members of a nation whether they like it or not—and the political borders must be adapted to this situation if possible. Arabic, as the original "sacred language" of the Quran and rich in tradition, was particularly suited to postulating a sublime "soul of the people" (*Volksseele*) in Herder's sense. With reference to the Quran, it was also possible to skillfully emphasize the Islamic heritage that many Islamic scholars correctly saw was threatened by nationalism.

As with all forms of ethno-nationalism, the Arab version is strongly fed by imagination that, depending on the situation, can flourish or dry up. Benedict Anderson has elegantly described nations as "imagined communities."[15] Modern ethnologists such as Wolfgang Kaschuba call the ethnic group, the skeleton of the ethno-nation, a "fictive reality."[16] Despite all of this, the affective power of the unreal can become real on the social level—so real that it triggers political consequences. Unfortunately, there is no room here to delve into the long debate of scholarship on nationalism as to how real or constructed an ethnic group actually is and how it should therefore be treated.

A brief hint of this paradox should suffice in the Arab case. The Arabic language, the main component of the "Arab nation," has developed in so many different directions in everyday life that Arabs from different regions can barely understand each other. For example, Moroccans who visit friends in Syria often resort to French for their conversations. There is a standard Arabic language (*fusha*) that dominates in the print media and news broadcasts, but the colloquial spoken language is characterized by a large number of dialects (*amiyya*). Although many Arabs do not speak classical Arabic, this does not represent a major problem. If one compares this with what is today called the Serbian, Croatian, and Bosnian languages, one becomes aware of the irony. These languages have been scrupulously distinguished and deliberately developed apart by ethno-nationalists after the collapse of Yugoslavia. The idioms belong to three different nations although they are so similar to each other that one has to use grammatical sophistry to locate the differences. Serbs, Croats, and Bosnians have no problems understanding each other—at least linguistically. The South Slav movement, a counterforce to ethno-nationalists, used to stress the commonness among the Balkan population (the common language was known as Serbo-Croatian). Pan-Arabists play a similar role in Arab countries. It simply depends on where the emphasis is placed. The motives are of a purely political nature. Nowadays the differences have prevailed in the Balkans. In the Arab world, contradictory developments are taking place. One could point to the new mass media, particularly the Arab TV news broadcasters, which create a stronger world of common experience with their content and the use of standard Arabic.

Another provocative question for Arab nationalists is whether some religious groups in the Arab region could instead be defined as ethnic groups. Here we come back to the basic difficulty of defining the term "ethnicity." Academic literature so far has not been able to deliver a clear answer. But if it has to do with a common origin and lineage, as ethno-nationalists advocate, one could claim that the Druze now constitute an ethnic group of their own. They are a relatively small group whose members for centuries have married only among themselves according to strict rules. It would be far easier to ascertain their lineage than the larger group of the Arabs, for example. But such discussions resemble shadow boxing, since from Ibn Khaldun to Max Weber and up to today, all serious scholars have stressed that actual lineage has no importance in the end, for people *think* themselves apart or together.[17] It is all about a *feeling* of community (*assabiyya*).

In spite of all the paradoxes, this feeling of community, as well as the Arabic language itself, are the pillars of pan-Arab ideology. The French concept of the nation, in which language has a less ideological importance in the formative stage, did not appear to come into question at all for the Arab region, since initially there were no Arab states in the modern sense and only later were their borders drawn by the Europeans. Nevertheless, the concept of a democratic nation of citizens can be found in individual cases among Arab thinkers. It is no coincidence that they lived and wrote only a few decades after Napoleon's expedition to Egypt in 1798. In his concept of the nation, the Egyptian Rif'a Rafi' Tahtawi, who had studied in France, linked values such as patriotism, equality, and justice in a liberal, democratic sense. It was the first time that an Arab had spoken of the nation in a secular sense.[18]

When Muhammad Ali went from Egypt to Syria in 1831 and took over rule there, the region further opened up to European influences. His son Ibrahim Pasha continued his father's policy of reform and the first generation of nationalists grew up in the Levant. The protagonists were mostly men of letters and Christian Arabs. They were influenced by American Protestant and Russian Orthodox missionaries who promoted translations into Arabic and the printing of books. The philologist Boutrus Boustani (1819-1883) for the first time linked the renaissance of Arab literature and culture to the idea of a national union of Arabs. He worked at the Syrian Protestant College, an institute that was founded by American missionaries and later became the American University of Beirut (AUB). Today, AUB is still *the* intellectual window to the West for students in the region.

The Arabic language, with the help of Western missionaries, became the source of modern pan-Arab thinking. Bassam Tibi writes, "The revival of the national language signified a revitalization of the national culture and with that the creation of a new, *national* identity that pushed the previous religious identity—the substance of the Arabs' loyalty to the Ottoman Empire—into the background."[19] The rather apolitical literary revival turned into a more and more distinct ethno-national current among intellectuals. Their views were, at the same time, in contrast to traditional Islamic thinking and also connected to it. Thus, the Islamic scholar Abdul Rahman al-Kawakibi (1849-1903) stressed that only Arabs were legitimate representatives of Islam. He called for the caliphate to be moved from Istanbul to Mecca and entrusted it to members of the Arab Quraish tribe. People like Kawakibi or Jamal al-Din Afghani strove for the modernization and strengthening of Islam, partly with reference to Western ideas and experience. They were less concerned with a political movement against the Ottomans. Although a Turkish-Arab dichotomy did begin to take shape and some people called for more cultural autonomy, until shortly before the collapse of the Ottoman Empire there was no pan-Arab national "awakening" or political mass movement for independence. The champions of nationalism were intellectuals as well as the administrative and military elites, with people in the countryside scarcely taking part in its development. Broader forces were not mobilized until the Great Arab Revolt started in Mecca in 1916, although its primary aim was to preserve Islam.[20]

There had been no ideological differences worth mentioning between the Arabs and the Ottoman administration for four centuries. The reason for change and the fact that Islam increasingly lost its bonding power lay mainly in developments at the Bosporus itself. For a long time the Ottoman Empire had been the model anti-nation, where minorities lived relatively undisturbed and enjoyed the right of self-administration (millet system). Neither did the colorful mixture of languages present any obstacle to the neutral state administration. Kurds and Arabs felt integrated into the empire as Sunnis, just as Christians or Jews found their places as Muslim protégés (*dhimmi*) with plenty of freedom in place of being second-class citizens.

However, the huge empire stretching from Bosnia to Baghdad and Mecca increasingly lost power and internal stability from the nineteenth century onwards. Ethno-national uprisings and secessions shook the Balkan provinces. European nations interfered more and more ambitiously in the internal affairs of the empire as "protective powers" for the minorities. Reforms (*tanzimat*) aimed at modernizing and centralizing the administration and education system showed only initial success. However, a new generation who grew up during this period of reforms became the champions of either Turkish or Arab ethno-nationalism.

The Young Turks under Kemal Ataturk (1881-1938) gained increasing influence in the Ottoman Empire beginning in the early twentieth century. They had also read the German Romanticists and promoted an extreme ethno-nationalism called Turanism. It culminated in the thesis that Turks were of Aryan descent and thus came from the pre-Islamic, central Asian cradle of civilization (which incidentally the Hindu nationalists as well claim for themselves).[21]

Such an ideology in the Ottoman Empire conceptually excluded a lot of ethnic groups and religious minorities, including Arabs. Most Young Turks looked down on them with contempt and in their own circles described them as "the dogs of the Turkish nation."[22] At the same time, this nationalism was, as in other parts of Europe, a vehicle for democratic ambitions against the *ancien régime*, as last embodied by Abdul Hamid II in the Ottoman Empire.[23] In 1909, when the Young Turks overthrew the sultan, they could still count on the help of Arab officers. Even an "Alliance of Arab-Ottoman Brotherhood" was established but was dissolved again only eight months later as tensions between the two sides rapidly increased. From Istanbul, the revolutionaries began to "Turkify" the Arab provinces in an authoritarian manner by means of language and education policies. This increased the displeasure of many Arabs toward the Ottomans. More and more people began to see the Turks as an occupying power.[24]

The secular Young Turks also undermined the pan-Islamic embrace as they regarded language and culture rather than religion as the national binding factor. On top of this, Ataturk abolished the pan-Islamic caliphate in 1924, offending many Muslim believers. Until then the caliph had been regarded by most Sunnis as the highest religious authority.[25] The focus thus increasingly shifted from the distinctively religious idea of a pan-Islamic community of believers (*umma*) or an Islamic nationalism (*umma* as nation) to political units of nation-states (*watan*) or pan-Arabism (*'uruba*). After the collapse of the Ottoman Empire, the short-lived Syrian King Faisal Ibn al-Hussein said in 1919, "We are Arabs before being Muslims, and Muhammad is an Arab before being a prophet."[26] Pan-Arab nationalism was in direct opposition to Islamic forces because of its increasingly secular and later socialist coloring. Many Islamists rejected any form of nationalism—not only the pan-Arab one but also that of nation states—as incompatible with Islam.

Islam was also of secondary importance for Sati al-Husri (1882-1968), the most influential pan-Arab ideologue. Husri, who was born into a Syrian family, spent his youth in the Ottoman Balkans. Ironically, he mastered Turkish and French before he learned Arabic, thus speaking the core language of his ideology with a Turkish accent.[27] His thinking was also strongly marked by the German philosophers and Romanticists. He admired Fichte, Hegel, and Herder, and his key ideological role in the Arab world earned him the nickname of "the Arab Fichte."[28] Accordingly, Husri put forward an organic understanding of the nation with common language as its backbone. In his thought, there was no place for the individual, as individuals were completely absorbed into the pan-Arab nation that, in his view, stretched all the way to the Maghreb. This was a new idea, for since the Napoleonic invasion, Egyptian nationalists defined themselves in terms of a nation-state (*watan*). Husri strongly influenced the new educational curricula in Egypt, Syria, and Iraq in its various functions.

Ethno-national ideas of this kind were not so far from the racist Nazi ideology. Because Germany was not a colonial power in the region, but an enemy of England and France in both world wars, many pan-Arabists sympathized with Germany (as did Hindu nationalists for the same reasons). The strongest influence of pan-Arabists was first witnessed in Iraq in the 1920s and 1930s when Hitler rose to power in Germany. In 1941, Husri supported a fascist coup in Baghdad, though in this case everyday politics likely played a more important role than ethno-nationalist ideology. In an alliance with the axis powers Germany and Italy, the Iraqi pan-Arabists aimed to expel the British colonial power.[29]

Pan-Arabism especially offered new opportunities for non-Muslim minorities in the Middle East. "Arab Christians, when they thought in a nationalist way, could free themselves from the status of a tolerated minority—as Arabs they could regard themselves as equal to Muslims,"

Gerhard Schweizer writes.[30]

The main ideologue of the subsequent Baath Party in Syria was himself a Christian (however, he reportedly converted to Islam shortly before his death, although this has never been confirmed). Michel Aflaq was born in 1910 in Damascus and went to Paris to study philosophy at the Sorbonne University. There he found the idea of Arabness in Western literature, as had many others before him. He viewed Islam as an essential part of the Arab socio-cultural heritage, but thought that it had become obsolete as a political means for Islamic nationalism. It had now been superseded by pan-Arabism with Islam as a humanistic foundation.[31] However, neither Aflaq nor other proponents of the ideology were able to eliminate the basic contradiction between Islam, which is a stranger to nationalism and does not differentiate between ethnic groups, and ethno-national pan-Arabism, which refers to Islam rather as a national heritage.

This lack of logic was compensated for by the political agitation of the pan-Arab ideologues. For Aflaq and his supporters the idea of Arabness was mixed with anger from the humiliation of colonialism. When Aflaq was a boy of six, England and France planned to split up Greater Syria (*bilad ash-sham*) between them in the secret Sykes-Picot Agreement. It became evident that the Arabs were being led up the garden path, particularly by the British. During World War I and following the struggle against the Ottoman Empire, the British government had promised a uniform and independent Arab kingdom under the rule of the Hashemite King Faisal (1883-1933). The betrayal soon came to light, and in 1920 and 1921 the colonial powers realized their plan against the will of the Arab population. Palestine and Jordan (Transjordan at that time) were placed under English occupation and today's Syria and Lebanon under French occupation. Faisal was fobbed off with a semi-sovereign Iraq (formerly Mesopotamia) under English mandate after the French had expelled him from Syria after a regency of only five months. That was not all. One year after the Sykes-Picot Agreement, the British guaranteed the Zionists the establishment of a Jewish "homeland" in Palestine in the Balfour Declaration of 1917. These decisions were a severe blow to the Arabs and sowed the seeds for the persistent conflicts in the Middle East that are still far from resolved today.

The persecution and extermination of European Jews by the Nazis and subsequently an increasingly aggressive Zionist immigration to Palestine with the approval of Great Britain gave an additional boost to pan-Arabism. Eberhard Kienle holds that "had it not been for the massive Zionist immigration to Palestine which increasingly exacerbated Arab sensitivities, and the uprising of 1936-9 which definitely became the key issue of Arab politics, Arab nationalism might not have survived as a unifying ideology aimed at the creation of a political entity encompassing the entire Arab world."[32]

Tibi sums up the ideological development as follows: "While the Arab nationalism of pre-colonial times, as formulated by the Syro-Lebanese Western-educated intellectuals, strove for the introduction of liberal freedoms and a citizens' democracy after the Western model in a secular Arab nation-state, it has become an apologetic, reactive, *völkisch*, and sometimes aggressive ideology under colonial rule." Husri and Aflaq, in particular, paved the way for this change. "Arab nationalism, once Francophile and partly Anglophile, has changed with English and French colonization and became anti-English, anti-French, and Germanophile."[33] Adeed Dawisha considers this nationalism to be inherently authoritarian—an ideology that does not know any civil liberties but only freedom from colonialism, indifferent toward domestic conditions and social progress. According to him, this "illiberal character" of nationalism à la Husri and Aflaq is partly to blame for the failure of the pan-Arab movement because they did not set up any institutions that could have supported them in times of crisis.[34] The neo-Baathists tried to correct this defect and managed to implement some social changes, but in the end they remained authoritarian.

Aflaq did not conceal his enthusiasm for Hitler.[35] He became a history teacher in Damascus, and in the 1940s he led a movement called the Arab Revival (*harakat al-ihyā' al-'arabi*) together with his Sunni colleague Salahadin al-Bitar. In 1945, the movement merged with a party that had borne the name Baath ("Rebirth") five years earlier. It had been founded by the Alawite Zaki al-Arsuzi from Antakya who had subsequently withdrawn from politics in frustration. The role of the philosopher and linguist Arsuzi is disputed among Baathists. Arsuzi was not rehabilitated as the spiritual father of Baathism until 1966, by Hafez al-Asad among others.[36] Incidentally, all three teachers—Aflaq, Bitar, and Arsuzi—had studied in France and after their return fought the French occupation in various places in Syria.

The first party conference of the new Baath Party was held in Damascus after independence on April 7, 1947. In November 1952, the organization merged with the Arab Socialist Party (ASP) to become the Socialist Party of Arab Rebirth (*hizb al-Baath al-'arabi al-ishtiraqi*) with the slogan "Unity, Freedom, Socialism." The ASP was the first peasant movement in Syria. Thus the Baathists considerably extended their social base and political program. Rural players, especially from the middle class and influential families, began their march through the Baath institutions.[37]

This new start took place in turbulent times. World War II had just ended; the Cold War and the Soviet socialist period had begun in Eastern Europe; the Arab League was founded as the first practical result of pan-Arab ideas; and in 1946 the last French soldier left Syrian soil. Finally, a hopelessly overtaxed England surrendered its mandate over Palestine to the United Nations like a hot potato. In 1948, the UN decided to divide the piece of land and pave the way for a Jewish-Israeli state.

The Baath Party was not the only secular voice in independent Syria. There were communists, socialists, Syrian nationalists (many of whom also thought in pan-Arab categories), and naturally conservatives and Islamists in the other camp. But Aflaq and Bitar's organization became more and more powerful, especially after the 1954 elections regarded as the first free ones in the Arab world.[38]

In the years after independence, hopeful democratic intermezzi and military coups alternated at a rapid pace. Syria became the synonym for instability and chaos in the region. As A.R. Kelidar joked, "It was a time when all the Syrian officers had to get up in the morning at the same time, otherwise one of them would initiate a coup."[39] On March 8, 1963, it was the Baathists that jumped out of bed a moment earlier and staged a putsch in Damascus.[40] This date is still a national holiday today.

Particularly young people from minorities such as the Alawites, Druze, or Ismailites were attracted to the Baath Party. Its radical pan-Arab ideology and social reform agenda gave them an opportunity to integrate into the young nation. Uprooted Alawites from the province of Alexandretta (the area around Iskanderun and Antakya), which France had ceded to Turkey in 1939, and Palestinian refugees—both victims of imperialist policies— saw their political home with the Baathists.[41] The Baathists were also able to win the support of those who were tired of the old elite and critical of the encrusted and unjust social conditions.

The main driving forces in Syria in the 1950s and 1960s were a combination of pan-Arab ideology and the struggle for an overdue land reform. The Baath Party skillfully combined the two elements, which broadened its base and mobilized the peasants according to the national agenda. The national revolution therefore became, in turn, a social one. Those who prospered were the small and medium-sized farmers who profited significantly from the redistribution of land.[42] The Baath Party today still has a significant number of rural supporters, in addition to workers, students, and members of the lower urban middle classes. Even though the economic benefit of the land reform, which dragged on for two decades, is controversial among scholars, it did in fact fulfill its social and political purpose. "Without it," writes Raymond Hinnebusch, "Syria would probably be ruled today by the kind of military regime in alliance with the landed class against the peasant masses found in many areas of Latin America."[43]

Pan-Arab nationalism and socialism, however, have two very different grounding social principles. As already described, pan-Arabism and Syrian nationalism are rooted in ethno-national thinking where members of the nation are classified according to primordial characteristics, i.e. according to external and a priori principles based on lineage. In contrast, socialism takes social classes that come into being through socio-economic development as a starting point. In spite of this contradiction, the Baath Party incorporated both Arab nationalism and socialism in a difficult balancing act.

Socialism was only the vehicle of Arab nationalism, as the founders of the Baath Party themselves admitted. Michel Aflaq wrote, "Our socialism is thus a means of building up our nationalism and our people, and it is the door through which our Arab nation will make its new entry into history."[44] The Christian Aflaq was, of course, irreconcilably opposed to atheistic Marxism. In this context, socialism was scarcely more than a diffuse but understandable call for social justice.

The very issue of socialism soon threatened to split the Baath Party. On one side were Aflaq, Bitar, and their supporters who advocated moderate socialism with democratic liberties, and who primarily followed their pan-Arab program. This also included a revival of Syria's union with Nasser's Egypt that became reality in 1958 only to fall apart three years later. On the other side were the more radical young intellectuals who saw Marxism and Leninism as the main pillars of the Baath Party. For them the social revolution in one country had priority over the distant goal of a pan-Arab state. Thus representatives of Greater Arabia were lined up against supporters of a social-revolutionary "Syria first" vision.[45]

In 1966, the old guard around Aflaq and Bitar were driven from their positions of power in a bloody internal coup in the Baath Party staged by the officers Salah Jadid and Hafez al-Asad. The left-wing neo-Baathists now had a free hand for their "revolution from above." Its motor was set in motion by a quasi-Leninist cadre party.[46] They went ahead with the land reform, nationalized banks and firms, and the monopoly for international trade was given to the state. These measures won the neo-Baathists support from rural and urban lower classes but antagonized businessmen and traders in the urban middle class. Also as "representatives of the Palestinian cause," they adopted a sharper tone toward Israel. But, as already mentioned, an accelerated secularization in the Marxist-Leninist sense did not go far beyond rhetoric.

A year later, the Arab countries experienced a traumatic defeat in the Six-Day War against Israel. Another year later, the branch of the old Baathists staged a coup in Iraq. After some hesitation, Aflaq emigrated to Baghdad in 1970 and became secretary-general of the Iraqi Baath Party. He was Saddam Hussein's deputy for a time. The all-embracing National Command (*al-qiada al-qawmiyya*) of the Baath Party had degenerated into a farce. Since that time, the power in Syria has been held by the Regional

Command (*al-qiada al-qutriyya*). The "national" level of the Baath Party still exists. As an institution it might be roughly compared to the idea of the Communist International, maintaining its pan-Arab claim only symbolically.

The schism between the old guard and the neo-Baathists increased due to the personal enmity between the two stubborn egos of Hafez al-Asad and Saddam Hussein. It was also about regional power politics and about who blazed the trail of the Baath ideology in the Arab world. This was a crucial question of internal legitimacy, especially for the Syrian regime. Paradoxically, this brotherly hatred between Syria and Iraq only ended in the last years and months before the Anglo-American attack on Iraq in 2003.

The enmity of the Baath regimes lingered on even after the so-called socialist revolution in Syria suffered another setback. In 1970, Hafez al-Asad from the nationalist wing, a pilot and head of the Syrian Air Force, finally emerged the winner of the power struggle among the leading Baath figures, consisting of, above all, the Alawite, Druze, and Ismailite military. He dismissed President and acting Prime Minister Nureddin Atasi, who held doctrinaire neo-Marxist views in what was termed the progressive wing of the Syrian Baath Party, but had adopted a less militaristic and irreconcilable stance toward Israel. At that time, nobody would have foreseen that it would be the last coup in Syria till this day. Asad did not call it a coup but merely a "corrective movement" (*al-harakat at-tashihiyya*).

Asad, the clever son from a mountain farming community, mainly corrected the socialist economic policy, thus forming an alliance with the bourgeoisie. In the 1970s, Syria experienced an economic boom by opening up its market to the outside world (*infitah*). In the following years, Asad went ahead with industrializing the country. He invested in infrastructure, urban construction, the health sector, and the education system. This contributed to create a relatively broad middle class, increased Syrians' economic mobility and drastically reduced illiteracy.[47] Asad turned the Baath Party into an organization with mass appeal. The number of members skyrocketed from 65,398 in 1971 to 374,332 in 1981, and 1,008,243 in 1991 in a country that had approximately thirteen million inhabitants in the early 1990s.[48]

After his coup, Asad initially began a limited liberalization of domestic politics and reduced the powers of the feared secret services (which, however, lasted a short time only because of the confrontation with the Muslim Brothers). Most Syrians welcomed the changes with great relief. In 1971, Asad had himself elected president by an appointed People's Council of Baathists, Nasserists, and communists with 99 percent of the vote. A new era had begun.

Since then, the country has been marked by pragmatism aimed at maintaining power and stability both in domestic and foreign policy. Lobmeyer writes, "Since November 16, 1970, Syria's politics has been largely de-ideologized and Baathism has declined into a mere ideology of justification and a reservoir for propagandist phrases."[49] The initial euphoria disappeared and was soon tempered by a hard line in domestic policy. Instead of liberalization, Syrians experienced a "presidential monarchy."[50] Asad fostered a gigantic leader cult. Streets and squares were dominated by statues and posters of the "leader throughout all eternity" (al-qā'id ila al-abad).[51] "In the end it was his personal authority and that alone which held the country together," writes Asad's biographer Patrick Seale. "He was the only pole that held up the tent."[52]

It was therefore not self-evident that the tent would not collapse on June 10, 2000, when Asad died of leukemia. But the death of the "leader" and "constructor of modern Syria" again threw open a question that had been smoldering for a long time: What actually happened to the ideology of the Baath Party? What about its two substantial components: pan-Arabism and socialism?

The answer is simple as far as state socialism is concerned. It went bankrupt after the collapse of the Soviet Union and the Warsaw Pact. It is true that Syria still offers a touch of communist nostalgia in dusty government offices, subsidized food and medicine, five-year plans, one-party rule, an inflated civil service, government propaganda, shaky Soviet military jeeps, and other anachronisms such as US vintage Chevys from the 1950s that create a Cuban-like atmosphere (due to once horrific import duties on automobiles). But this is only a distorted picture of an increasingly modern and capitalist reality. Pragmatic as always, Hafez al-Asad had already started looking westward as the Berlin Wall fell in 1989.[53]

Most of the members of the communist opposition in Syria have long since changed direction and now call themselves secularists or humanists. Apart from elements of a planned economy, the main thing that remains from Baath socialism is in fact Syrian secularism—or let us call it the qualified social liberalism that is so remarkable for the Middle East. However, it also runs the risk of getting worn down. Even the socialist facade is crumbling more and more. Since mid-2004, the state media no longer refers to leading members of the Baath Party as "Comrade" but simply as "Mister."

The balance sheet does not look much better where pan-Arabism is concerned. In spite of its claims, the Baath Party has never grown beyond its role as the Syrian national party. Pan-Arab ambitions have failed. The union of only two Arab states—Egypt and Syria—ended in a debacle. Other union plans did not come into being in the first place. The Baath brothers Iraq and Syria ground each other down in jealous competition and symbolic trench fighting. Finally, with the Iraq war in 2003, pan-Arabism—the second historic pillar of the Baath Party—ceased to exist altogether. Arab states have always formed temporary political alliances, even against each other with the help of non-Arab states, as was shown particularly in the Gulf War and, of course, in the Iraq war. The principles of behavior among Arab states are based on the sovereignty of nation-states and on independence from pan-Arab stipulations. Petro-dollars count more than revolutionary pipe dreams. In its history, the Arab League has more often been the stage for inter-Arab disputes than for pan-Arab cooperation. Neither has there been talk of Arab unity in the Palestinian issue or on a comprehensive policy toward Israel.[54]

One positive effect of Baath ideology today is less pan-Arabism and more nationalism, which serves as a common umbrella for religious minorities who can feel integrated into the state concept. The majority of Sunnis who reject a sectarian policy also equally identify with it. However, the idea of "common Arabness" ignores the problem of ethnic minorities such as the Kurds. Here is a predetermined breaking point in the ethno-nationally connoted "Arab Republic of Syria" that has begun to creak, especially since the recent war in Iraq.

Bashar al-Asad is aware of the ideological crisis of the Baath Party. He lacks his father's charisma and therefore needs all the more institutional and ideological foundations. Party committees have been set up at various levels to discuss the role of the Baath Party in today's Syria. Observers report fierce debates between the president and other Baath functionaries, where Bashar is said to have often appeared openly frustrated. What is surprising is that even opposition members from the Civil Society Movement have been invited to these debates. The big question in Damascus remains whether a reform of the Baath ideology is possible despite its many inherent contradictions.

Apart from the intellectual debates about direction and ideology, critical voices also question the party base. Baath member and former friend from Bashar's youth, Ayman Abdul Nour, points to increasing contradictions within the Baath Party as well as a lack of leadership. "In the Baath party are Muslim Brothers, intellectuals, businessmen, trade unionists, soldiers and what have you. It's not a party but a collective movement. There is no ideology anymore."[55] Yet, the party should not be underestimated as a power factor, warns analyst Samir Altaqi. "The ideological role of the party is weakened, but the party is still the main kitchen for cooking up loyalty."[56]

Recently, during the Iraq war, pan-Arab ideology has gained support from an unexpected corner. In search of a direction for his foreign policy, Bashar has used the Anglo-American attack on Syria's neighbor to revive pan-Arab rhetoric. It is debatable whether this has helped or hindered him. Many people wonder how Hafez al-Asad would have acted in this situation. Some consider Bashar's policy to be even more ideological than his father's in this respect, for in the end most Syrians were glad that Saddam was overthrown.[57] Why should Syria have suddenly lent support to the Iraqi dictator, its Baathist archrival? Michel Kilo is convinced that "Hafez al-Asad would have avoided the conflict with the United States. Now this can only mean the last battle."[58]

It is too early to say if Bashar is really more ideological than his father. His hard-line position on the Iraq issue may possibly be more an expression of a search for a political orientation that would most benefit Syria, a learning process concerning foreign policy rather than an entrenched ideology. It is scarcely surprising that it was the Baath cadres in particular that are said to have advised Bashar to adopt such a strict pro-Iraq and anti-American position. For them it was a welcome opportunity to begin to replenish the empty reservoir of the Baath ideology in a time when they are otherwise running out of answers.

Hinnebusch justifies Syria's stance with ideological raison d'état: "Opposition to the US was a collective decision that would have been taken by any nationalist leadership in Damascus. Not only did the invasion threaten vital Syrian interests in Iraq, but it was also an egregious affront to the Arab nationalist values so ingrained in Syrian thinking." After all, the invasion of Iraq was also in Israel's best interest.[59]

Syria's critical position in the Iraq war is also embedded in a wider context. 9/11 has had fatal repercussions in the Arab world. "The September 11 attacks hit us Muslims as much as it did the United States," said Minister Buthaina Sh'aban. "It was the most terrible thing that has happened to our region."[60]

Of course, first of all 9/11 was a severe blow to Americans that caused great pain, physically and psychologically. But by overreacting to the attacks in rhetoric and action, which is felt as a collective punishment to the Islamic world, the Bush administration has provided terrorists with the platform they need to gain broader support for their Islamist hate campaigns. In addition, US policy has caused many moderate Muslims to lose their orientation, as they are wavering between revulsion toward the September 11 attacks and indignation at Washington's perceived insensitive, "neo-colonial" policy.

The neo-conservatives in the White House and the Pentagon, whom George Packer describes as "fevered minds" in the prelude to the Iraq war,[61] have advocated an explosive blend of policies. It consists of a glorification of violence and military options linked with blindness or unwillingness for deeper policy analysis, a tendency toward "groupthink"—a dangerous auto-dynamic where decisions are taken without critical minds having the possibility or the guts to question basic assumptions[62]—, a simplistic, dualistic, and state-focused division of mankind into "good guys" and "bad guys" reminiscent of the Cold War, and the conviction that the United States has a historical, religious mission as a "chosen people." This often includes a morally overloaded egocentrism. In addition, an uncritical stance toward the politics of the Israeli government and its settlement policy has estranged the US from many Arabs who are by far not all Islamic radicals. The leading policy advisers and neo-conservative policy makers have not shown any effort in incorporating knowledge of Islamic culture or taking into account the deeply entrenched social and political grievances in the Middle East. The result has been an approach devoid of any sensitivity or serious political diplomacy, at least during Bush's first term in office.

These factors have given a boost to a new pan-Arabism today. It is a pan-Arabism of a much stronger Islamic or even Islamist hue fed by anti-Americanism. An ideology believed to be almost dead has returned to the political agenda with Washington's help. Arab politicians are exploiting it in order to distract people from their own contradictions, weaknesses, and unresolved problems.

Syria finds itself in this interplay of forces, in which the Baathists have to perform another ideological bridging feat. If they want to swim with the tide of Islamic neo-pan-Arabism, they will have to play down their secular concept of pan-Arabism that grants Islam a cultural role only. This shows how watered down—or flexible if expressed in positive terms—the Baath ideology has become.

The big question in Syria is: Will this neo-pan-Arabism cum anti-Americanism be sufficient to give Bashar al-Asad the backing he needs to negotiate the many crags of domestic and foreign policy that lie ahead of him? Or will pragmatism prevail in the end?

8

OPPOSITION, ISLAM,
AND THE REGIME

He took up office as a liberalizer. People were hopeful and many cheered in the streets. They were relieved to shake off his predecessor's authoritarian rule. The new statesman brought momentum to the economy by opening up the country, restricted the power of the secret services, eased the use of martial law, released political prisoners, held fair local elections, and promised further political liberalization in which other parties could also participate. The new president promised an alliance with the people and the restoration of the citizens' "freedom and dignity."[1] The term "Damascus Spring" made the rounds.

All this happened in late 1970 and early 1971. The new figure on which all hopes were pinned was Hafez al-Asad. The situation was repeated in 2000; this time the Great White Hope was Bashar al-Asad.

In both cases, disillusionment soon set in. But the difference is that hope has still not been abandoned in today's Syria. The tug-of-war between the hard-line Baathists and the liberalizers has yet to be decided. Furthermore, there has been movement in the foreign policy arena. Nevertheless, some observers are beginning to wonder if history is not repeating itself.

Dangerous parallels exist between the elder Asad's relationship with the opposition and his son Bashar's approach to his critics. In the 1990s, the Baathists systematically eliminated any moderate forces, as well as conservative Islamic ones such as the People's Party and the National Party. The strong Sunni urban bourgeoisie became politically homeless. "For this reason, the social base of the Muslim Brothers broadened considerably," concludes Lobmeyer. Hafez al-Asad lashed out and fought not only the Muslim Brothers but the secular opposition as well, eliminating them in 1980. For a while, the only option for opposing the regime was to support the radical Islamists.[2]

Today, it may prove to be a similar big mistake that Bashar has left moderate forces such as the Civil Society Movement out in the cold. Up to now, the regime has treated Islamists and secular opposition figures more or less the same, apart from some cyclical fluctuations. But, as in earlier times, the regime puts forward the fear of the Islamists as the reason for delaying the opening up of the country. The Damascus Spring of 2000-2001 may have presented a unique opportunity to bring the regime and the secular forces in the country closer together—but both sides missed it. The highbrow Civil Society Movement could have been strengthened and used as a counterforce to populist Islamists, which would have been in both Bashar and the reformers' interest.

The secularists

The opposition in Syria can be roughly divided into two currents: left-wing secular forces and Islamists of various nuances. The secular Civil Society Movement has already been frequently mentioned in this book, as it is the most talked about movement in the semi-public debate, and its members publish quite a lot. The movement is a kind of amorphous network of intellectuals, journalists, actors, doctors, attorneys, and professors with a colorful range of opinions. Nobody knows how many people support it. They use mobile phones in place of conferences, personal contacts instead of legal statutes, form working groups instead of boards of directors, and manage websites instead of index cards.

Especially after the arrest of several key activists during the Damascus Spring, Michel Kilo has filled the role of the Civil Society's spokesman. A Christian, Kilo studied several years in the northern German town of Münster and speaks fluent German. His philosophy of a grassroots democracy stems from that time, and he prefers a plethora of small initiatives to a large party, which makes persecution by the state machinery more difficult. The former communist describes himself as a humanist. "The regime has to accept that freedom is the greatest principle in life," he says. "In a modern society you can no longer separate state and society because the free human being is the central principle." Kilo is convinced that every ideological party in power will enter a period of crisis because real life is much more complicated than any *Weltanschauung*.

While Kilo has assumed the role of a front-line activist in writing petitions and articles, Sadiq Jalal al-Azm is more the philosophical mastermind of the movement. A Sunni by birth, Azm has a Marxist background and is known as the "Heretic of Damascus." A professor of philosophy who completed his doctorate at Yale University, where he also taught, Azm has stood for a strict separation of religion and state throughout his life. His father, who belonged to the high aristocracy of the Ottoman Empire, was an ardent supporter of Ataturk. Azm wrote about Immanuel Kant and called upon Arab Muslims to take the European Enlightenment as a model for their reforms. In 2005/06 he returned to the United States as a visiting professor at Princeton University.

Azm made most of his enemies after the Six Day War with *Self-Criticism*

After the Defeat, published in 1968. In the book, Azm held Muslim Arabs responsible for their disastrous defeat by Israel, blaming outmoded traditions, insufficient modernization, and a lack of societal progress. He also criticized the strong influence of conservative Islam that obstructed scientific learning. Finally, he accused the Arab states and societies of avoiding self-criticism. Only one year later his collection of essays titled *Critique of Religious Thought* (*Naqd al-Fikr al-Dini*) created one of the biggest literary scandals in modern Arab history. Azm lost his teaching position at the American University of Beirut and went to prison, but was freed after only a few days. The "Azm Affair" made him into one of the most controversial symbolic figures in the contemporary Arab world.[3]

Another ideologue of the Civil Society Movement is Ahmed Barkawi, professor of philosophy at the University of Damascus. He is the author of leading discussion papers about the path to freedom and democracy in Syria, the role of civil society, nationalism and democracy, women and democracy, and many other fundamental issues. The Civil Society Movement is supported by many nationalists, communists, and other left-wing groups—often splinter groups formed out of the bigger block parties that are coupled with the Baath Party in the National Front.[4]

Hardly had Baghdad fallen when the members of the Civil Society Movement saw their opportunity to turn up the heat in Damascus. Their first action was a petition, designed by Kilo, and presented to the president in May 2003. The text emphasized the new strategic "challenges and perils" for Syria following the occupation of Iraq. As a common denominator with the regime in Damascus, the opposition figures mentioned the "aggressive, racist, egotistical, and evil policies and ideology" of the Bush administration and Israel. "Honorable President," the petition continues, "our country faces this looming danger without being prepared for it. [Syria] must strengthen itself against [this danger] and enhance its ability to confront it, after having been weakened by cumulative mistakes that distanced the nation from public issues, exhausted the country and society, and exposed them [to dangers] like never before."[5]

The signatories call for "sweeping reforms," including the lifting of the state of emergency that has existed since 1963, curbing the power of the security machinery, permitting freedom of the press, freedom of speech, and freedom of assembly, as well as the freedom to be politically active, move around the country freely, and travel abroad. There was no official reply from Bashar.

The opposition continues to strive for a new Damascus Spring, and international pressure is providing them with arguments. In their petition, they call on the president to act before the United States does, arguing that only a free state is able to withstand such pressure from outside. There are indications that in this difficult situation the regime is seeking discussions with the Civil Society Movement, though on an unofficial level. Some members of the opposition report that attempts have been made to win them over as collaborators or to convince them of the wisdom of the government's policy. It is at present hard to judge if this is an attempt to co-opt parts of the opposition or a step toward greater intimidation.

Azm once received a personal summons from the head of the Mukhabarat, Suleiman. Azm's supporters reported the tenor of the meeting. "Syria is currently in greater danger than you think. You must rein in your criticism!" This message was a serious warning meant to reach the Civil Society Movement as a whole. The fate of Riad Seif and other prisoners of the opposition was ever-present. The regime tries to exploit the common denominator shared by government and opposition: the danger lurking from outside, the threat to the home country, pressure from the United States and Israel.

The regime blows hot and cold. At the moment when everybody is holding their breath, the opposition is suddenly given encouragement by the government. Michel Kilo has experienced this several times. In February 2004, a member of the regime close to the president called upon Kilo to publish his critical articles not only in Lebanese newspapers but also in Syrian ones. "He promised me that not a single word would be left out," rejoiced Kilo. In March 2004, he was allowed to appear on a talk show on Syrian television for the first time. He was filmed live as he criticized the delay in reforms in the presence of a government representative, saying that "Syria needs a different beginning than that of March 8," referring to the day in 1963 when the Baathists staged the coup and took power.

After the broadcast, Kilo was given a tumultuous welcome in the popular Café Rawda opposite the parliament building in the modern business quarter of Damascus. During countless evenings, the journalist meets there with various acquaintances and whiles away the hours with them at the small tables with the apple-tobacco scent of the waterpipes and the clicking of chess and backgammon pieces on wooden, mosaic game boards. The noise level is so high in the large, covered inner courtyard that a spy could scarcely eavesdrop. "People hugged me, clapped me on the shoulder, and kissed me when I came into the café," Kilo remembers. "They told me: 'You said exactly what we think. We would never have thought that one day we would see this on Syrian television.'" The program was not broadcast live, but nothing was cut. Then-Minister of Information Ahmed Hassan had taken full responsibility for the experiment. Kilo was pleased that afterward the state newspapers also jumped on the bandwagon and praised the critical discussion that had taken place on the talk show.[6]

Hassan also made it possible for a British-Syrian media conference to be held in April 2004 at the initiative of the BBC. Observers were surprised at the Syrian journalists' frankness and their cutting criticism of the situation in their country and of their own way of working. Journalists from the state media even expressed their criticism more sharply than some from the opposition.[7] After all, the dusty state media and the professionally disastrous regime reporters are to blame for the fact that almost all Syrians switch to satellite TV for their news. Nobody trusts information from the state channels anymore now that Al-Jazeera can be received in Syria.

The pressure is building to allow more freedom of speech, and it is coming from unexpected quarters. As already mentioned, Mahdi Dakhlalah, the former editor-in-chief of the state newspaper *al-Baath*, surprisingly underlined the importance of freedom of speech and human rights, though in harmony with the Syrian constitution. More importantly, he said that the Baath Party and the smaller parties in the National Front have to approach civil society. In the same month, the independent political magazine *Aswad wa Abyad* (Black and White) criticized the suppression of freedom of the press in Syria in a similarly blunt manner. The author of the magazine article stood up for a liberalization of the strict publishing laws. Shortly before that, the magazine had stuck out its neck by calling for the martial law to be eased. Interestingly, the paper is published by the son of the new defense minister, Hasan Turkmani.[8]

Fear of government reprisals for speaking your mind is fading and gradual concessions by the government are the rule of the day. This has led to the formation of new alliances. The secular opposition is marshalling its forces. At the beginning of 2005, twelve non-licensed parties and groups united to form a committee for the "national coordination of the defense of basic and human rights." Among them are members of the Civil Society Movement, human rights activists, communists, and Kurdish activists.[9] Without a doubt, the political debates in Syrian life have become more colorful and lively. Yet the opposition regards such surprising leeway with skepticism and sees it as a maneuver to distract attention from dictatorial government practices.

Apart from the Civil Society Movement, other Syrian opposition figures are operating abroad. Among them is Farid al-Ghadry, who plays more or less the same role as the dubious businessman Ahmad Chalabi did in Iraq before he fell into disgrace with the Americans. The thirty-five-year-old Ghadry has been built up by the United States as "the opposition leader" and the American media has promoted him. In Syria, on the other hand, the head of the Syrian Reform Party is barely known. So far he has no backing among the population or in other opposition groups at home. Some observers claim that Ghadry's father, Nihad, who publishes a newspaper and lives in Lebanon, has collaborated with the CIA. However, Nihad has fallen out with Farid over politics and says that his son was used by the United

States. Ghadry senior adds that Farid is so distant from Syrian affairs "that he thinks Aleppo is located in Sudan."[10]

Kilo gets angry when he speaks of the US-based Syrian opposition. "They want the same as we do, only under American patronage," he says tersely. Kilo would have preferred it if the Europeans had adopted this role.

Following the Iraq war, the opposition in exile has been gathering forces. In June 2004, the European Union organized a meeting of various groups and protagonists in Brussels, where Farid al-Ghadry acted as spokesman. This, in turn, affected the activists in Syria itself. "Because of it [the joining of forces abroad] our voice has become much louder and bolder," admits Kilo. "The regime will have to give us more leeway since they're afraid we'll join up with supporters abroad. We have threatened to do so. We have to become even more aggressive!" Kilo is convinced that the regime can take no action against the present leaders of the Civil Society Movement. "It would also strengthen the Syrian-American opposition. This is a battle that Bashar can't win."[11] On the other hand, by inviting Ghadry to a hearing in Brussels in mid-March 2005, the Europeans annoyed many Syrian opposition members, and the Syrian ambassador to the EU, who wanted to participate in the meeting, cancelled his visit in protest. "This was a big mistake," admits a European diplomat in Damascus regretfully.[12]

Despite such fickle relations between opposition figures in Syria and in exile, domestic activists continue to count on the indirect effect that the US-supported opposition abroad has on the regime in Damascus. They hope to profit from the fear of those in power that "it could be worse," and thus extract concessions. However, their agendas and personalities differ to such an extent that it is unlikely that they will join forces to topple the regime at home. The mistrust of the domestic opposition also arises from the fact that those in exile would likely take the leading positions in government if the Iraqi model of toppling the regime through US military intervention was followed.

By contrast, at home a historical step toward a more unified opposition has been achieved through the Damascus Declaration of October 16, 2005. For the first time, all major opposition groups—reaching from the secular Civil Society Movement to Kurdish activists, moderate Muslims, and even the outlawed Muslim Brotherhood in London—issued a broad call for democratic change in Syria. The lengthy document calls for an end to the emergency laws and other forms of political repression, for a national conference on democratic change, as well as for a constituent assembly that is to shape a new constitution "that foils adventurers and extremists."

The signatories bluntly condemn the policies of the regime "that have brought the country to a situation that calls for concern for its national safety and the fate of its people." They also criticize "the stifling isolation which the regime has brought upon the country as a result of its destructive, adventurous, and short-sighted policies on the Arab and regional levels, and especially in Lebanon." Directed at the Baathists as well as at radical Islamists, the document calls for "shunning totalitarian thought and severing all plans for exclusion" and underlines that "no party or trend has the right to claim an exceptional role. No one has the right to shun the other, persecute him, and usurp his right to existence, free expression, and participation in the homeland." The aim is the "adoption of democracy as a modern system that has universal values and bases, based on the principles of liberty, sovereignty of the people, a state of institutions, and the transfer of power through free and periodic elections that enable the people to hold those in power accountable and change them." The signatories do not intend to spur on a revolution but reach out to progressive forces of the present regime and invite them to take part in the proposed national conference for democratic change.

The Damascus Declaration calls for a "new social contract" which leads to a "modern democratic constitution that makes citizenship the criterion of affiliation, and adopts pluralism, the peaceful transfer of power, and the rule of law in a state all of whose citizens enjoy the same rights and have the same duties, regardless of race, religion, ethnicity, sect, or clan, and prevents the return of tyranny in new forms." The principles of that society ought to be "moderation, tolerance, and mutual interaction, free of fanaticism, violence, and exclusion, while having great concern for the respect of the beliefs, culture, and special characteristics of others, whatever their religious, confessional, and intellectual affiliations, and openness to new and contemporary cultures." Acknowledging the Muslim Brotherhood's contribution, the document reads: "Islam—which is the religion and ideology of the majority, with its lofty intentions, higher values, and tolerant canon law—is the more prominent cultural component in the life of the nation and the people."[13]

Regarding the broad alliance of highly heterogeneous signatories, the Damascus Declaration's far-reaching political demands, its conciliatory tone, its denouncement of any form of violence as well as social and political totalitarianism, particularly its vision and readiness to incorporate all kinds of "contemporary cultures" and beliefs, makes this document among the most remarkable papers of Arab political culture today. Beyond its humanistic and ideological value, however, it remains an open question whether the Declaration will have a political impact in Syria. Observers doubt that it has strengthened the opposition or that it represents a bulwark that could hold together the different oppositional streams if dramatic political change should occur. Already, only a few months later, the alliance between the defected Khaddam and Sheikh Bayanuni of the Muslim Brotherhood in

London has gained momentum since both participate in the new National Salvation Front that has become a rallying point for opposition figures in exile. This has driven a wedge between the groups within Syria, who despise Khaddam, and the exiled Brotherhood. The difficult rapprochement in the name of "national unity" between secular and moderate Muslim groups in the country and the Brotherhood in exile is about to be disrupted altogether. A unification of secularists, moderate Muslims, and the purged wing of the Muslim Brotherhood, which could have had a moderating effect and been a model for other Arab countries, looks less likely once again. The opposition remains fractured. Moreover, opposition figures abroad who are now about to rally behind the Khaddam-Bayanuni tandem will sabotage themselves and lose credibility at home.

By contrast, a boost for the local secular opposition in practical terms could turn out to be the release of Riad Seif and M'amoun al-Homsi in January 2006. Some already see a possible revival of the Damascus Spring. For hardly out of prison, Seif boldly announced the formation of a new political force under the name of National Liberal Party. The founding of an independent party (in parliament, at that time) was exactly the point where he had crossed the red line in 2001 and the reason why he was incarcerated. Déja-vu five years later: Seif is challenging Bashar. Now the president, who felt strong enough or pressed enough to release a key and charismatic opponent, must find a strategy to show that times have changed and that Syria is ripe for pluralism. He knows that a second arrest of Seif will not be possible without high political costs.

While defying Bashar and the Baath monopoly, Seif carefully follows the moderate line of the rest of the heterogeneous Civil Society Movement. In his first interview after his release he emphasized: "We honestly seek to change the regime in a very peaceful way…not by overthrowing the current regime. There are many clear indicators to the incapacity of the Syrian regime to go on or achieve reform. ... If President Bashar al-Asad decides to accept the change and real democracy, ... then the transition toward democracy would be easy, at a very low cost, and achievable by the end of his term in 2007. President Bashar al-Asad would go into history as the man who took a nationalistic [i.e. patriotic] position and spared his people from a lot of anguish."[14]

Even though the secular opposition has reinforced its ranks with Seif and Homsi, it still lacks organization, coherence, and broad popular following. Also, Seif as a businessman is not an undisputed figure among mostly highbrow intellectual Civil Society activists. A consensus on a roadmap for an efficient and prudent political transition is far from established. It will depend on both sides of the table if a transition can really be achieved at "low cost" as Seif hoped.

The Islamists

The most widely known Islamist group in Syria is the Muslim Brotherhood, the organization that had nearly driven the "Alawite heretic" Hafez al-Asad out of office. Since 1980, membership in the banned organization has been punishable by death. The leaders live in exile in Europe, but numerous sympathizers have sneaked into the Syrian system, among them intellectuals, members of the military, and even members of the Baath Party.[15]

As the Damascus Declaration demonstrated, some representatives of the Civil Society Movement and of today's Islamists are by no means irreconcilably opposed to each other. There are even regular personal contacts between them, as a member of the Civil Society Movement in Damascus told me. Islamists have also signed some of the secularists' previous petitions. They are both pursuing the same end: democracy, at least in words.

This surprising compatibility does not stem from opportunism only. There is also a more profound intellectual dynamic behind it, in contrast to the Kifaya Movement in Egypt where, since the end of 2004, hardcore Muslim Brothers and staunch secularists have marched side-by-side in the streets against Husni Mubarak's unending reign, but without any common goals beyond *kifaya!* (enough!) Another difference between Egypt and Syria is that Kifaya attacks the president directly, whereas in Syria this is still not the main focus of the opposition.

One reason why Civil Society activists and Islamists in Syria get along is that the Syrians have developed a movement of political Islam that is more moderate than in neighboring countries. Many people recall with horror the Muslim Brothers of twenty-five years ago and the situation in Syria that resembled a civil war. Radical Islamism would probably have no broad following in Syria, not even with the Sunnis, at least at present. Another reason lies in the many decades of secular experience under the Baath regime and earlier.

However, something extraordinary and seemingly contradictory is taking place under American pressure. For the first time since the 1982 bloodbath in Hama, the Syrian regime is cautiously seeking talks with the Muslim Brothers. True, Bashar stressed to American journalists in May 2004 that no apologies would be made for the action in Hama. Yet a month before, he had met with leading Islamists from neighboring countries who have connections with the Syrian Muslim Brothers. The late Mufti of Damascus, Ahmed Kuftaro, and a member of parliament, Muhammad al-Habash, acted as mediators. Reportedly, the government has meanwhile established contact with Syrian leaders of the Brotherhood. However, details are difficult to uncover because of the delicacy of such developments, and the information is partly contradictory as well.[16] At any rate, Habash is a leading advocate of abolishing the death penalty for members of the Muslim Brotherhood in the name of national unity.

Whatever the exact circumstances of these contacts, there are increasing indications that something remarkable is happening. The political scientist Salam Kawakibi sharply criticizes this move. "The regime is now doing all it can to survive. This includes approaching the Muslim Brothers. It is trying to curry favor with everyone except the secular Civil Society Movement. From the beginning the other secular forces have been the Baath Party's greatest enemies."[17] Some fear that the regime is slowly but surely abandoning the foundation of secularism in Syria. Observers see the temporary arrest of the intellectual Nabil Fayyad as one indication of the growing influence of Islamist forces on and within the government. Fayyad had written about the spread of radical Islamists in the country.

Bashar is playing with fire. Anti-Americanism and the isolation of the regime are bringing pan-Arabists and Islamists closer together. When it comes to foreign policy, the once-hated Alawites in the Damascus regime have become the Sunni extremists' best option. The Syrian ambassador to the United States, Imad Moustapha, who is known for unconventional statements, went even further than Bashar when he said what was previously inconceivable: Hama had been a "tragic event." It was not so long ago that the Syrian government had enveloped Hama in a mantle of silence. Moustapha's statement adopts a new tone that might be a small step toward national reconciliation. Many former members of the Muslim Brothers have been permitted to return to Syria after examination of their individual cases. However, one of the conditions for their return is that they must apologize for Hama.

Sheikh Ali Sadr ad-Din al-Bayanuni, who lives in London, has been head of the Syrian Muslim Brotherhood since 1996. Encouraged by the Damascus Spring, the movement published a statement in May 2001 that seemed to announce a significant change of direction. In it, the Muslim Brothers committed themselves to democracy, free elections, the primacy of law without reference to the Sharia, separation of powers, and a pluralistic modern state. "The time is gone when one party claims it is the homeland," the statement says, and goes on to assert that each party is entitled to present itself only in accordance with the power it has derived from free elections. The conflict between secular Arab nationalism and Islamism was "a stage in history that is now past."[18]

In an official statement the Syrian government declared that the Muslim Brothers only wanted to distract from their internal crisis, to create for themselves a new identity, and to regain influence in Syrian politics. The Islamists remained a "terrorist organization" who believed that there was now a political vacuum in the country that they hoped to fill.[19] That the Muslim Brothers had become active again after years of silence increased Bashar and the reformers' anxiety, who feared that their reform policy could get out of hand. Maybe this was the decisive reason why the Damascus Spring was ultimately crushed.

The parallels are striking. The Syrian Islamists were initially blamed for the bomb attack in Mezzeh in April 2004. An alternative theory was that the attack had been staged to conjure up the potential danger of Islamists. Members of the Civil Society Movement immediately feared that this could suffocate reform, similar to the Kurdish riots the previous month.

In August 2002, the Muslim Brothers met again in London to convert their 2001 statement into a national charter. Opposition figures from the left-wing and nationalist camps were present this time. However, the new document contained slight differences from the previous statement: the role of Islam with its "noble objectives, sublime values, and perfect legislation" was emphasized more strongly. The passage stating that Islam may also be understood merely as a "cultural affiliation" was deleted.[20] Such a statement would have meant that the Islamists were suddenly on the same wavelength as Baath founder Michel Aflaq!

In November 2005, al-Bayanuni reiterated his pragmatic stand and emphasized that the Muslim Brothers were not interested in a violent coup in Syria, nor in a revenge campaign against secularists and Alawites. "We want a civil and not a religious state," al-Bayanuni vowed.[21]

Pragmatism is nothing new for the Muslim Brothers. In the struggle against Hafez al-Asad, the Islamists had displayed contradictions and breaches in their ideology, although Asad himself was no more consistent. In the 1940s and 1950s, the Muslim Brotherhood sympathized with socialist ideas, even with secular elements of socialism, and later with a capitalist economic system coupled with the call for political liberties and human rights. It had the quite worldly objective of getting rid of a dictatorship in the interest of the bourgeoisie. Their arguments were influenced by the overall political mood of the time, and for strategic considerations.[22] Nowadays, the Muslim Brothers, not only in Syria but in almost all authoritarian Arab states, have discovered popular issues, most of which are commonly associated with Western-style democracy. They converge with the secularist opposition movements on four key issues: the call for human rights, emphasis on encompassing humanist elements in Islam, respect for an ideological and political pluralism, and the guarantee of freedom of speech.

This pragmatism has made the new Islamists acceptable to the rest of the opposition. The Christian Kilo even compares some of them to European Christian Democrats, or the ruling moderate Islamist party in Turkey, AKP

(Party for Justice and Development), under Prime Minister Erdogan. "I believe they are a moderate force with a strong democratic tendency," says Kilo. "Therefore we won't give the regime the chance to play us off against each other." The readiness for dialogue "is a basis for the time being to challenge the power of these people [the rulers]." Political change is the first priority. "If my opinion is the expression of a civil and secular democracy and theirs is an Islamic one, this is all right as long as we have democracy as a common denominator. We will accept the Muslims coming to power through elections, provided that they accept the democratic system."[23] Similarly, as Riad Seif put it after his release from prison: "We have no problems with Islamic groups and organizations. I mean when the Islamists become democrats, they won't frighten us anymore."[24]

Islamic currents in Syria have traditionally rejected the radicals in Saudi Arabia and elsewhere. Especially after the terrorist attacks on September 11, 2001, Kilo is convinced that "Saudi Arabia has no more credibility in the Islamic world." Neither does Iran serve as a model even for faithful Muslims. Sadiq al-Azm agrees. "Radical Islam has been in decline worldwide since September 11." This holds true for Syria as well. "If there were a regime change, a moderate Islam of the merchant middle class would prevail," Azm says. But only a strong civil society could act as a "shock-absorber" against conservative Islam and dampen the possible fears of religious minorities against oppression by the Islamic majority.

The pragmatist lawyer Anwar al-Bounni shares this view. "Of course, there is a danger when Islamists are allowed to return to the country. But the Syrians will not put up with a second dictatorship, with a transition from a nationalist to an Islamist one. Syrians don't want to become a second Afghanistan. I'm not afraid of the Muslim Brothers. Syrians have always had a loyal relationship among each other. Even if the Muslim Brothers came to power, they would not be as radical as in Egypt."[25]

Of course, Sadiq al-Azm admits that doubt exists. "But I think the risk is worth taking." The regime only uses the fear of radical Islam as an excuse for not changing anything in the encrusted system, he says.[26] Tayyeb Tizini goes a step further. "The regime has sometimes actively supported the Islamists because they wanted to keep them as a visible danger to the secular opposition: 'Just look, this is the danger. Either you have us or you get them.'"[27]

Azm's relaxed attitude toward political Islam is all the more remarkable since the philosopher has often disparagingly called Islam a "backward folklore" and repeatedly warned that "the Islamists are always in favor of democracy when they know they have the political majority behind them and against democracy when they are afraid of losing the elections." In Syria not only the Islamists but also the left-wingers have come a long way.

The moderate line taken by the Muslim Brothers' political leadership in London has also led to rifts in the movement itself with the political wing opposing the so-called Jihadis. While the moderates would even be willing to close ranks with the United States in order to put pressure on the regime in Damascus, the Jihadis, some of whom live in exile in Saudi Arabia, demand that anti-Americanism be more emphatically stressed than anti-secularism. One of the radical Jihadi figures is Sheikh Mohsen al-Qaqa who holds his hate sermons in an Aleppo suburb. He calls for an Islamic state in Syria and openly supports the Iraqi resistance to the United States. His CDs laced with anti-American slogans find an enthusiastic market in Baghdad and other Sunni cities in Iraq.[28]

The fundamental policy disputes among the Islamists are far from resolved. Meanwhile, the moderates get increasing support from Sunni entrepreneurs. Observers see this group distancing itself from the government because the latter can no longer ensure a profitable environment. The moderates are also turning away from Islamic rhetoric, realizing that it is not credible to pursue a policy of liberalization with Islamic populism that demonizes the West in general and the United States in particular. The more radical Muslim Brothers, for their part, no longer have their social base in the Sunni business class and are looking for support in the lower urban classes and the urbanized country population—exactly where the Baath Party had always anchored their social base!

Naturally, there is also disagreement within the Civil Society Movement about the question of how to assess the Muslim Brothers. Not everybody follows Kilo's strategy of chumming up with them. The economic historian Ali Saleh, for example, warns that "the risk of political Islamization will exist as long as the country doesn't have a secular constitution that is accepted also by the Islamic forces. As it was in Algeria, as soon as the Islamists come to power, they will want to have an Islamic state and an Islamic society because it's Allah that is the supreme master for them."

Already in the 1980s, Muslim Brother ideologists admitted that democracy was only a means to their ends. One of their leaders asserted that "the Islamists are fighting democracy in the world ... [but] democracy is a suitable means to prepare the way for an Islamist victory."[29]

Therefore, Saleh stresses that AKP politicians in Turkey are forced to keep to the laicist constitution, although they themselves may be strict Muslims. Unlike in Turkey, however, the Islamists in Syria have a leg up on the left-wing intellectuals. The Islamists have an already existing infrastructure of numerous Quranic schools and mosques. Meetings of more than five people in public places are forbidden by martial law. "This applies to us in the Civil Society Movement," says Saleh, a Sunni by birth. "But nobody forbids people to go to the mosques in crowds and assemble for talks."[30]

Even Christians and communists sometimes sneak into the Muslim Friday prayers just to meet unrecognized, and in large numbers, members of the opposition report.

Salam Kawakibi, who himself comes from a famous family of Islamic scholars, offers criticism. "Nowadays there are hundreds of mosques in Damascus but not a single meeting hall for secular people. This says everything. The truth about the Islamists will come out once they're in power." According to Kawakibi, they pretend to be moderate on the outside but they preach intolerance and missionary zeal inside the mosques. The problem is, he says, that the Islamic forces consist of two pillars: narrow-minded theologians and ignorant masses.[31] The secular historian Abdullah Hanna also warns that "the religious opposition is stronger than the secular one. At present, the Islamists are operating under the cover of a ritual exercise of religion. But the ground has been prepared for an explosion once the lid is lifted."[32] Tizini adds that "this state is a band of robbers. Of course, the Islamists would win [in the case of democratization] because they do everything for their masses. The state doesn't do anything."[33]

Indeed, the question must be asked: in the case of an abrupt regime change, who would be able to fill the power vacuum more quickly—a bunch of mainly elder intellectuals who represent Western secular philosophy and a modern civil society, or an Islamist movement, possibly supported by Saudi petro-dollars or by the more radical Muslim Brothers in Jordan and Egypt? If a violent upheaval takes place, those who seize the reins of power will write the constitution. In this case, it will not have a corrective function. This is an argument in favor of a cautious transition, which is what most Civil Society activists (and also moderate Muslims) are striving to achieve.

The new Islamic alternative

Apart from the purged Muslim Brothers, another Islamic force has surfaced in Syria that presents itself in an even more moderate manner. The focal point of this current is Sheikh Muhammad al-Habash, director of the Islamic Studies Center and grandson-in-law of the long-serving Mufti of Damascus, Ahmed Kuftaro.

In March 2003, Habash was elected to parliament with the largest number of votes among the independent candidates from Damascus, according to the official count. An Islamic scholar, Habash sees the late Kuftaro and himself as "chosen by God" to counteract religious fanaticism and intolerance, which he tries to convey to Muslims in his writings, with the help of appropriate *suras* (chapters) from the Quran. In Habash's view, state and society are in a "harmonious relationship" in "secular" Syria. Nevertheless, he complains that more radical forces are also gaining ground. They revile him as a heretic, sometimes as a Christian, and sometimes as a "secular Imam." Habash does not even find the last two titles offensive.

Habash draws his ideas about the renewal of Islam exclusively from the Islamic sphere itself. The forty-three-year-old scholar was educated in Quranic schools in Damascus, where he concentrated on recitation of the Quran. At the age of twenty, he started publishing writings on Islamic law, which distinguishes him from those past and present reformers who have tried to renew Islam using religious and non-religious elements.

The telephone is ringing constantly in Habash's office pavilion, located in the garden of his institute in the Rukneddin quarter of Damascus. The institute is humming with conferences, interviews, and publishing ventures. Habash is a man in great demand. Dressed in a dark suit, he sits in front of a wall of bookshelves filled with Islamic volumes with golden calligraphy on their spines. After the interruption of every telephone call, Habash picks up the thread of thought again exactly where he had left off.

"We regard Islam as one among many religions," he says, knowing that this provokes the ire of the largest number of Muslims. "We reject the idea that Islam has superseded all religions that existed before. We are against a monopoly of the doctrine of salvation. You are a good person when you do good, no matter in what religion." Even for moderate Muslims it is hard to swallow that redemption should be possible without believing in the prophet Muhammad, which is what Habash is implying.[34]

Habash just as boldly criticizes the schizophrenic Muslim view of women either as "saints or whores." According to him, this has a destructive impact on Muslim community life. Habash writes that women were endowed by God with intellectual and spiritual abilities that they should use freely, and that they should be able to decide their own fates and what happens to their bodies. Nevertheless, Habash conforms with Islamic restrictions such as no sex before marriage, no free social intercourse between the sexes, and "moderate clothing" for women.

Habash is convinced that Muslims can only correct their relationship with God if they change their relationships with other people. This contrasts with the belief of the extremists who try to fix their relationship with God by breaking off their connections with others who do not agree with such a monopolization of Islam, be they Muslims or non-Muslims. In Habash's view, only dialogue can rescue Islam from its internal crisis. Islamic critics accuse him of wanting to merge all types of faith into a new religion.[35]

Habash believes in an inclusive cosmos where everything is interrelated. This brings him close to Sufi-inspired teachings such as those of the great Islamic mystic and philosopher Ibn Arabi, who was born in Andalusia in

Spain in 1165 and died in Damascus in 1240. Habash's beliefs also evoke parallels to the Indian Mogul ruler Akbar (1556-1605), who strove for a lively spiritual exchange between the various religions in his kingdom and even envisaged a common religion, the "divine faith" (*ad-din al-ilahi*). Akbar, too, ceased to be regarded as a Muslim by many.[36]

Looking around the world today, there are several Islamic scholars who advocate dialogue between the religions and cultures as well as the importance of a secular state. Among these scholars are Abdul Rahman Wahid, the former president of Indonesia (1999-2001) and chairman of the Islamic organization *Nahdatul Ulama'* (Renaissance of the Religious Scholars).[37] Habash personally knows Wahid and other like-minded Islamic figures such as Iran's Shi'a philosopher Abdolkarim Soroush or Turkish Prime Minister Erdogan. "We consider ourselves of the same stream of renewal," Habash says. "We have individual connections but we don't form a big common movement. Our main focus in Syria is domestic politics."

Habash himself likens his ideas to those of the European Enlightenment. Whereas early Islamic pantheism defined human beings as Allah's passive creatures, Habash is among the ranks of rational Islamic thinkers, such as the Mutazilites, who ascribe to human beings a large amount of freedom to determine their individual fates.[38] Democracy is Habash's political objective. But in his view caution should be exercised on the way toward it: "Our priority is to bring about an Islamic renewal before we move toward democracy. We have to first correct our ideas of Islam."

The Islamic faith is a "collection of ideas over the course of history," says Habash. "We can choose from a large number of ideas." According to him, conservative Muslims interpret the Quran selectively for their purposes. Habash has particular aversions to Saudi Arabia, which in his opinion sends a radical message of Islam out to the world. In a letter to Crown Prince Abdullah in April 2005, Habash expressed his frustration over a new translation of the Quran published in the birthplace of the Prophet that uses the most radical way "out of more than one million traditions" of interpreting the *suras* and *hadiths*. "Why do we translate the Quran in such a way and then send it to England or the United States? If Westerners read this, of course they will want to fight us," he says scornfully. "The misunderstanding of Islam is not only the fault of the Western people, but also Muslims' responsibility when we convey a misguided understanding of Islam."[39]

His pragmatic interpretation of Islam had even alienated Habash from Kuftaro, who died on September 1, 2004, at the age of eighty-nine. Kuftaro had issued a written statement saying that Habash no longer spoke for him. Habash attributes this to the "conservative people" around the Mufti in his old age. Other voices had also expressed the criticism that Kuftaro was spreading an increasingly conservative brand of Sunni Islam. He had also called upon Muslims worldwide "to use all means and martyrdom operations to defeat the American, British, and Zionist aggression on Iraq."[40] Thus, Kuftaro had once more shown himself true to the political line of the Syrian regime.

Habash, on the other hand, is even "more secular" than the Syrian constitution, for he rejects the Sharia as a law for everyday life. The Syrians have always been a people with a will of their own, he says, as shown by the difficulty the French had in establishing colonial rule. "Now we have the risk of another kind of colonization: Islamist movements from outside."

Two things are especially important for Habash. First, the state should remain neutral and not dictate to its citizens any public dress code, including the veil. Second, radicals have misinterpreted the Islamic jihad, which in fact merely means defending oneself, one's family, and one's homeland, not fighting other religions and forcing their members to convert to Islam.

On the one hand, Habash thinks in the cultural and dogmatic paradigms of Islam. In one of his books, he condemns the West's "spiritual emptiness" and idealizes Islamic societies as "clean areas" with peace, no crime, alcohol, or rape. On the other hand, he also expresses sharp criticism about Muslims in the West who see their host countries as "a pasture for their lusts and desires and a market for their profits, without feeling loyalty toward the land that protects or welcomes them."[41] On the one hand, Habash hopes for a growing Islamic influence in Europe. On the other hand, he preaches tolerance and rejects religious zeal. Habash regularly holds religious services in the Az-Zahara Mosque in Mezzeh and is pleased about the good attendance. "More than five thousand people come every Friday."

One of his mentors is Jawdat Said, a liberal sheikh from the Quneitra region. This popular old man, whose trademark is a pointed fur hat, champions vehemently for democracy, even if the Syrian majority would decide against an Islamic form of society. He likes to use the European Union as a model for the open dialogue between peoples and a balance of interests between the various countries. According to him, the Arab world should take the EU as an example of how to live in peaceful coexistence with ones neighbors instead of fighting with each other. "We need education, not nuclear bombs," Said insists. "We must use our brains and the Internet, not weapons." The old sheikh runs his own website. He is a humanist through and through who likes to refer to Plato's cave parable in conversation, where the human being frees himself from darkness and sees the light of truth at the end of a difficult path. Said opposes the dogmas of monotheistic religions. At the same time, he openly says how disappointed he is with the US and also with the Europeans who were once "the nation of discoverers and thinkers." With regard to the current Middle East policy of Western countries in Iraq and Israel, the old man laments that "today there are no more values. Only muscles and violence count." This applies to both sides, he says self-critically. The phenomenon of Islamic violence is the result of an unresolved intellectual crisis in the Islamic world, Said holds.[42]

In the moderate Islamic camp, there are also businessmen pressing for an economic opening up of the country. One of their spokesmen is Ihsan Sanqer. "In Syria conservative Islam is only a reaction to socialism, a reaction to the regime," he says. "It doesn't belong to our culture." The stocky, energetic, almost bald fifty-one-year-old runs a financial empire with his family in Damascus. He is an agent for DaimlerChrysler, Porsche, Siemens Nixdorf, and other international firms in Syria, and owns a food-processing company. When the corrupt regime protégé and businessman Rami Makhlouf schemed to take over the Mercedes agency, the Stuttgart company backed Sanqer. DaimlerChrysler accepted the consequences and was barred from importing new cars to Syria for a period of three years. Officially, the ban was lifted in January 2005, and the Sanqer family was supposed to be able to deal once again with the limousines with the Mercedes star. It seemed that the businessman had won a long legal dispute. But "administrative burdens" and sudden "new taxes" imposed on Sanqer have prolonged this war of nerves. It is difficult to advance in Syria once one is a public enemy of the Makhloufs.

Certificates, pictures of Syria's sights, and a photo showing Sanqer with Hafez al-Asad hang next to the heavy bookcase in Sanqer's office in the central Damascus quarter of Baramke. The businessman occupied an independent seat in parliament from 1990 to 1998. He is a committed supporter of a social market economy. "When I read German post-war history and Ludwig Erhard's concepts, it reminds me of our history," he says, alluding to the German minister of economy and later chancellor, who has become a symbol of the model of the social market economy and the economic boom in Germany in the 1960s. "This is in line with our culture."

The word "culture"—above all with an Islamic connotation—frequently occurs in his lively flow of speech. Sanqer holds that something of this culture should resurface in politics. "Turkey is a very good example for the whole of the Middle East," Sanqer is convinced, looking at the AKP government. "For this model doesn't leave religious people abandoned but gives them a political umbrella. Like the Christian Democrats in Europe, these forces can absorb the conservatives. This has nothing to do with Islamic fundamentalism. On the contrary, they can draw the Muslim population into the moderate center." Syria, too, needs such a party to compete with the Baath, says Sanqer. Islam might be an integrating factor: the mostly

Sunni Kurds, who feel excluded by the pan-Arab ideology, could find their
political home in such a party. Sanqer hastens to say that the party should
be so moderate that it could also attract Christians. "My feeling is that
the president wants to allow such a party but he isn't able to because the
pressure from outside is so great at the moment." No doubt about who
would found and lead such a party—Sanqer himself. "I'm just waiting for
the chance, for I don't want to burn myself too early," he says impishly and
quotes an Arab proverb. "Put the honey in the store so that it increases in
value." One like Riad Seif was enough to overstretch the bow during the
Damascus Spring.

Sanqer stresses that he certainly favors reforms. "But here we have the
problem that people still act too much with emotions. This is dangerous."
In such a society, democracy must come slowly and from above to guarantee
a "soft landing." The businessman shows a great grasp of reality when he
insists that "we have to carry out reforms before there is peace between
Israel and the Palestinians so that we are prepared. For it will only be after
peace that the economic problems will begin."[43]

Habash, Said, and Sanqer are friends and support each other politically.
They also have contact with Civil Society activists on the other side of
the political spectrum. Both sides invite each other to meetings and give
each other space in their publications. Habash's position in relation to the
government is typically ambivalent. On the one hand, his institute works
illegally because the Baath ideology allows no room for such Civil Society
institutions outside the official associations. On the other hand, he has
"good relations" with the government, he says. Habash sees himself as
following the same line as the president with respect to democracy as his
long-term goal (this is where he differs from the Civil Society Movement
who want it faster) and in the fight against radicals.

Sheikh Habash is definitely a person with a sense of power. Sharp
tongues have even called him Machiavellian. In order to gain influence,
he does not shy away from making pacts with those in power. In the
parliamentary election in 2003, Habash snubbed supporters by forming
an alliance with a list of candidates with well-known associations among
the parasitic business class. Muhammad Hamsho, a former teacher who
became rich with a range of firms that supply state institutions, was also
on the list. Hamsho represents the mobile phone manufacturers Sony and
Ericsson in Syria, among other companies. During the elections, Hamsho
promised a free mobile phone to anyone who delivered a certain number
of voters for him.

Skeptics see both the Great Mufti and Habash as the regime's accomplices.
With the Kurdish Kuftaro, who was the state-recognized authority of
the Syrian Sunnis from 1965 on, the ruling Alawites tried to whitewash

themselves of the charge of neglecting Islam, to shake off their heretical image among Sunnis, and to broaden their constituency. The Asads could always count on Kuftaro. In 1991, the sheikh declared the reelection of the president to be a "national obligation and religious duty."[44] Habash is also welcome to the Baathists since he emphasizes the national Arab character of Islam, unlike Sanqer, for example. Thus, Habash strengthens the historically weak link between religion and pan-Arab nationalism.[45] Similarly, Kuftaro's successor, Ahmad Badr Eddin Hassoun, has signaled a willingness to bridge the gap between Arab nationalism and Islam, playing into the hands of the Baathists' present agenda.

However, despite all criticism, it can be considered progress that the Baathists—for whatever reasons—have created an environment where such a liberal Islam has not only established strong institutions but has also found committed followers. This is a valuable social and political asset, especially since 9/11.

Hassoun seems to be more progressive than the old Kuftaro. When Hassoun took office in July 2005, he criticized the kidnappings and suicide attacks in Iraq. Within the Syrian *ulam'a* he is not alone in this opinion. Already in January 2004, the Syrian Islamic scholar and university professor Muhammad Said al-Bouti made a controversial statement, describing the killing of American civilians as "un-Islamic" and the calling for the death of Americans as "ignorant." Bouti, too, wants to found an Islamic political party, but the regime has so far refused to allow him to do so.[46] Some consider him to be too conservative. Yet another protagonist, the Syrian author and engineer Muhammad Shahrur, uses very moderate arguments. He calls for the Quran to be interpreted in a new and pragmatic way for each epoch instead of centuries-old interpretations being constantly held up as eternal truths.

In the case of a political change or an opening-up of the system, sympathizers of Habash, Hassoun, Sanqer, or perhaps even Bouti, who are not strained by a past record of radicalism and violence like the Muslim Brothers, could actually become the true Islamic "Christian Democrats." Habash estimates that half of the Syrian population is secular-minded and the other half is religious. According to him, 80 percent of the religious Muslims are conservative, 20 percent identify with the "enlightened trend," and 2 percent are radicals of whom less than 1 percent are ready to use violence.

Thus, a moderate Islamic party would have the potential and also the ability to catch traditional Muslims before they turn to more radical pied pipers. The party would have appeal for those who are looking for some connection to Islam in politics without wanting to Islamicize politics. This is the constituency to which the "infidel," secular Civil Society activists could hardly appeal.

Habash has started political efforts to create inroads into the large conservative crowd. In April 2005, he stood for election as the president of the conservative Syrian League of Islamic Scholars (*rabitat al-ulama*). To his own surprise, and the surprise of others, he was elected. Habash's explanation is interesting. "The conservative direction in Syria has no political agenda at all. They prepare for life after death and observe strict traditions and values. That's all. It's very easy to influence the conservative direction in favor of Islamic renewal. But they can as easily turn to Islamic radicals for the same reason!"[47]

With pressure on the regime increasing, the status quo only benefits radical Islamists. The government is playing with fire by suppressing Islamic initiatives across the board, including on a local level, for at the same time it is making concessions to radical preachers who are stirring up hatred against Western politics. How long will the regime be able to play with Islam without losing control? They don't have to permit any exclusively ethnic or religious parties that would quickly tear any political community apart. Yet new ways are needed to give a fresh social and political value to moderate Islam in Syria in order to provide a counterweight to the radicals. Possibly the Baathists are more afraid of the moderates becoming a strong force than of the extremists who serve as a welcome deterrent.

9

SYRIA THE ROGUE STATE?

The Palestinian issue

As dawn breaks, a rumble drifts over the desert, quickly approaching. The hands of the clock show 4:30 AM on October 5, 2003. Two F-16 jet fighters fly over the border of the Golan Heights and reach the Syrian capital in less than half a minute. People are fast asleep, including in the town of Ain Saheb. The Israeli pilots fire three missiles into the small town, only fifteen kilometers north of Damascus, then turn back and disappear as fast as they had come. One person is injured. It is the first time in thirty years that Israel had attacked Syrian core territory.

At 2:14 PM the day before, Hanadi Jaradat, a pretty Palestinian lawyer, had buckled on a belt loaded with explosives and had gone to the Maxim beach café in the northern Israeli city of Haifa. There the twenty-nine-year-old in jeans and head scarf pulled the ignition, killing herself and twenty-one other people, including two families spanning three generations, three children, and a baby. Five months earlier, Hanadi had lost her brother in the West Bank city of Jenin. Her lover had also been killed by Israeli soldiers for coordinating an attack on Jewish settlers.[1]

What did the incidents in Ain Saheb and Haifa have in common? Israel took the suicide attack as an occasion to establish a direct link to Damascus. As Israel and the United States read it, Palestinian attacks are planned in Syria and assassins trained there. In the Israeli government's view, this must also have been the case with Hanadi. The spiral of violence had assumed interstate dimensions. For a moment in October 2003, observers feared that a new war between Syria and Israel could no longer be ruled out. Press releases from the Israeli government ticked away on fax machines in the offices of correspondents. The statements claimed that the missiles had hit a training camp of the Islamic Jihad. Israel had the right to take measures in "preventive defense." The Syrian authorities hushed everything up. The terrain, now with a gaping crater in the ground, was cordoned off. Not until a week later did the Syrian government hold a press conference. By that time, hardly anyone was interested in the subject anymore—a typical example of the lost media war.

In reality, the rockets fell on a long-abandoned camp where members of the General Commando of the left-wing Popular Front for the Liberation of Palestine (PFLP-GC) used to train. It had since been turned into a sports ground, where children took swimming lessons, residents of Ain Saheb reported.[2] The camp had not been used to train Palestinians for several years. Israel merely wanted to teach the Syrians a lesson and demonstrate their vulnerability. At the same time, Israeli Prime Minister Sharon presented a map of Damascus and announced that more attacks would follow on targets in the Syrian capital. As he put it, he intended to destroy the offices of Palestinian organizations in Damascus in the same way it had been done in the West Bank or in Gaza. A few weeks before the attack on Ain Saheb, Israeli jets had attacked Syrian positions in Lebanon and had flown low over Bashar's summer residence in the Syrian coastal town of Lathakia. The examples of humiliation do not stop there. US troops destroyed the Syrian trading center in Baghdad during the war and even encroached on Syrian territory in June 2003, taking Syrian soldiers to Iraq as prisoners.

It is true that the Syrian regime sees itself as an advocate for the Palestinian cause and sometimes uses aggressive rhetoric. As previously mentioned, Syria grants hospitality and freedom of movement to members of Palestinian organizations such as Hamas, Islamic Jihad, and the PFLP. These groups have established a network of hospitals, schools, and welfare institutions for Palestinian refugees in Syria. However, this does not necessarily mean that Damascus has become the center of command for suicide attacks in Israel. Any evidence is lacking so far. In fact, there is always some residual uncertainty as Syria treats military matters with the utmost secrecy. But if Israel had had a better target, it certainly would not have fired on Ain Saheb. Based on the present level of knowledge, the regime in Damascus can no longer be charged with systematically training Palestinian "terrorists" or "resistance fighters" as it did in the past. A woman like Hanadi does not need training in Syria when her life is marked by the cruelties of the Israeli occupying forces, the spiral of violence of the Intifada, and radical Islamist slogans about paradisiacal martyrdom. It does not require sophisticated training to pull the trigger on a belt of explosives.

On the other hand, the Syrian regime has taken every opportunity possible during the past thirty years to create a fog of anti-Israeli propaganda. Thus, in parallel to the hardliners in Israel, the Syrian regime has built an atmosphere that has created considerable obstacles to peace between the peoples of the region. An example is Syria's school textbooks, which describe Zionism across the board as racism without going into the various historical currents in Jewish nationalism such as early socialism or Marxist Zionism. Anti-Semitic clichés and conspiracy theories about Judaism can be found in the books, as well as the statement that Zionism is the real reason for Arab backwardness and the prevention of pan-Arab unity. The books also contain a glorification of the martyr's death in the "holy war" against Israel. This is a grotesque manipulation since these Islamist ideas conflict with the secular Baath ideology.[3]

It is equally contradictory that, on the one hand, the textbooks speak about the relentless struggle against Israel until all land that was unlawfully taken is returned to the Arabs, while on the other hand they describe peace with Israel—as long as it is "comprehensive and fair"—as Syria's "strategic choice." This could be interpreted in such a way as to pave the way to new circumstances, such as peace negotiations with the supposed archenemy, in the minds of the next generation. Incidentally, in 2004 the eight block parties in the National Front under the leadership of the Baath Party proposed deleting the section in the Front's National Charter that prohibits negotiations with Israel or a recognition of the Israeli state. Instead, reference is made to UN resolutions, the Madrid peace process, and even the wish for peace with Israel. Furthermore, the proposal suggests that the term "war economy" should be replaced by "economic growth" in the charter and the "unitary" political structure of the country replaced by a "pluralistic" one.[4]

It must be pointed out as well that the so-called regional peace process, starting with the Madrid conference in 1991, has found a place in more recent school textbooks in Syria. But the books also contain the criticism that the United States is using this opportunity to give Israel preferential treatment. Only since 1991 have the Syrian textbook authors used the name "Israel" rather than "Zionist entity." In contrast, the elder Asad since the 1970s had insisted on calling Israel by its name and had never questioned its sovereignty, even in interviews with the Syrian military magazine *Jaish as-Shaab* (People's Army). This is a remarkable contrast to the official former Baath wording.[5]

In a nutshell, the new school textbooks use a more conciliatory language than their predecessors. Even when the authors complain that the United States misuses the term "terrorism" and that the Zionist occupation violates international law, they do not represent a particularly aggressive or exclusive Syrian position.[6]

What propaganda sticks in peoples' heads depends on a variety of factors. Young Syrians, whose modern world consists mainly of satellite television, speak with a touch of humor about their education at school and university. "I'm good at lying," one student told me. "That's why I always got top grades in 'nationalism.'" After numerous conversations, it became clear to me that many people see through the Baathist propaganda or even reject it. Stirring up hatred in school textbooks is one of the greatest dangers for long-term peace. But propaganda does not necessarily translate into public opinion out-and-out, and certainly not when the state has lost its monopoly over the media through satellites and the Internet. Even Israeli television can be received without problem in Damascus, and Jews watch the news in Hebrew every day. Many Syrians have been exposed to a traditional Islamic education and therefore do not know religious hatred for Jews, but rather integrate them into their worldview as an ancient scriptural religion. They separate this fact surprisingly clearly from Zionism as a worldly, modern, and political problem in spite of the cruel pictures that emanate from the Occupied Territories each day.

Since 1979, Syria has continually been on the United States' black list of countries. Syria is a "supporter of terrorism" in the eyes of many other Western states as well. But, paradoxically, Syria is the only "rogue state" with which Washington has normal diplomatic relations and from time to time even exchange political opinion at a high level. This is despite the fact that President Bush counts Syria as part of his extended "axis of evil."

The problem of assessing Syria as a "rogue state" is twofold. Part of the issue has to do with distinguishing the past from the present. The Baath regime does have a record of proxy wars and international terrorism, but the last incident took place twenty years ago. Some actions subsumed under terrorism were supported by secular-nationalist Palestinian groups who conducted attacks against Arafat's PLO in the late 1970s and early 1980s. Moreover, Syria linked up with both radical Palestinian and Lebanese groups in Lebanon who carried out attacks against Lebanese, Israeli, and Western targets following Israel's invasion of Lebanon in 1982. This was to prevent the Lebanese government from signing a peace treaty with Israel. After Israel provoked Syria by intercepting an airliner carrying Syrian officers and shooting down two Syrian fighters in Syrian airspace in 1985, Asad attempted to blow up Israeli jetliners at airports in London and Madrid in 1986. Both operations failed and caused severe international reactions. After that, Asad followed a more indirect approach.[7]

The second problem in assessing Syria is the fact of widely varying definitions of the term "terrorism." The definition is far from clarified despite several political and scholarly attempts worldwide.[8] Israel's cleverest move after 9/11 was to extend the term to include anything connected with Palestinian resistance—even when such a resistance is directed at an occupation that violates international law and does *not* exclusively consist of suicide attacks against Israeli civilians. With this use of rhetoric, the Israeli side has managed to drive their archenemy Syria into a corner on the international level.

The ideology of the regime in Damascus is diametrically opposed to that of Sunni Islamist movements such as Hamas. Hamas developed out of the Palestinian Muslim Brothers, who at that time were supported by

Israel as a counterforce to Arafat's PLO in an attempt to drive a wedge between the Palestinians. Hamas was not even allowed to open an "agency" in Damascus until a few years ago. As mentioned, Syria has for many years made great efforts to combat the activities of Islamic extremists. Instead of making use of these fundamental differences, the United States and Israel have brought Islamist forces and the Syrian regime closer together—even Hamas, the secular PLO, and other Palestinian groups in Damascus—by condemning all of them across the board as terrorists and, at the same time, narrowing political options for Syria. After Arafat's death, the joining of forces between different Palestinian groups with diverging ideological outlooks was sealed with the Cairo Declaration in March 2005. The groups agreed to develop the PLO to include all factions and as the sole legitimate representative of the Palestinian people. This aim, of course, was challenged by the sweeping victory of Hamas in the Palestinian parliamentary elections in January 2006.

The bonding between Damascus and Palestinian groups is one reason why the new Hamas leader Khalid Mash'al could feel relatively safe in Syria after the murder of his predecessor. "Syria has adopted a courageous attitude," he said frankly in an interview at the end of April 2004. "It isn't putting any pressure on us."[9] This changed, however, after Syria felt more pressure regarding Lebanon, and after a Palestinian suicide attack took place in the Negev desert on September 1, 2004, for which Israel again threatened Syria with retaliation. Three days later, Mash'al was reported to have left Syria, although the government denied any official order expelling the Hamas leader.[10] Meanwhile, Mash'al has again made public appearances in Damascus.

In the rapprochement between Syrian secularists and Palestinian Islamists the Palestinian cause is more than ever a unifying bond. For the former it is a vehicle for legitimizing Syria's domestic policy and a welcome opportunity to use pan-Arabic phrase-mongering. For the latter the worldly nationalist struggle is a means of reinforcing the ideological religious agenda of Islam. For both it has become a synonym for a new anti-Americanism.

The rhetoric from Washington that puts the Syrian regime, the Palestinians, and al-Qaida into one boat of "global terrorism" is far off the mark. This is a kind of propaganda that had already proved to have little substance in Iraq—although it became a self-fulfilling prophecy in the post-war chaos (even the official US report of the 9/11 Commission finally conceded that there was "no evidence" of a "collaborative operational relationship" between al-Qaida and Iraq. "Nor have we seen evidence," it continues, "that Iraq cooperated with al-Qaida in developing or carrying out any attacks against the United States").[11] On the contrary, Syria has long been cooperating with the US secret service, especially after the 9/11 attacks. It was no coincidence that George Tenet, who resigned from his position as head of the CIA, was, with his organization, one of the few moderating voices with regard to the Syrian regime within the US administration. Many long-wanted terrorists and Iraqi Baath members were caught with the help of Syria. On at least three occasions, Damascus has furnished information that prevented terrorist attacks against US interests, including planned strikes against Navy bases in the Middle East. Al-Qaida has issued a warning to its members not to travel through Syria since the risk of arrest or having large sums of money confiscated is too high.[12]

Just a year after the attacks in New York and Washington, the US State Department praised Syria for having saved "American lives." After that, the relationship again cooled down. Washington complained that the source of information in Damascus was drying up. It is not surprising that Syria was not too enthusiastic about cooperating in the "war on terrorism" with a country that reviled it as being "terrorist" itself. Snubbed, Syria finally broke off any intelligence collaboration with the United States in May 2005 (the Syrian embassy in Washington said that it was the US government that was no longer interested). Only two months before, Damascus had handed over Saddam Hussein's feared half-brother, Sabawi Ibrahim al-Hassan, in an effort to appease the United States after the Hariri killing. At the end of April, Syria formally acceded to a UN treaty designed to cut off funding for "terrorist activities." And at the beginning of 2005, the government was reported to have closed two al-Qaida facilities in Aleppo and Homs run by sheikhs.[13]

Washington has not understood how to separate the fight against fundamentalist al-Qaida terrorism from the Palestinian Intifada. The United States has been roped in by Israel in this matter and, at the same time, has fallen right into Usama bin Laden's trap. During most of his life, bin Laden had not shown any great interest in Palestine. However, he used the one-sided US Middle East policy, among other things, to justify the 9/11 attacks. In the fight against al-Qaida terrorism, Washington has estranged valuable allies, among them Syria.

Iraq and the border issue

It is certain that arms were supplied by—or at least through—Syria to Saddam Hussein's regime before the war in Iraq. Even a cousin of the Syrian president was arrested in Paris and extradited to Syria on charges of arms smuggling. Bashar reacted swiftly: he had him put under house arrest and gave orders for his cousin's arms cache in Lathakia to be destroyed by tanks.[14] However, supplying arms can hardly be defined as terrorism, and many Western states have done the same. It may be called "supporting terrorist regimes," which would in the case of Iraq also apply to Western countries, including the United States, at least periodically.

It is true that no other Arab head of state has criticized the United States' Iraq policy as harshly as Bashar, who even called the violence of Iraqi rebels "legitimate resistance."[15] This was open provocation for the stumbling occupiers and poured fuel on the flames. Moreover, Iraqi rebels now and again flee from US troops into Syrian territory. It is no secret that both Islamist and pan-Arab activists from Syria infiltrate Iraq to fight there (unofficial sources speak of some fifteen thousand and Syrian sources of about three thousand.) Officers in the Syrian intelligence service are said to have taken bribes from fighters in exchange for allowing them to enter Iraq.[16] The US administration accused the Iraqi embassy in Damascus of issuing cheap visas to fighters. According to the Americans, the Iraqi diplomats in Syria have been reluctant to recognize the new order in Baghdad.[17]

However, there is no indication that the Syrian government systematically sends "terrorists" or "resistance fighters" to Iraq as a matter of policy. Instead, Syrian troops have built a sand wall along the border. Many people have been arrested when trying to cross the border or after their return from Iraq. Several Arab nationals have also been held and deported to their home countries. Within Syria, Islamists can only be active at great risk to themselves, so they would rather take their chances in Iraq. This issue illustrates how external pressure dovetails with domestic politics. The Syrian government has to weigh costs and benefits. Because of its compromised position, the government cannot afford to make more enemies on the domestic front than it already has. Thus its hands are tied in clamping down more harshly on radical elements in Syrian society. This affects many aspects of life and politics in Syria today. With regard to the border issue, one can fairly guess that the government does not go beyond certain efforts to curtail the movements of extremists, preferring to see radical Islamists and thugs leave Syria before they mess up things at home. Some cynics also point out that US troops even perform a valuable service for Damascus by killing the radicals for them. At the same time, the government in Damascus admits that the six hundred-kilometer-long desert border to Iraq cannot be made watertight.

After the creation of Arab nation-states, members of the same or affiliated tribes still cross this desert strip in regular course. In his speech before parliament on March 5, 2005, Bashar complained that the United States demanded the impossible from Syria. "Of course we don't claim that the borders are completely controlled. Usually, the Americans say they cannot control their borders with Mexico. Yet, they tell us to control our borders. It's a strange argument."

Syria has not been obstinate or resentful in spite of all its bitterness and criticism of US policy in Iraq. After the United States withdrew its administration from the Tigris in the summer of 2004, the ice began to thaw between Damascus and Baghdad. It was by no means a matter of course that Syria would recognize the new Iraqi government so soon, but the pragmatists prevailed. When the temporary Iraqi Prime Minister Iyad Allawi visited Damascus in July 2004 for the first time, the two sides agreed on a resumption of diplomatic relations, which had been broken off in 1982. Asad and Allawi set up a joint committee to improve the controls of their shared state borders. A railway connection is planned to be opened again between Aleppo and Mosul. At the end of September 2004, an Iraqi aircraft landed at Damascus airport for the first time in twenty-two years. In January 2005, the regime even permitted exiled Iraqis to vote in the first democratic Iraqi elections—while residing within the Syrian dictatorship. Some twenty thousand Iraqis made use of this opportunity.

Interestingly, the government in Damascus has adopted a less ideological stance than some of the opposition, who wrote a letter of protest over Allawi's first visit to Syria, saying that Iraq was the tool of an occupying power, controlled by the Americans, the Israelis, and foreign secret services. Michel Kilo and Haitham Maleh were among the signatories.

The Golan and Lebanon

Syria's link to the Shiite organization Hezbollah in Lebanon is another thorn in the side of Western politicians when it comes to the discussion about "terrorism." According to Damascus, Syrians only grant "moral support" to the organization. But in reality Syria is the hub for arms supplies from Iran to Shiite fighters. Hezbollah was founded as a response to the Israeli invasion of Lebanon in 1982 and is supported by Iran in particular.

One argument from Damascus to justify its support of Hezbollah is the continuing Israeli occupation of a tongue of land, the Sheb'a farms in southeast Lebanon. The twenty-six square kilometers of land is Syrian territory that was occupied by Israel when it took the Golan Heights. That is why Israeli troops kept the farms when they withdrew from southern Lebanon in 2000. But the Sheb'a farms are only a pretext that Israel could easily invalidate by withdrawing its troops from this tiny piece of land, especially because Syria has toyed with the idea of handing it over to Lebanon as part of a new border agreement.[18]

It was a clever strategy on the part of the elder Asad to stand up to Israel in a proxy war in southern Lebanon with the aid of the Hezbollah militia, without entering into direct conflict with its neighbor, who is clearly superior in military terms. At the same time, Syria is the only regional power that is able to control Hezbollah. Bashar has continued this policy. Hafez al-Asad was highly indebted to the Shiites. After the coup that brought him to power in 1971, he received a religious legal statement (*fatwa*) from the Shiite High Council, led by Musa Sadr, confirming that Alawites are Muslims. This was significant because many Sunnis consider Alawites to be heretics, and the Syrian constitution insists that the president be Muslim.[19]

In the past few years, Hezbollah has concentrated on Lebanon and branched out far into society by providing welfare organizations and social services that the weak and fragmented state cannot deliver. In 1992, the Party of God (*hizb 'allah*) entered parliament and took part in elections recognized by the West as democratic. Hezbollah's participation in politics presents a dilemma for the West. How can democratic states such as the United States or Israel ignore other peoples' democratic wills and dismiss their choices in general as "supporting terrorism"? The victory of Hamas in the Palestinian territories has further aggravated this dilemma. This question must be tackled despite the fact that observers report that some votes for Hezbollah are not freely cast votes, but are made under social constraints.[20] This is a serious problem. But how can this social pressure be measured and included in the assessment of democracy worldwide? This aspect is alien to the classic theories of democracy, for the societies of ancient Greece and later England and other Western countries assumed that individuals acted with self-determination and free will to make their own choices. But are western voters always more self-determined individuals free from social constraints? This is a fundamental discussion that must be held on a societal and political level.

In a recent turn of policy, it seems that even the United States has accepted as unavoidable this deeply entrenched position of Hezbollah in Lebanon. After the assassination of Hariri and Hezbollah's subsequent efforts to galvanize support for Syria, the US signaled its readiness to speak to the Shi'a movement for the first time ever. Getting rid of the secular regime in Damascus, or at least driving a wedge between the Syrian government and Hezbollah, seems to be more important to the US than shunning an "Islamist terrorist organization," as Washington labels it.

Hezbollah's reorientation as a Lebanese political party is not undisputed within the movement itself. A more moderate tone has become the rule, at least among the leadership. The spiritual leader of the organization, Hassan Nasrallah, says that "the Islamic state is not the end but a means of achieving justice. If there is another realistic means available and this way is the only possible one, it will be supported by Islam. This is not a contradiction to Islam." According to Nasrallah, this is the case in Lebanon, where a number of strong religious minorities have to live in one state.[21]

Hezbollah lived up to this philosophy after the Hariri killing when it struck electoral alliances with Jumblatt's Socialist Progressive Party and the *Tayar al-Mustaqbal* (Currents of the Future) movement led by Hariri's son Saad. Hezbollah has attempted to ensure that the resistance against Israel remains a national endeavor and not a sectarian one. Hezbollah leaders know that the organization will face hard times now with the Syrians gone, and that the pressure to disarm according to UN Resolution 1559 will increase. The head of the Hezbollah foreign relations unit, Nawaf al-Musawi, made it clear in June 2005. "I believe that by striking these [electoral] alliances we have managed to close the door to disputes of a sectarian nature. [...] I believe we have made significant success in showing how the resistance is part of the national defense mechanism."[22] Nevertheless, the religious groups are split on this issue. Most of the Christian Maronites favor the disarmament of Hezbollah, whereas 31 percent of the Sunnis and 79 percent of the Shi'as oppose it.[23]

It was the nascent Hezbollah movement that introduced the practice of suicide attacks in the 1980s.[24] This is the frequent argument for those who see in Hezbollah a problematic partner for Syria. On the other hand, this was more than twenty years ago, and in a conversation with Western scholars in February 2004, Nasrallah clearly condemned violence against civilians as a means to achieving goals in domestic policy.

Dressed, as always, entirely in black with turban, cloak, and trimmed beard, the spiritual figure sits reflectively in a deep armchair and speaks calmly in a gentle, low voice. Small glasses of sweet black tea are on the table. The shutters are down in the small lounge situated in a guarded enclave in a suburb of Beirut. "Defining terrorism is currently one of the most difficult problems worldwide," Nasrallah admits. "But it's clear that resistance must be excluded from the definition of terrorism. [...] Israeli soldiers are aggressors when they go into Lebanese territory. Do you expect us to offer them coffee? [...] Therefore this war is legitimate resistance and certainly not terrorism. By contrast, it is terrorism when someone, for instance in Lebanon, pursues a domestic policy goal by killing people—men, women, and children. If someone parks a car loaded with explosives in the middle of a market or in front of a cinema and blows it up, this is an instance of terrorism, even though the political objective may be perfectly legitimate and just." Thus Hezbollah has adopted a different strategy in comparison to Islamists in Egypt or Algeria, who have worn themselves down in direct confrontation with the authoritarian regimes.

Nasrallah is younger than he looks on the propaganda posters that are common in the streets, especially in southern Lebanon. They show the forty-four-year-old with bulky plastic glasses and a Kalashnikov in his raised hand, the Dome of the Rock in Jerusalem shining golden in the background. This is the message that frightens Israel and the West. Nasrallah does not distance himself clearly from suicide attacks in Israel. "It's up to the Palestinians themselves to define the limits of their resistance," is how he cautiously formulates it, "be it in the land occupied in 1967 or in the territories of 1948 [in today's "Israel proper"]. Our responsibility is merely to help them."[25]

Syria is double-dealing. On one hand, it has lowered its head since the Iraq war and stresses its willingness to hold peace talks with Israel. On the other hand, Damascus naturally intends to keep as many options open as possible. "We don't need any nuclear bombs," someone told me in Damascus. "Our atomic bombs are Hamas and Hezbollah." From a Syrian point-of-view, it is clear that they cannot afford to give up Hezbollah as their right hand in Lebanon because of their own military weakness. This is even more obvious after the withdrawal of Syrian troops. After all, the Israeli-Palestinian conflict is far from resolved. Encouraged by the war in Iraq, Israel has adopted an increasingly aggressive strategy that has included the bombardment of Ain Saheb as well as the outspoken intention of integrating large West Bank settlements into Israel and doubling the number of settlers on the occupied Golan Heights.

From an Arab point-of-view, peace negotiations with Israel are always a vague affair because of the "democratic uncertainty factor." Israeli political opportunism based on election strategies has again and again led to the revision of previously agreed upon negotiation results. It would be oversimplifying matters to attribute an obstructive attitude exclusively to the "evil dictatorship" that is threatening a "good democracy." The progressive Israeli historian Avi Shlaim joins the criticism that "the Middle East peace process is being held hostage to the vagaries of Israel's internal politics."[26] Deep rifts cannot be overcome by merely changing short-lived majorities.

This became clear in the negotiations between Syria and Israel in January 2000. According to American participants, Hafez al-Asad had made exceptionally far-reaching concessions in security issues and in matters of normalizing relations (diplomatic exchange, open borders, trade, etcetera). But his counterpart, Ehud Barak, sensed among the Israeli population a growing opposition to the return of the Golan Heights to Syria. Barak backed down in this crucial issue and no longer wanted to commit himself to a complete withdrawal to the borders of June 4, 1967. Syria saw this as a betrayal. The negotiations in Shepherdstown, USA, were a missed opportunity. In Geneva in March 2000, US President Bill Clinton once again attempted on Barak's behalf to persuade the terminally ill Asad to surrender land east of Lake Genezaret that belonged to Syria before 1967, and according to the international borders of 1923. Hafez al-Asad had splashed around in that lake as a child. He remained unbending in the final big decision of his life. He refused to participate in any further discussions and in a rage flew back to Damascus where he died three months later.[27]

The issue of the Golan Heights gives Syria a reason to maintain its relationship with Hezbollah, which, in a vicious circle, has lent the country the image of a supporter of terrorism. Bashar, likewise, referred to national security to justify Syrian troops stationed in Lebanon. In 1982, Israel invaded Lebanon, reaching the Syrian border in just forty-eight hours. Their troops stood some twenty kilometers away from Damascus. Even after its withdrawal from Lebanon in May 2000, Israel has repeatedly encroached on Lebanese air space to spy or bombard Hezbollah or Palestinian targets. This had served Bashar as an argument for making the pullout of his troops from Lebanon dependent on the Middle East peace process. Syria's fear has not been allayed that Israel may again try—as it did in the 1980s—to win over the Lebanese Christians and turn Lebanon into a satellite state. This was another vicious circle until the assassination of Hariri turned the tide irrevocably against Syria.

The Syrian bargaining position has not improved since the breakdown of the negotiations in Shepherdstown. Powerless, Syria accuses Israel of using the Golan as a nuclear waste dump and building extensive settlements there.[28] Israel can feel secure with its unqualified American backing. For the first time, the neo-conservatives in Washington have set up conditions for Syria even to participate in the peace process at all. Among those conditions are demands to expel the Palestinian militant factions from Damascus, to cut off support for Hezbollah, and—until 2005—to withdraw from Lebanon. Damascus was not invited to negotiations on the Road Map in the Egyptian beach resort of Sharm as-Sheikh in June 2003. Washington's intention was to knock Syria's diplomatic cards out of its hand and subject the country to conditions dictated by Israel, criticizes Raymond Hinnebusch. The Middle East expert quotes Shlomo Gazit, former head of the Israeli secret service, that the Syrians would not be able to accept such a situation. If they accepted such preliminary conditions, it would be a "public surrender to Israeli-American dictates."[29]

Apart from tightening the screws on this front, the United States has also used Lebanon as a tool for eroding the regime in Damascus. For a long time, the Syrian regime underestimated the seriousness of the situation, failing to recognize the U-turn in US policy. The demand to withdraw from Lebanon could have been made years ago. But a Syrian military presence in this fragile state was in American and even Israeli interests. "Better a politically administered Lebanon than an unhindered point of crystallization for terrorists," as the opposition figure Kilo puts the argument (although he and other Civil Society activists were in favor of a withdrawal and reiterated this stand in a press communiqué about one week after Hariri's assassination).[30]

Because of this rigid conviction and sudden change in the paradigm, many Syrians experienced a sense of injustice, which the Syrian ambassador to the United States, Imad Moustapha, expressed, alluding to Israel's practices in the Palestinian territories. "I just want to remind you that Syria went to Lebanon to end a bloody civil war that cost almost one hundred thousand lives. We did not annex a single square kilometer of the Lebanese territories. We did not impose our social, political, or economic system on Lebanon. We did not build any settlements in Lebanon, we did not demolish houses there, and we did not, of course, build a wall deep into the Lebanese territories."[31]

It was a fruitless lament because priorities had changed, and Lebanon once again served as a gameboard for greater interests. Here, the US and French interests diverged. Both supported UN Resolution 1559, but France was interested in Lebanese sovereignty and democratization, which would also increase its historical influence on the country. The United States aimed at weakening Damascus and had no further stakes in Lebanon itself.

But if Syria was the guarantor of stability in Lebanon, it failed in its role when Rafiq Hariri was assassinated on February 14, 2005. This is the mildest reproach that the regime in Damascus has to accept. Of course, a majority of public opinion in Lebanon and abroad did not stop here, but blamed Syria much more directly. The professionalism of the assassination and the strength of the explosion hinted at a well-organized and well-backed enterprise in a country that was suffused with Syrian military and intelligence. Bashar's personal fallout with Hariri a few months earlier fueled the speculations. The exact circumstances of Hariri's death remain unclear, even after the report of the UN fact-finding team, headed by German prosecutor Detlev Mehlis, was published on December 15, 2005.

Mehlis made it clear that he was convinced that Syria was involved in Hariri's murder. But he did not go so far as to blame Bashar al-Asad directly. In an interview with the newspaper *As-Sharq al-Awsat*, Mehlis was asked, "Do you feel you are on the right track? Do you feel Syria is definitely behind this [Hariri's] killing?" Mehlis answered, "Yes."—"The Syrian government?"—"Well, let us say Syrian authorities."—"How high up [in the government] do you go?"—"Well, that is speculation so I cannot comment on this."[32]

Whatever will turn out to be true (if ever truth will come to light), Mehlis' investigation has left scars on the face of the Syrian regime. In October 2005, the spectacular death of Interior Minister Ghazi Kan'an added to the tension. It boosted speculation that not only the Syrian Mukhabarat was involved, but Syrian government representatives, too.

Consequently, it would be less likely that Bashar had known nothing about the developments.

Kan'an's death is also linked to the subsequent defection of former Vice President Khaddam at the end of 2005. Both men, together with former Chief of Staff Hikmat Shihabi, were rumored to be plotting against Bashar because they considered him incompetent, and because they wanted to secure their own economic interests in Syria and Lebanon against the Asad family. At the least, Kan'an and Khaddam were the only men powerful and politically resourceful enough to represent a realistic threat against Bashar. The president was well aware of this.

The sixty-three-year-old Kan'an was a key player in Lebanon for nineteen years as Damascus' military intelligence chief there until Bashar removed him in 2003. From this time on, Kan'an's authority started to crumble. He finally felt cornered by the UN fact finding team and by rising accusations of bribery. Kan'an had been interrogated by Mehlis and denied any involvement in Hariri's murder. In the summer of 2005, Washington froze Kan'an's American bank accounts. (His children studied in the US. He even used to have good ties with US intelligence officials and had interceded with kidnappers to release Western hostages in Lebanon.)

Shortly before noon on October 12, 2005, Kan'an, who was one of the last living Alawi strongmen from Hafez al-Asad times, once again denied on Lebanese radio that he had accepted bribes from Hariri, or ordered the man's death. He concluded ominously: "This is the last statement I can make." An hour later, the Syrian news agency SANA announced his suicide. According to reports, he shot himself in his office. Rumors started to circulate that he was murdered as a scapegoat for the Hariri assassination or because he simply knew too much. Of course, Kan'an had many enemies within the regime's growing internal power struggle. In particular, relations had soured between Kan'an and Syria's new military intelligence chief, Asef Shawkat (Bashar's brother-in-law), whom Mehlis also listed as a suspect. Various other factors might have played a role but, given the timing, a link to the developments in Lebanon seemed unavoidable.

The question of "who killed Hariri?" is, of course, a component in assessing whether modern Syria shows the traits of a "rogue state." The answer is not so easy because of a complex mix of factors.

On the one hand, it is clear that Syria is the main loser in these events, at least in the short term. It has lost Lebanon as its political and military backyard and, therefore, has to reassess its security policy in the region. Political options have narrowed and Syria's image has been shattered. The words from the mouth of a US official make things clear. "It doesn't matter [who killed Hariri]. Why are you worrying about the fact there's no empirical evidence for who killed him?...It doesn't matter what reality it is.

It's—Syria did it. That's all we say and that's all the world wants to believe and that's it."[33]

Before following the bloodline to Damascus, several counter-arguments stand in the way. The brutal and spectacular assassination of a personal enemy is far from Bashar's style, judging from his prior political and personal behavior as well as from his educational background. In addition, Hariri was a moderate and cooperative politician who had supported Syria in critical times. Damascus will miss his capacity for compromise and his skill at integrating the diverging interests of Lebanon. Other figures were much more outspoken and radical anti-Syrian mouthpieces, especially the old protagonists from the civil war such as Druze leader Walid Jumblatt or the exiled Christian General Michel Aoun. The Maronite Patriarch Mar Nasrallah Sfreir also joined the ranks of those who called for the implementation of Resolution 1559. If there was a plan to assassinate adversaries, these figures would have made a good, if not better, target according to this logic. The counter-argument to this is that Hariri was the only Lebanese politician who could have really challenged the Syrian regime, and with his money and charisma he could have gathered broad support to rule Lebanon on its own for the first time after more than thirty years. If someone in Syria wanted to prevent this from happening, it was Hariri who had to be erased from the scene. In addition, he was an ally of Bashar's rival, Vice President Khaddam, who represented a threat to Bashar from within the regime.

The core issue in this context points to domestic Syrian politics and the pluralization of power centers. If Hariri was killed by Syrian hands—be it in cooperation with Lebanese intelligence, Hariri's business rivals, or others— the question falls back on Bashar. If Syrians were involved and he was not consulted or even informed, it would be the final proof that he has lost control. The same logic would apply if he got wind of it but couldn't prevent it. If Bashar condoned it or even ordered the murder, it is even worse. This puts him in a lose-lose situation, for he is blamed either way.

Several facts seem to indicate direct or indirect Syrian involvement in Hariri's assassination. According to a well-informed and leading Syrian opposition figure, the reshuffle of positions in the Syrian and Lebanese Mukhabarat six months before the assassination could be interpreted as having prepared the ground for this big event. Moreover, a media smear campaign was launched to chip away at Hariri and other anti-Syrian voices. Hariri was exposed to repeated personal threats from Syrian officials in Lebanon, according to the source. This escalated to the point that, in a sense of anticipation, Hariri told Jumblatt that "it's either you or me."[34] Only two weeks later Hariri was dead.

Certainly, creating an atmosphere of hatred is as much or as little evidence that Bashar killed Hariri as concluding that Benjamin Netanyahu was guilty of the 1995 assassination of his opponent, Prime Minister Yitzhak Rabin. However, this remains a question of *political* responsibility. And it rests on Bashar's shoulders. Khaddam's allegations from his exile in Paris that Bashar was not only involved in intimidating but also in killing Hariri are the most serious attacks the president has faced so far. But Khaddam, a staunch hardliner and corrupt politician, has several personal accounts to settle with Bashar and has always had ambitions to play the leading role in Syria himself.

Nevertheless, with or without Khaddam's accounts, more details raise concern: according to the same Syrian oppositional source cited above, Asef Shawkat, widely regarded as the second most powerful man in Syria, traveled to Paris a few days after the assassination. There the French confronted him with Russian evidence that the ammunition powder used in the attack had been delivered by Russia only two months before. According to this information, Syria was the only country in the region that used the powder.

Most people, even in Syria, believe that a complex combination of interests and actors from the political and possibly business arenas led to Hariri's death, and hardly anyone wants to bet on the fact that no Syrian hand was involved. At least, public wisdom holds, the feared Syrian intelligence chief in Lebanon, General Rustom Ghazaleh (Kan'an's successor in this post), must have been in the picture. Others also point to the June 2, 2005, assassination of the liberal Lebanese journalist Samir Qassir, who was a staunch critic of Syrian influence in Lebanon. He was killed shortly after the pro-Syrian director general of internal security in Lebanon, Jamil as-Sayyed, was forced to resign. Sayyed happened to be Qassir's political and personal enemy. The time for settling accounts had begun and it is far from over as the murder of the politician and leading critic of Syria, Gebran Tueni, in December 2005 made clear.

In the months after Hariri's assassination, speculation on its causes and implications for Lebanon and Syria were only bolstered by a loose collection of facts. Part of the puzzle is the view that Bashar's uncle Rif'at al-Asad masterminded the disaster in order to further weaken the president. Maybe Rif'at is preparing for the role of "savior" and is waiting to be invited to end his exile and take over the family business in Damascus. Rif'at could be backed by parts of the military, because especially in military circles doubt is rising whether Bashar will be able to save the country from more disasters.

Another version is that Israel could be behind it all. It would not have been the first time that Israel was involved in liquidations in Lebanon and Syria. Both Israel and the United States have a long record of finalized or planned assassinations of political opponents, be it in the Middle East, Latin America, or elsewhere. If this were the case, the Mossad or the CIA would not have used ammunition powder from Israel, of course, but from Syria. Not surprisingly, this version had most of its adherents in Syria itself, although US intellectual rebel Noam Chomsky also uttered this view. Interestingly, also Khaddam blamed Israel when he was still Syrian vice president. The logic of this theory goes that the Hariri killing and the following military withdrawal weakened Syria. Thus it reduced Syria's cards in possible peace negotiations with Israel, dimming the prospects of recuperating the Golan Heights. The findings of the Mehlis investigation, however, make this version appear as rather one of many conspiracy theories in the Middle East.

Mehlis himself focused on nineteen Syrian and Lebanese intelligence officers and tried to track the chain of command high into Syrian regime circles. This sent Syria into yet another pressure cooker of international dimensions. UN Resolution 1559 that had been pressuring Syria was now replaced by Resolutions 1595 and 1636 that called for Syria to cooperate with the UN fact finding team. Otherwise, Syria would face tighter sanctions or even worse. The regime was accused of failing to cooperate, of having destroyed evidence and intimidated witnesses, and of trying to discredit the work of the UN team. However, in a gesture of good will, the Syrian government later issued travel bans for figures listed as suspects by Mehlis. It also agreed to conduct its own investigation, just as the members of the UN Security Council had asked Syria to do.

Mehlis' list of interviewees, apart from high-ranking Lebanese Mukhabarat officials, reads like a who's who of the Syrian powerful. Reportedly, the list also included the name Asef Shawkat, but he was spared an interview for the time being after negotiations between the Syrian government and the UN. Some of the men on Mehlis' list were interviewed in Damascus, like Vice Foreign Minister Walid al-Mu'allim, a former friend of Hariri, who until a few days before his assassination had tried to convince Hariri to change his political course and not work against Syria. Others had to face Mehlis in Vienna, chosen as neutral ground because the Syrians refused to come to Mehlis' office in Lebanon. Among those were General Bahjat Suleiman, former chief of Syria's internal intelligence, General Rustom Ghazaleh, who was Syrian intelligence chief in Lebanon when Hariri was killed, General Jam'a Jam'a, Ghazaleh's assistant in Beirut, General Abdul Karim Abbas, head of Syrian intelligence's Palestinian section, and General Zafer Youssef, head of the intelligence's communications and Internet section. The list did not include Bashar's younger brother Maher, head of the Presidential Guard, who was originally named along with Shawkat in a copy of Mehlis' interim report to the UN Security Council. Bashar's close family circle has been spared—for now.

Actually, Mehlis' second report was generally less coercive than the interim report two months before. That is why Lebanese critics suspected a secret deal between the Syrian government and the international community, including the United States. Reportedly, the decrease of international pressure on Damascus was due to a joint initiative launched by Saudi Arabia and Egypt, which called on the US, France, and Britain to give Syria a grace period to fulfill the demands of the international community. The Arab League also had a role in easing pressure. Even British Prime Minister Tony Blair said he was prepared to open a conditional dialogue with Syria if Damascus cooperated.[35] Much more importantly, a surprising and radical shift in Israel's policy toward Syria took place at the end of 2005. Tel Aviv dissuaded Washington from implementing further sanctions against Syria despite the Mehlis findings.

This is why, against common expectations, the Mehlis report has not had any serious implications for Syria so far. To the contrary, the failure to impose further sanctions on Syria has strengthened Bashar's position.

On the technical level, the Syrians criticized Mehlis for obvious reasons. In his report they saw a biased political statement and no judicial investigation based on evidence. That Mehlis was called inexperienced in the Middle East and unfamiliar with the players and customs in the region was still one of the milder reproaches that could be heard in Damascus. Grist for these mills was the fact that one of the witnesses that Mehlis had interviewed turned out to be a liar who was bought out, a second one was equally unreliable, and that witnesses had to sign a summary account of their interview translated in English that they were unable to read. Critics were also puzzled as to how an investigator could release the statements of his witnesses before the investigation was concluded, which violates the principle of confidentiality. In addition, neither the CIA, nor the Mossad, nor the French secret service contributed much to help the investigation, which disappointed Mehlis.

However difficult and maybe flawed the investigation was, at first glance it seemed a remarkable victory of international law: a prosecutor sent by the UN to investigate a political murder had the power and international backing to force a reluctant regime to cooperate. This, however, only works if a state is already softened up. The miffed Syrians, supported by others in the region and beyond, correctly pointed out that many more occasions existed worldwide where it would be justified to send a Mehlis to investigate. Experts on international law criticized that the investigation confused the solving of a crime with the *political interest* of powerful countries to isolate a state and its regime. These experts worried about the nexus created between a judicial interest to solve a murder or several murders and UN resolutions that threatened a whole country and its population with sanctions or worse. This, they said, runs counter to international law. It all boils down to the fact that Syria's overall standing in the international community has suffered after the Iraq war to such an extent that it can be cornered by a single public prosecutor from Berlin.

Already before the Lebanon disaster, the transfer of power from the elder Asad to his son had resulted in a weakening for Syria in matters of foreign policy. Nevertheless, the regime still benefits from the heritage of the deceased president, who transformed Syria from a pinball in the political game to an independent force in regional politics. Its influence on Lebanon, too, will remain high, not least because of economic ties, the infiltration of Syrian intelligence, and even Syrian influence on the Lebanese administration. It is unlikely that Bashar will simply give in and follow the Libyan example voluntarily. In such a case, the regime in Damascus would hardly have a chance of survival in domestic politics.

Instead, Syria's motto in its relationship with the United States can be summed up as, "cooperation as much as necessary with as much restraint as possible. Go into hiding and wait until the storm has passed." An analyst in Damascus says that "the Syrian regime's biggest trick is to live from the crisis and on the edge of the crisis, to play the role of a stabilizing factor but to let the crisis simmer." This is a dangerous gamble that may go wrong with George W. Bush on the other side.

In principle, the whole question as to whether Syria is a "rogue state" or not revolves around the Palestinian-Israeli conflict, the root of political chain reactions. On this issue Syria is simply on the "wrong" side of the conflict, on the weaker side of realpolitik, although on the side of international law. If Syria had been on the "right" side, for example, the United States would not have cared if Syria had a foothold in Lebanon.

Those who are on the "right" side can count on a blind eye from the US with regard to human rights violations and other rogue manners. Just take Mubarak's Egypt. When it comes to the realities of the political system, Egypt hardly resembles a democracy, but is closer to today's Syrian model in many ways. A neverending martial law is only one example. This holds true despite Mubarak's hypocritical "multi-candidate" election in the fall of 2005. Pointedly, one could say that Egypt was granted the title of a democracy by the West mainly because it showed the boldness and vision to sign a peace treaty with Israel. It almost appears forgotten that Egypt has a long record of arbitrary and collective arrests, high numbers of political prisoners, torture, extreme levels of corruption, an impoverished society controlled by the strong secret service, and press censorship. Currently there are 20,000 political dissidents behind bars.[36] This is more than thirteen times the estimated number in Syria. Even if Egypt's population of eighty million is taken into account, the number of political detainees is still proportionally almost four times higher than in Syria. Comparing the numbers with other Arab states and Turkey, Joshua Landis comes to the conclusion that Syria is doing quite well, even with regard to Turkey.[37]

In the end, the assessment of Syria on this level is decided by the current definition of terrorism and for what actions the Syrian government can be held directly accountable. There are Palestinian acts of violence against Israeli civilians not much different to acts of al-Qaida or former European groups such as the Red Army Faction (RAF). Particularly, suicide attacks against Israelis fall into this category and are definitely a form of terrorism. But there are also conventional Palestinian actions as resistance to an occupation that violates international law, such as the struggle for freedom, land, and basic human rights in the West Bank and formerly the Gaza Strip. On the other side there is a phenomenon that could be called Israeli "state terrorism" that affects and terrifies innocent civilians in the same way with its method of collective punishments as well as the bombardment and flattening of residential areas with many civilian casualties. If all these factors are taken into the equation, the overall picture looks more differentiated.

Shibley Telhami found the right words pointing to this dilemma of hypocrisy and the loss of credibility of the West:

> "Although they [the Palestinians] have a right to seek freedom, they have no right to use terrorist tactics that inflict so much horror on many innocent people. The ends can never justify the means. This is a worthy moral position. Then we turn to the Israelis as we watch the horror that they endure in the face of suicide bombings. We understand that they must respond in some way, but we act as if they can respond in any way they choose. We do not impose the moral limitations of demanding such actions must not be sweeping, that they must be less hurtful to the hundreds of thousands of innocent Palestinians who suffer the consequences. In fact, we take no moral position and appear to give a blank check. Our global moral authority is underminded as a result."[38]

The key to an effective struggle against politically motivated violence against civilians in the whole region lies in a just and permanent solution to the Israeli-Palestinian conflict. Because of its military power and special relations to Israel, the United States is and remains the decisive actor in this theater.

10

CONTRADICTORY US POLICY

In the spring of 2004, confusion spread in Damascus. It was not the first time mixed signals had come from Washington, but the contradictions were becoming more and more striking. On one hand, US President Bush for a long time had postponed sanctions against Syria. Reconciliatory tones could be heard praising Syria's efforts to stop rebels from infiltrating Iraq. On the other hand, US officials again accused the regime of not doing enough to seal its borders.

"There is a feeling of anger, despair, and outrage. We don't know whom to believe," said Muhammad Aziz Shukri, an expert on international law. The most common explanation is that the State Department under former Secretary of State Colin Powell and the Pentagon under Defense Secretary Donald Rumsfeld were pursuing two contradictory policies toward Syria. Minister Buthaina Sh'aban made it clearer. "Colin Powell is a very sensible person. If he could decide, he would continue the dialogue with Syria."[1] His successor, Condoleezza Rice, by contrast, turned up the heat again in 2005 and has tried to enlist Syria's Arab neighbors to pressure Syria, citing the Iraqi border issue as the main concern.

But also, after Powell, signals toward Syria have been mixed despite the pronounced goal of regime change. A more recent example: whereas US ambassador in Iraq, Zalmay Khalilzad, said in September 2005 that "our patience is running out with Syria" and "all options are on the table," including military ones, in November 2005, Alberto Fernandez of the US State Department surprisingly stated that the US did not expect Syria to change its regime but to change its behavior.[2]

In fact, a full-fledged military attack on Syria similar to what happened in Iraq is something only a few people hold probable in Damascus—although nobody wants to exclude it completely. Compared to Iran, Syria is a much lower hanging fruit. But it seems that a gradual undermining of the Baath regime has become the strategy, pressuring it on all levels, narrowing its political options, and weakening it with regard to its regional influence and its confrontational potential toward Israel. Most of the time, the US has openly advocated a coercive regime change in Damascus, but without any indication as to what is to follow subsequently.

If the Syrian political system collapses in a heap of noise and dust, however, it could cause considerable instability in Syria and beyond. Israel's more cautious approach toward a regime change in Damascus since the end of 2005 reflects this concern for the first time in the camp of Syria's enemies. With Hezbollah deeply entrenched in Lebanese politics, Islamists of all kinds and colors on the advance in Iraq, Iran being ruled by a religious fanatic, the Muslim Brothers gaining hold in the political process in Egypt, and Hamas on the rise in the Palestinian territories, Israel seems to have realized that a violent regime change in Damascus may turn out to be against its national interest. This Israeli U-turn adds a new dimension to Syria's situation and to the premises of Middle East politics. It is a change of paradigm after the war in Iraq. Possibly, the US may come to a similar conclusion. But after such heavy rhetoric and a stick-only policy toward Damascus, it will be difficult for Washington to change its stand and to offer carrots again. In any case, the strategy toward Syria will also depend on Israel's domestic political developments after Ariel Sharon.

Until now it is hard to tell what long-term strategy the US administration has been pursuing. Flynt Leverett, a former member of the US National Security Council, correctly points out that the US policy toward Syria lacks profound analysis and is far from coherent.[3] The Baath regime has always been a guarantor of stability in Syria—whether in the negative or positive sense since, before the Baath came to power, Syria had been the country with the highest number of military coups in the Arab world between 1949 and 1970. The United States can hardly be interested in a second Iraq. Even a superpower can easily overstretch its capacities, especially with such a normatively loaded political agenda. Many other challenges are emerging for the neo-conservatives, like an increasing number of moderate leftist and populist leftist governments in Latin America, the United States' traditional backyard, possibly soon to include Mexico. Anti-Americanism was no incidental common denominator during the first Arab-Latin-American summit in Brazil in May 2005.

In the long run, the war in Iraq could backfire against Israel and the United States with regard to regional alliances, too. Turkey, Iran, and Syria have shouldered up because they share the concern over a politicization of their Kurdish minorities bordering Iraq. Mistrust is rising with each report that mentions Mossad activities in the Kurdish regions. Israeli-Turkish relations have additionally soured because the AKP government has become more outspoken against Israeli human rights violations in the Occupied Palestinian Territories. Moreover, relations between the new, Shi'a-dominated regime in Baghdad and Teheran may turn out to become friendlier than both the United States and Israel wish. In any case, Iranian Foreign Minister Kamal Khazzeri enjoyed a warm welcome in Iraq in mid-May 2005. Both countries signed an agreement to end hostilities between them, and both agreed that the Iraq-Iran war in the 1980s was the fault of Saddam Hussein. Part of the pact was renewed criticism of Israel. Instead of celebrating American liberators, the Iraqis could soon become self-conscious critics of US policy and friendly neighbors to US and Israeli enemies. Also, Syria's relations with Iraq have improved. For the US, the costs of the Iraq war could turn out to be very high on the diplomatic front in addition to everything else.

Also, developments in Iraq's domestic politics have not taken the direction US policymakers had hoped. The illusion that Iraq would turn into a modern democratic model state has been destroyed. The new Iraqi constitution is framed along Islamic principles and the Shari'a, much more than any Western politician could have wished or what even secular or moderate Muslim forces could have wanted. Women's rights in everyday Iraqi life have fallen behind the years of the Saddam Baath regime and will continue to be curbed in the future, also because of the precarious security situation.[4] The unity of the country is still pending while Shiites and Kurds try to secure their slices of the political pie and economic privileges like oil reserves. Iraq will remain a troubled state for some time to come and a danger to stability for the region.

Against this background, US policymakers have not been conscious enough of the probable costs of a forced regime change in Syria. Moreover, Washington has lost Damascus as a valuable and experienced ally in the fight against Islamist terrorism after 9/11. The true reason for the persistent pressure on Damascus so far was that Syria is a thorn more in Israel's side than in the United States'. Together with Iran, Syria remains Israel's most awkward neighbor in the region. But Israel has shown little interest in easing the tensions with its neighbors. The Oslo Peace Accords have been broken. The construction of Jewish settlements in the Occupied Territories has continued. The Road Map has become nothing more than a slogan. Unilateral disengagement as a strategy, with Israel setting all the conditions, dictates to the Palestinians rather than cooperates with them, and thus will not lead to an enduring peace with a viable Palestinian state. Unilateral ceasefires, even from Hamas, have not led to a resumption of political dialogue.

The United States and the entire world are facing two major policy problems. One entails fighting global Islamist terrorism and the other involves solving the Israeli-Palestinian conflict. Both problems are not intrinsically connected as some in Israel and the US want to believe (the gradual religious radicalization of the Palestinian people and the use of suicide bombings are a consequence of that conflict and not an intrinsic and ideological part of it). Provocative as it may sound, the neo-conservatives in Washington have put the *unconditional* support for Israel higher on their list of priorities than the fight against Islamist terrorism and thus the security of their own country. The war in Iraq and its chaotic aftermath are a product and an illustration of this agenda. The strongest connection between these two policy problems is a causal one: Global Islamist terrorism will not be defeated if the Israeli-Palestinian conflict continues to smolder.

So far Syria has not been part of the Islamist terrorist problem (similar to pre-war Iraq), but it is part of the downright political and secular—not religiously fanatic—Middle East conflict. Since the US has made the latter issue a higher priority despite 9/11, Syria has been sidelined. But the uncompromising stance against Syria has not led anywhere and the US has more or less exhausted its political options. One side effect of this approach was that in their predicament, opponents from extreme sides of the ideological spectrum in Syria have discovered common interests. Secular nationalist and Islamist movements—that is the Baath Party and the Muslim Brothers—are moving closer together in an attempt to protect themselves from a US agenda in the Middle East. This is a self-fulfilling prophecy.

US administrations have never shown particular interest in the cultural and social realities of the countries on which they exerted political pressure or in which they intervened. More important were overriding strategic or economic interests. It is well known that the United States has nourished some of the very forces that threaten them today: Islamist fighters in Afghanistan, among them Usama bin Laden, to counter Soviet influence, some of whom merged with the nascent Taliban movement; initially, until 1997, the Taliban themselves as a force of "stability" and a bastion against Iran's influence;[5] and Saudi Arabia, the country from which opulent funds have flown to the most radical Islamists in the world outside and inside the US. Also, Washington condoned the civil war in Syria which was unleashed by the Syrian Muslim Brotherhood in the 1970s and 1980s and militarily supported by Israel and Jordan at that time.[6]

By contrast, US policy has remained noticeably cool toward social players who tried to defy *both* religious fundamentalism *and* authoritarian regimes. This especially applies to Algeria, Jordan, and Egypt. According to the US anthropologist Augustus Norton, the prospects of strengthening civil society have dimmed in these countries as a result. Violations of human rights have increased under the authoritarian regimes in the past few years, without much protest from the United States. These regimes were only too happy to jump on the bandwagon of the "war on terrorism" and, in its name, batter the tender shoots of civil society growing within their countries. Critics and human rights activists were silenced and liberal reforms shelved. This has been the result of the Western states having exchanged their human rights agenda for an anti-terror agenda.[7]

It remains to be seen if the Bush administration in its second term, with neo-con hardliner Condoleezza Rice having replaced the last remaining pragmatist in Bush's cabinet, will shift to an even more missionary stance or become more circumspect and multilateral in her approach. Even though she has embarked on a campaign to regain credibility in the Middle East by emphasizing the value of democracy and more sharply criticizing friendly dictators in Egypt or Saudi Arabia, she has had a hard time convincing the skeptical local audiences, judging from the media echo in Arab newspapers.

The United States has ruined its moral and political credibility in the Arab-Muslim world after 9/11 to such an extent that any future foreign policy and public diplomacy will have an extremely hard time combating the tide of anti-Americanism. With little surprise, the low attitudes toward the US in the Arab world are closely linked with the US government's bias toward Israel, the Iraq war, but also, more generally and more problematically, with the perceived "American treatment of Arabs and Muslims," according to a poll conducted in 2005.[8] Instead as a victim of terrorism, the US has become widely perceived as arrogant and anti-Muslim, as a report of the Washington based Brookings Institution concedes. "What the United States calls a 'war on terrorism' is broadly interpreted as a 'war on Islam' by the world's Muslims," Hady Amr writes in this report. "This credibility gap is worrisome not just in itself, but also because it presents real complications for the success of our foreign policies, ranging from seeking cooperation in the pursuit of terrorists to supporting the expansion of democracy." This problem has turned into a security issue, as Amr emphasizes. "The paradigm through which America chooses to answer this question of 'why do they hate us?' and how it responds will be crucial to national security in the decades ahead."[9]

Francis Fukuyama points out the contradiction that, according to results of another poll in the UN Arab Human Development Report, many Arabs still admire the US and would emigrate there if they could. Fukuyama concludes: "We are disliked or hated not for what we are, but rather for what we do."[10] If US actions are the problem and not Americans as such, the US image can be improved again by counter actions, especially by a more thoughtful foreign policy and a more considerate disposition vis-à-vis possible partners and international law. Some signs in this direction are discernible in different polls that indicate a slightly better view of Arabs toward the US in 2005 compared to 2004. US favorability rates have risen over-proportionally in Lebanon after the withdrawal of Syrian troops.

But the overarching trend is that during the past few years, the reckless neo-con policy has become a boomerang for Washington and contributed to the forming of new counteralliances, be it in the Arab world, Latin

America, or even parts of Europe. Damage control will take more and more energy away from proactive policy potential, just as paying interest rates on one's debts takes away budgetary room for maneuver. With regard to the Muslim Arab world, this is damage that can last for generations, a grave fact that has yet to be realized by US policymakers. Apart from repercussions for US interests in the region, including rising material costs, US policy has also dragged down democratic activists in those countries because they have become weak and vulnerable victims of Islamist hotheads and also victims of the cheap populism of the authoritarian regimes riding on the Islamist tide, who impute to the activists an American agenda.

US diplomats have uttered hopes that if freedom and political reform do expand in the region, the current US image crisis among Arabs would quickly become a thing of the past. But the crisis of credibility adds a more fundamental dimension to the so-called "war on terrorism": a "war of values". A lot of damage has piled up and first correctives like the new US law against torture enacted in December 2005 still must be tested in everyday practice. Consciously and systematically ignoring international law and conventions on human rights in the "war on terrorism," with memos on torture and the Geneva Convention written by the president's counsel Alberto Gonzales and others (thus making torture a systematic tool with the blessing of the Pentagon, the Justice Department, and the White House), and with indefinite detentions without trial, the United States has allied with the crude methods of authoritarian regimes in the Middle East and elsewhere. Apart from well-known scandals such as torture incidents against captives in the Abu Ghraib prison or in Guantánamo, the United States has outsourced torture, as suspects have been sent to countries where mistreatment is notoriously used as an interrogation practice. For this purpose, the CIA used a Boeing 737 in clandestine missions that carried detainees to distant interrogation facilities, including Afghanistan, Egypt, and Jordan. Until 2002, US officials sent al-Qaida suspects even to Syrian dungeons.[11] With this behavior, US reputation has sunk so low that even one of the worst dictators of our time, Saddam Hussein, can claim that US authorities tortured him during his detention in Baghdad without the whole world bursting into laughter.

Instead of political engineering, the neo-conservatives in Washington have pursued a policy of primarily military orientation. With its excessive and insensitive use of blunt force, lack of context analysis and expertise on the ground, the US has gambled away the initial goodwill of many moderate Iraqis vis-à-vis US troops and the US as such. This became especially clear in the aftermath of the Iraq war when the US administration lacked an effective plan for social and political reconstruction.

Likewise, the United States has shown little noticeable interest in the

Civil Society Movement or other democratic forces in Syria. Where a relatively broad secular base exists, political engineering suggests itself. Leverett acknowledged that US policy did not permit the fostering of civil society forces in Syria, for it is in principle forbidden to let public money be paid to countries that support terrorism according to the US definition. "This prevents us from engaging and empowering reformists in Syria," he complained.[12]

The undifferentiated approach and lack of knowledge about developments on the ground lead to bitter incidents. For example, the moderate Muslim intellectual Mohammed al-Habash of all people was not allowed to enter the United States in spite of having a valid visa. He was forced to turn around at Dulles Airport in Washington and fly back home in December 2004. "The Americans are not making any distinction between conservatives and the path of renewal that I follow," criticized Habash. "Unfortunately, they treat us all the same, as if we were all followers of Usama bin Laden."[13] After his protest to the US embassy in Damascus, he was re-granted a visa and finally traveled to the United States in April 2005.

Instead of supporting Islamic moderates, secularists, and reformists, some people that I spoke to in Damascus claim that the United States is entertaining contacts with the Muslim Brotherhood. This would be a dangerous déjà vu. "The Americans want to build on popularity," said a confidant of Bashar's. "Good people who have clever ideas, such as Michel Kilo, don't serve their purpose because they have no mass basis." Other people outside the government also hinted at the possibility that the Washington-London-Damascus triangle is beginning to work.[14] A high-ranking Syrian government official abroad, however, dismissed these claims and told me that if contacts between the US government and the Syrian Muslim Brotherhood existed, they were rather "superficial." More than anything else, such contacts would cause a serious rift within the Brotherhood movement and represent a massive challenge to their credibility among radical Islamic and anti-American followers. Nevertheless, if it is true, it remains to be seen if the Baathist call for national unity against an American agenda will appeal more strongly to the courted Muslim Brothers than Washington's possible effort to rope them in as a counterbalance to the Baathists. Apart from this, Washington has not been able to connect with a workable opposition, except with shady figures in exile or such lacking local expertise and a political following like Farid al-Ghadry.

Criticism of this strategy also comes from within Washington. Leverett draws parallels of failed attempts to use external opposition to bring about regime change, citing the cases of Iraq and Cuba.[15] Meanwhile, Syrian opposition groups have cast to the winds Ghadry's call to form a united front with his Reform Party and rejected any intervention from the United States.

Alluding to the US record of supporting "benevolent dictators" from the Middle East to South America, the Syrian human rights activist Haitham Maleh does not count on American involvement of any kind. "Take your nose out of our affairs and out of this region. Don't support any dictatorship. This would automatically help us."[16] This shows once more that the loss of trust in its intentions has become the single biggest burden for the United States in the region.

On the one hand, in the market places, one can hear Syrians utter the view that "our corrupt Arab regimes are much worse than the United States." This is how it was summed up by a young carpet merchant in the Old City of Damascus who goes to the mosque five times a day for prayer. On the other hand, most Syrians are convinced that the Americans do not really want to bring democracy to the Middle East when they talk about a "new order" in the region, but aim merely at creating a more favorable political environment for Israel and the securing of oil fields. Doubts about Bush's Middle East policy do not only exist here, but also to an increasing extent surround the US president at home. The Republican foreign policy expert and former National Security adviser to Bush Sr., Brent Scowcroft, doubted that the Americans really wanted to bring democracy to the Middle East since it would be unrealistic and dangerous. "The reason I part with the neocons," he said, "is that I don't think in any reasonable time frame the objective of democratizing the Middle East can be successful. If you can do it, fine, but I don't you think you can, and in the process of trying to do it you can make the Middle East a lot worse. [...] I'm a realist in the sense that I'm a cynic about human nature." Right-wing hawks, by contrast, criticize Bush for his inconsequence in bringing democracy to the Middle East—and thus come to the same conclusion. Robert Kagan holds that "if the Bush Administration isn't willing to let Islamists, even radical Islamists, win votes in a fair election, then Bush officials should stop talking so much about democracy and go back to supporting the old dictatorships."[17]

On the other side of the spectrum, Hinnebusch opines that democracy is a meaningless word when it comes from the Bush administration. What the United States really wants is "compliant regimes," possibly with a democratic tinge, but with an authoritarian core like in Egypt, Jordan, and perhaps also in Iraq. "If these regimes are really to become democratic, they will have to combat social inequality and Islamist movements," concludes Hinnebusch. Therefore, the United States prefers pluralization to democratization and their goal is to establish "liberal oligarchies." "If democracy were to be promoted [in the Middle East], Washington would evoke the very forces that are against US interests."[18]

The Libyan case supports Hinnebusch's thesis. After long, secret, diplomatic negotiations, the United States made an unexpected deal with the former "rogue state" under Muammar al-Qadhafi in December 2003. Libya agreed to stop developing weapons of mass destruction (which is, of course, a good thing as such). In return, the authoritarian and potentially dynastic Qadhafi regime received the United States' blessing. Suddenly, there was no more talk of a democracy project. Nothing will change in the areas of human rights and political participation. A tamed Qadhafi is better than a free Muslim-Arab people going to the ballot box to cast their votes in anger.

After the tipping of Libya and the fall of Iraq in the "axis of evil" domino game, a chance exists that Bush's plan for "transforming military force into political power" may become reality, as the German political scientist Herfried Münkler suggests.[19] One could add hopeful developments where democratic elements seem to have a chance, like in Lebanon after the Syrian withdrawal, in Egypt where, for the first time, several candidates could run for president (though rather as a matter of window-dressing with nearly insurmountable obstacles), or more incremental reforms in Morocco, Bahrain, Qatar, or even Saudi Arabia.

But it is the political motives of the United States that are a matter of dispute in the region and beyond. Moreover, looking at Iraq, the price to be paid has been extremely high. Not only is international law, painstakingly established over centuries, at risk with far-reaching consequences for future conflicts when the doctrine of unilateral preemptive war sets a precedent. Part of the balance sheet of the Iraq war includes tens of thousands of dead civilians, destruction of infrastructure, land contaminated with uranium ammunition for generations, and a feeling of helplessness on the part of many Arabs who are reminded of colonial times. It is this perception that matters, even though US troops and the decision-makers in Washington have repeatedly pointed out that they are not pursuing a colonial agenda since their aim has been to hand over Iraq back to Iraqi leaders.

For many people, joy at Saddam's fall cannot compensate for the deterioration in the quality of their lives. Islamic fanaticism all too often provides a safety valve for this frustration, which will last much longer than a war. This closes the vicious circle by creating a hotbed for the current form of terrorism. In the meantime, independent studies have confirmed the obvious, namely that Iraq has become a fertile ground for al-Qaida fighters *since* the war, and that global terror has increased instead of decreased after 2003.[20] This is a bill that will be further paid over many years and by many people and countries.

Not only France and Germany but also the Syrian regime felt justified in hindsight on their position against the invasion of Iraq. By opposing Washington's policy they profited by gaining political credibility among their populations. "For the first time, the United States has turned into a source of instability instead of stability. The war in Iraq has unleashed a hatred that is finding an echo in terrorism," said Syria's president, summing up the situation in European newspapers. Sectarian groups have gained momentum, weapons are being smuggled through Syria, extremists are getting a boost, and the streets are filled with an unprecedented amount of anti-Americanism. These are points that Bashar enumerated in an interview in May 2004. Most Europeans and even many Americans would hardly disagree.[21]

Despite these obvious setbacks, the US administration could have taken advantage of a great opportunity to at least partly restore their credibility in the Muslim-Arab world—and not only there. Qadhafi of all people provided Washington with this chance. Leaving aside the democracy project, the American administration could have used Libya as an important component for introducing a change of paradigms in the fight against weapons of mass destruction, starting with the Middle East as a free zone. But for this to work, Washington would have to measure everybody with the same yardstick and call for the nuclear power Israel to comply with these standards, knowing that in case of emergency Israel would have the backing of the United States with all its military potential. This also applies to conventional warfare, of course.

Syria signed the Nuclear Non-Proliferation Treaty in 1969. Israel, by contrast, refuses to place its nuclear plants under the supervision of the International Atomic Energy Authority, in violation of UN Resolution 487. The head of the organization, Muhammad al-Baradei, confirmed in July 2004 that there is no evidence that Syria has atomic weapons.[22] Syria has so far neither denied nor confirmed that it possesses biological or chemical weapons. Many analysts are convinced that Damascus possesses them, and meanwhile this has become conventional wisdom. Syria has not signed the Chemical Weapons Convention. Nevertheless, Syria, unlike Iraq, has never used such weapons. Some observers believe that those weapons could be in a dismal state anyway and that the regime would be happy to get rid of them. Looking at the rest of Syria's military, this seems not too far off the mark.

If the Middle East is to become a region free of weapons of mass destruction, the Syrians would have to put all their cards on the table, too. They showed a willingness to do so and emphasized this once again in December 2003 when they drafted a UN resolution for the Middle East as a region free of weapons of mass destruction (after Iran in 1974, Egypt in 1985, and Syria in 1989 had already made unsuccessful attempts in this direction). But the United States did not show any interest at this time either, and so Syria voted the resolution postponed until "a better time." The neo-conservatives are instead pursuing a unilateral disarmament of

Syria that, as the weaker party, is only left with the option of counting on the United Nations to put pressure on Israel. If all the countries, including Syria and, more urgently, Iran, would disclose or disband their weapons' projects if Israel did, another domino would fall to the benefit of the United States and the whole world—without anymore bombs.

Washington's unconditional political and economic pressure on Syria has been successful to a certain extent, culminating in the Syrian withdrawal from Lebanon. But the ultimate goal remains in the dust. Regime change as an end in itself does not work alone. Military action is no guarantee for peaceful elections, elections per se are no criteria for democracy, and democracy per se is no criteria for good governance. Even US diplomats in their fortress-like embassy in Damascus, who are familiar with the situation on site, are not enthusiastic about their government's stance because they see the consequences for Syrian domestic politics, as discussed above. This is no secret among diplomats in Damascus. "Bush and Sharon presented a gift to the hardliners," said Alan George, quoting a liberal Syrian intellectual.[23] US pressure on Syria tends to lead to a "circle the wagons" mentality for the regime rather than to a readiness to open up. The analyst Samir Altaqi also speaks of a defensive stance. "The pressure helps to preserve the status quo and paralyze the process of reform. It makes it impossible for the regime to embark on any adventures."[24] Bashar, of course, has not failed to use the unstable situation in the region and other security concerns as reasons for the sluggishness of the economic and political reform process.[25]

A presidential advisor points to possible social repercussions, warning that "the greatest danger for secularism is Bushism." The US president's "with us or against us" slogan has polarized people. "The mere question about whether you are black or white is inept for Syria, a country that has lived with different shades of gray for centuries." American pressure has given fresh impetus to the fear of a break-up of the Syrian mosaic of minorities and to the specter of radical Islamism.

The Civil Society Movement is split over the question of whether American pressure is a help or a hindrance. Some of the activists have adopted a wait-and-see approach. "The Americans won't come because of democracy. They have supported so many dictators in the past," attorney Bounni holds. "But their pressure is helping to get things to change in Syria." Without the US turning up the heat on Syria, more people would be sitting in prison today, he points out. "I would be the first," he says, laughing heartily.[26] With growing frustration, people may become more pragmatic and ready to make concessions to US pressure before it is too late. "They say we are not going to lose Syria for the sake of two families," an analyst puts it, alluding to the Asads and Bashar's sister Bushra's entourage.

But the majority of the opposition are afraid of a setback in domestic reforms under the present political climate. Concerning foreign policy, many regime critics are just as pan-Arab as the regime itself, sharing a basic skepticism toward US policy and any kind of Western interference. It will be crucial to see how the United States continues to manage Iraq and the Israeli-Palestinian conflict. However, no effort to restore American credibility in the Arab world will succeed as long as Washington continues to apply or tolerate political and legal double standards with regard to Israel and the Palestinians. The Syrian professor of political science, Imad Fawzi Shu'aibi, sums up the defiant mood. "We can agree with the slogan that democracy is the best system and that freedom is a basic right for human beings, but we can't accept it from someone who is violating this freedom and this democracy."[27]

11

POLITICAL OPTIONS FOR
THE EUROPEAN UNION

In spite of, or perhaps because of, the US embargo against Syria, the European Union has made it clear that it is making its own rules. The negotiations on the association agreement are evidence of this. Syria is looking for new partners. The EU, however, rightly does not make offers without conditions. Up to now, European diplomats in Damascus have pursued a dual strategy. On the one hand, they stress the issue of human rights and domestic reforms much more than the United States. On the other hand, the EU states are not shutting the door. They count on the tried and tested German-German principle from Cold War times (West Germany's strategy toward socialist East Germany): change through trade. Nevertheless, some Syrian opposition figures are critical of the Europeans, saying that they are by no means using all possible avenues for exerting pressure on the regime, especially concerning human rights.

Meanwhile, the EU has beefed up its efforts to underline the importance of human rights in cooperation with forces from within Syria. At the beginning of 2006, a human rights training center was opened in Damascus, financed in a joint effort by the European Union and Syrian human rights activists with 93,000 euro. It is led, out of all people, by human rights lawyer Anwar al-Bounni, who has become a painful thorn in the regime's side. The center is to train women's organizations, journalists, lawyers, and other civil society activists in the field of human rights. Operating without permission, the center was closed again by the Mukhabarat a few days later. Since then a tug of war has been going on between the Syrian government and the EU. This is an example of how European politicians and diplomats have started to press the regime at a weak spot while pushing it to its limits of tolerance. At the same time such a non-violent but highly symbolic measure contributes to strengthening civil society in Syria in the long run.

The irony of this context emerges when Samir Altaqi reflects that "the conservative bureaucratic hardliners in Damascus say that making concessions to the United States is much easier than to the European Union, because the Europeans demand real domestic reforms, the guarantee of human rights, and so forth. For the United States a superficial adaptation would suffice."[1] This again reminds one of the Libyan experience.

All in all, it seems that the EU policy operates in broader horizons. Part of the EU's long-term strategy is the integration of the mostly Muslim-Arab countries that border the Mediterranean into a common economic zone. This approach is similar to the one followed by former US President Bill Clinton with free trade markets in Central and South America. Like the European partners, Clinton recognized that trade was an important mechanism in a globalized world used to exert influence on the one hand and, on the other hand, to achieve political stability and thus social progress in the long run. Whether it succeeds depends on many factors, especially on the stronger trading partner, who can either abuse its political power or use it cooperatively. At any rate, this is the counter-program to the neo-con hardliners who prefer to enforce policies and regime changes with smoking revolvers at high noon.

The European Union in its Euro-Mediterranean Partnership speaks of a "strategic partnership" in its efforts to achieve economic and social progress in the Arab world. At a summit in Brussels in June 2004, the European heads of state and their respective governments stressed that reforms could only succeed if they came from the Arab states themselves. "They cannot and may not be enforced on them from outside," the participants stated in a draft document. This, of course, doesn't exclude a clear agenda for reforms and reform incentives by European states. The Mediterranean countries "are our neighbors," the signatories emphasized. The Europeans point out that peace and prosperity in the region will not be possible without a just and permanent solution to the Israeli-Palestinian conflict.[2]

Despite the overall positive direction of this approach, it is still suffering from a lack of momentum and particularly of a lack of Arab-European and Arab-Arab cooperation. Another problem is that the partners of the European Union are mostly those authoritarian, so-called secular regimes that are hiding behind the "war on terrorism" and the "danger of Islamism" in order to freeze their economic and political reforms, ignore human rights violations, and secure the power of the present clique or dynasty. Similar to the United States, many European policy makers are still blind to the societal developments within those countries, including secular and moderate Muslim civil society activists. Western politicians still have to develop policy tools designed to promote those forces without necessarily destabilizing given state structures to an extent that endangers chances of a peaceful transition.

Also, the lengthy process of fixing the association agreement with Syria continues to be a challenge for the European protagonists. As mentioned in the chapter on the Syrian economy, the initial rift within the member states occurred when a debate arose over the clauses in the draft document concerning weapons of mass destruction and human rights. When the debate was finally settled, the Europeans, pushed by France, threw another obstacle in Syria's path by attaching a condition to UN Resolution 1559. The EU would only ratify the agreement after Syria had withdrawn its troops from Lebanon. After Syria had fulfilled this condition faster than anyone could have hoped, some Europeans started to point to the second part of 1559, which is the disarmament of militias in Lebanon, most of all Hezbollah. Almost simultaneously, voices from the European Parliament advised the Syrian government to help the ratification process by releasing the Syrian ex-parliamentarians Riad Seif and M'amoun al-Homsi.[3] Others said that the findings of the UN report on the Hariri assassination could also block the agreement if Syria is found guilty.

"The EU should be very careful not to push it too much," criticizes a European diplomat in Damascus. "This is more grist for the mills of the hardliners who had argued from the beginning that the association agreement would only make Syria dependent on foreign powers and was a tool to interfere in domestic affairs. Syrians have come to think that it's a game and ask what the next condition will be." However, according to the diplomat, the danger that Syria will completely withdraw from association talks remains low because Bashar is committed to economic reforms.[4]

Despite the inconsistent and at times chaotic handling of the ratification process of the association agreement, the economic approach in general has another advantage. It throws the thesis of a clash of civilizations overboard and does not give a political platform to ethnic, sectarian, or cultural elements. This applies to both political practice and scholarship. Political scientists such as Herbert Kitschelt stress that Islam is not the cause of terrorism, but rather that specific regional developments that have taken place in the Middle East have created an atmosphere in which terrorism can flourish. Among Kitschelt's reasons for terrorism are authoritarian regimes that consume large portions of the national income with corruption, nepotism, and incompetent elites. Further factors include: the strong and often oppressive role of the state machinery (etatism); a wide economic and social rift between population groups, where the poor fail to benefit from economic progress and social reforms, thus fomenting frustration and anger, a growing education and knowledge gap between rich and poor, and between Arab societies and the West; sluggish economic growth; and the lack of institutions for the free exchange of goods with capitalist markets (such as in Muslim states in Asia, for instance).[5] Therefore, if the causes of terrorism are largely of a social, institutional, and economic nature, two possible reactions do not look sensible: first, exclusively military solutions to problems such as the US-led invasion of Iraq; and second, focusing solely on religion or culture as the cause of conflict, which only leads to growing polarization.

In its close partnership with the United States, Great Britain has failed to adopt its own approach. Due to its special role in Europe, it could have had greater possibilities than any other European state to exert influence on US policy. When British Prime Minister Tony Blair supported the war against Iraq, he need not have done so unconditionally. He should have made his collaboration dependent on a package deal that could have read as follows: "The war against Iraq is very much in Israel's interest. If the Baath regime in Baghdad falls, Israel's most aggressive enemy will have been defeated and this will shift the balance of power in the region in Israel's favor. Therefore, a second step has to follow after the Iraq war: now the Israeli government has the duty to support the peace process with the Palestinians and to stop the extension and construction of settlements." This did not happen. The pullout from the Gaza Strip in August 2005 was not part of such a coherent roadmap for peace, but a unilateral strategic step to strengthen Israel's grip on the West Bank. As a whole, after the Iraq war Israel has adopted an increasingly aggressive stance with the backing of the US administration that has regularly used its veto in the UN Security Council in favor of the Sharon government's violations of international law and human rights. By failing to link his support to such conditions, Blair issued Washington a blank check. He thus unnecessarily degraded himself to the stature of a henchman of the neo-conservatives in the White House, which ruined his popularity at home. Scandals of mistreatment by British soldiers against Iraqis made it even worse and aggravated the Arabs' suspicion of "Western values" as much as did the torture incidents of US soldiers. Finally, the admission that the reasons for the war were hyped-up and unfounded, as well as the failure of the peace process in the Middle East, are political burdens that have made life hard for the Blair-Bush tandem in their home countries.[6]

Now since disaster has struck in Iraq, it is, of course, in everyone's interest to help limit the damage as well as to ensure that similar political mistakes and failures are not repeated in the future. With regard to the Arab world and Syria in particular, the EU's alternative to the US neo-conservative policy includes, on the domestic level, a continued stress on human rights issues, insisting on substantial institutional and economic reforms as well as creating a nexus between them and further aid, and the development of a civil society in Syria with the help of carrots and sticks—not with sticks only.

On the international level, the EU should exert its influence on the United States and Israel to put an end to violations of international law, from illegal detention and torture methods to collective punishments and preemptive attacks, in an effort to win the "war of values" and to regain credibility, which is a precious political asset. Any country—even the "rogue state" Syria—whose territorial integrity is violated for reasons intolerable by international law (by the pretext of preventive or even preemptive self-defense), must at least obtain justice on the international level and thus symbolic compensation from the UN Security Council. This did not happen after the Israeli attack on Syria in October 2003. By using its veto in the United Nations Security Council, Washington halted any condemnation of Israel. President Bush justified Israel's action as self-defense and even added that "we would be doing the same thing."[7] In this case, the Europeans did not protest as harshly as they could have. If Syria turned its back on the UN in disappointment and the battered Baath regime saw itself forced to carry out a military counter-attack against Israel the next time, however suicidal this might be, it could have fatal consequences for the entire region, and for the world.

12

CONCLUSION

"Every Syrian considers himself a politician, one in two regards himself as a national leader, one in four thinks he is a prophet, and one in ten thinks he is God. How is it possible to rule such a country?" Former Syrian President Shukri al-Quwatli issued this warning to his Egyptian counterpart Jamal Abdul Nasser in 1958 on the eve of Syria's union with Egypt. These words have since become a proverbial saying throughout Syria. When Quwatli coined this bon mot, Syria had just gone through a brief and turbulent phase of democratic experiments. It was also a heyday of ideological politics and a struggle for self-orientation following colonial oppression.

The proverb is heard less and less following nearly four decades of Baath rule and the fading of civil society and many political ideals. However, Syrian society has not become silent. Be it in spite of, or because of, the domestic rigidity during the Asad years, Syrian society possesses a large variety of moderate forces, an intelligent opposition, and the capacity for religious tolerance—something that cannot be taken for granted in the Middle East region. Western states should consider these factors in their policy toward Syria, despite justified misgivings about the encrusted Baath dictatorship. A good foreign policy must more than ever consider social realities in addition to political aspects and actors on the political stage, for the new players in international conflicts, such as al-Qaida supporters and other terrorists, are also socio-cultural protagonists and not states.

Syria has good grounds for wanting to avoid both the Iraqi and the Egyptian paths. This means neither an abrupt regime change—with a collapse of the system of law and order and a primordialization of politics—nor that the country is bound to get into the predicament of oppressing an impoverished population, highly imbued with conservative and staunch Islamist thinking, while cloaking itself in a Western facade.

The Baath ideology had been watered down long before Hafez al-Asad came to power and has now almost completely faded. What remains from the pre-Baath and Baathist periods is a stable public order, a diffuse but widespread dislike of fundamentalist Islamic ideas, and a relatively secular social and political order. These are exactly the salient points of contact for a modern foreign policy after 9/11. Western states should not start with military action, but with political engineering. For anyone who hits the

Middle East with a hammer, as a Kurdish source warned, the action will have future repercussions and will not go unpunished. "If it can't defend itself, this region is used to swallowing aggression only to spit it out again later."[1]

So far, Syria has been able to keep its head out of the noose. After the Iraq war, it responded evasively to pressure from the United States in order to avoid a reason for war. Furthermore, it has been looking around for new alliances. Most importantly, the rapprochement with Turkey is encouraging. Ankara could also play an important part in a possible agreement with Israel, and in the dispute over water rights. Despite high risks, Bashar would surely welcome peace with Israel—if perceived to be just—from the point of view of domestic politics. However, this would require sacrificing a large number of sacred cows with regard to Baath ideology, thereby giving up an important pillar of legitimacy for the regime. School textbooks would have to be rewritten and the propaganda played down. But the fact that the state media is still controlled by the government could actually be helpful in this matter. There are many examples that already show that moderation can be decreed when it is politically opportune.

One new strategy is the courting of the Syrian Jewish community in the United States, in an attempt at reconciliation with Syria. The initiator of this extraordinary approach is the Syrian ambassador to Washington, Imad Moustapha. The dynamic professor of information science is a confidant of Bashar, and by Syrian standards very eloquent and skilled in handling the media. In May 2004, Moustapha organized a tour for Syrian Jewish emigrants to Damascus. Most of them had emigrated in the early 1990s. It was a very daring enterprise and at the same time full of emotions for the travelers who were personally received by Bashar. The guests were not only welcomed by officials but also by people in the streets. These Jews went to Syria in the face of harsh criticism from the Zionist Organization of America (ZOA). But the experiment proved successful and reduced distrust. One of the visitors who took part in the trip said with regard to a possible reconciliation of the archenemies: "If both sides asked us to be a bridge, we would gladly do it."[2]

Of course, there is also fear in Syria of what might happen when the external enemy can no longer staple together the rifts in its own population and conceal homemade problems. Israel faces the same problems and concerns at home. Unlike Syria, however, Israel does not need to fear open borders from an economic point-of-view. Syria's ability to make peace with its neighbor thus also depends on the success of Syria's political and economic reforms. This is another strong reason to support Syrian reformists and the Syrian economy.

The question that is currently haunting the Syrians is whether a deep-rooted change—that seems inevitable in the long run—can and should come from within or without. Opinions are divided in the oppositional camp. Some give credit to the United States that Syria has become politically and economically isolated and thus has to compromise. However, this isolation goes hand-in-hand with the regime's uninhibited suppression of opposition forces and their attempts to organize politically. Under these circumstances any critical word is considered national treason, as Michel Kilo complained. The majority of liberal opposition figures hold the view expressed in the petition of May 2003: the danger for Syria is looming not only from its own obsolete regime and the country's archenemy Israel, but also from the United States. Most people have doubts concerning Washington's methods and motives. Democratization cannot be achieved by stigmatizing the regime in an enlarged "axis of evil." Change must come from within, accompanied by moral and economic support from without. The secular opposition is counting, above all, on European support for this endeavor.

A three-fold strategy suggests itself. This includes support for the Civil Society Movement and other moderate forces, as well as expanded economic relations according to the concept of "change through trade." At the same time, it makes sense to step up the official political dialogue, with clear conditions and focusing on the president himself, who possesses sufficient legitimacy among the population and appears to continue to sympathize with many ideas of the Civil Society Movement. There is still a chance that Bashar can free himself from political brakemen and other personal rivals.

The Baath Congress in June 2005, when Bashar reshuffled most of the important posts of power, was a step in this direction. The Mehlis report that hints at culprits in Hariri's murder within Bashar's own family and closest power circle could provide Bashar a second—and maybe the last— chance to get rid of corrupt players. In a bold and painful move he could tear himself away from his family entourage and ally with the Syrian people who still pin their hopes on him. In any case, many of his most dangerous enemies are now either dead or in exile. At this critical moment it is now time for Bashar to show his ultimate intentions and capabilities, by which he will ultimately be judged. If, moreover, the United States released its unconditional pressure on Syria, Bashar would soon run out of excuses about wanting reforms but simply not being able to embark on them because of internal resistance or reasons of national security. This would be the moment of truth for Bashar. Time is clearly running out for him to deliver.

In the case of weakening or dismantling Bashar's regime, the prospects do not look rosy, at least when considering the traditional players that might take a grab at power. For instance, Hafez's brother Rif'at, who is linked to many acts of violence, could be waiting for his chance to overthrow his brother, although in June 2005 he declared that he did not wish to challenge Bashar's reign on his planned return from exile. The defected Khaddam has turned into a dangerous rival of Bashar, too. He may line up with Rif'at and other former regime protagonists now in exile, or the Sunni might even approach groups such as the Muslim Brotherhood in order to stage a return to Damascus and fulfill his biggest wish to become—at the least—interim president of Syria. Khaddam is a wily political heavyweight, but his sudden talk about pluralism, democracy, and human rights after he left Syria sounds hollow considering his dirty record of corruption and his continuous torpedoing of Syria's reform process. Other protagonists, many of whom are technocrats, do not have the charisma or political background to fill the vacuum after the Asad dynasty. It would be in no one's interest to see an old hardliner, who draws his legitimacy from the early Baath years and his involvement in wars against Israel, seize power.

In November 2003, rumors circulated in Damascus about a failed coup attempt at the presidential palace. "Politically speaking, these may be Bashar's last days," a liberal intellectual told me. Developments, he said, were threatening to throw Bashar off his guard. After the forced withdrawal from Lebanon, this comment had regained its chilling connotation. "Conflicts can no longer be resolved with the rules of the regime. A lot of people near the president say we may need a new corrective movement," the analyst said. Whether Bashar can be part of this correction or whether he would be washed away by it is an open question. However, there are also indications that the young president is getting better at consolidating his interests and making personnel decisions. Much of his success will depend on whether he can uphold or win back his credibility among the young population as a proactive politician and a real reformer with vision and power, and if he can prove himself skillful enough to successfully navigate the foreign policy cliffs that lie ahead. At least he has shown a readiness for compromise, and the regime, unlike Saddam's dictatorship, is showing signs of self-correction with measures like the planned new party law.

If Bashar wanted to pull off a major coup, he would simply call a popular election for president. He still has the chance of actually winning such a vote. After all, he would need only a 51 percent majority, and he has the support of the minorities who account for nearly a third of the population. "These people [the minorities] may be the most unsecular of all in their way of thinking," says a businessman in Damascus, "but they have to pretend to be secular because it is necessary for their financial and political survival." If we add 10 percent of progressive Sunnis to the minorities, we come to a secular base of 40 percent of the population. "Syria is perhaps the only country in the region that can regard itself as secular. Even Turkey and Israel are becoming less and less secular," the businessman continues. Nevertheless, Turkey has just demonstrated how well democracy can work in its effort to head off external political pressure. When the parliament in Ankara voted against supporting the United States in the Iraq war, even against the will of the Turkish government, Washington had no choice but to accept it grudgingly. The voice of the people had spoken.

The United States would also have to modify its tone toward Syria if it was led by a freely elected president, even if the country continued with its old foreign policy. But this is just hypothesizing. Bashar will probably not dare to hold a free election, let alone push it through the machinery of power. This would deprive Baathist rule and the entire political system of their foundations. An alliance with the people against the corrupt power elite, with or without elections, still seems too risky at this point. But if Bashar wants to remain part of a solution instead of being washed away by the political tide, such a popular alliance may turn out to be the only option for him to stay in power and maybe to protect Syria from worse. One day this may lead to the point that he has to risk his personal survival in order to ensure his political survival (or simply choose the former and give up power). Bashar's fate will also testify to whether in this region a person with a weighty heritage can stay in power without being an unscrupulous and brutal power politician himself.

Skepticism about an abrupt democratization is by no means only to be found in government circles. Many Syrians wonder: Is a society rooted in tribal thinking and religious ties that for decades could not gather any political experience not overtaxed by Western-style democracy? Wouldn't this inevitably lead to demagoguery and radicals currying favor with voters? After all, the subject of politics was taboo for thirty years for the average Syrian, meant only for an exclusive club of a few sheikhs and intellectuals.

Many members of the opposition use exactly the reverse argument: the encrusted structures cannot be changed unless there is democracy. Free political discussions and more self-criticism would bring new momentum to the country and lead to self-dynamic reforms in the administration and the economy. Corruption, vested interests, and privileges would have to give way to accountability and efficiency. One important thing is the design of the political arena: parties with an exclusively ethnic or religious orientation could and should remain banned, as was the case in socialist Yugoslavia, for example. On the other hand, the argument that Islam and democracy do not go together is qualified by enlightened Muslim representatives in Syria, not least because of the political practices in other predominantly Muslim states such as Turkey, Indonesia after Suharto, or even for some time in the history of Pakistan (although the question of whether Islam and democracy are theoretically compatible from the point-of-view of religious doctrine and the final legitimacy of political power is a fundamental and open debate among Muslims and non-Muslims alike).

Ironically, in comparison to other Arab states in the Middle East, Syria has good prerequisites for democratization. On one side, there is the potential for secular forces to come into play, as already mentioned. Possible rifts between religious and ethnic camps have not yet entered politics in Syria as in Iraq. The general level of education is satisfactory. Women enjoy considerable rights and would be able to exercise a perceptible political influence under the current conditions. The economic divide is not yet as great as in other countries, thus the danger of social tension is smaller. Non-state violence, such as theft and murder among the general population, is extremely low. Syria possesses a state machinery that functions down to the lowest levels: parking tickets are issued and generally paid, to list just one example that is far from a given in other Arab countries. In other words, internal stability—that was thoughtlessly destroyed in Iraq—gives the country the potential basis for a relatively fair and orderly transition to some form of political participation by the population.

There is another helpful factor: Syria does not have much oil. As Herbert Kitschelt and others concluded after evaluating data on several Muslim nations, the chances for democracy are greatest in countries with low oil reserves. Conversely, the staying power of authoritarian and predatory regimes is highest when those in power can fall back on rich oil resources, and/or when a large amount of oil wealth is accumulated in the hands of a few people. When lacking oil resources, the rulers have to look for a more differentiated constituency, including peasants, traders, and craftsmen. Neither are they able to pacify the population with endless acts of generosity. Kitschelt draws the further conclusion that there is no direct and compelling connection between Islam and an authoritarian form of government.[3]

In the Syrian case (as probably in many other cases), the black-and-white dichotomy between regime conservation and regime change (in the American way) makes little sense. Syria is changing from within, not as fast and as smoothly as most people wish, but the erosion of the Baath Party has long been underway. Ideologically, there is not much left of the Party, and as an organization in public life it has lost significance. Even though Baath members are still dominant in key positions, non-party members have been appointed to high posts like Najah al-Attar, Syria's first female vice president. Furthermore, the yearly celebrations of the 1963 Baathist takeover in Syria have been downsized from grand military parades to humble cocktail receptions. And public demonstrations are no longer initiated by the Party but by text messages from the Makhlouf mobile phone companies. Another sign that Baathism is on the wane is that Bashar now calls for national unity with the slogan "Bashar and Syria," without any mention of the Baath Party. Although still a career machine, the Party has become a very mixed salad bowl of different people and interests. One scenario could be that the Baathist structure disintegrates into different sub-factions and interest groups. Syria could then turn into a model of incremental pluralization. This would become more visible if the new party law is enacted. The challenges in the future would further shift away from ideology toward technocratic issues such as corruption, nepotism, and weak state capacity.

The example of Syria shows also that moderate Islamists and secularists are able to take great steps and approach each other respectfully, at least on an intellectual level. Their rapprochement, or at least their mutual acceptance of each other, is more than simply presenting a common front to the Baath regime. This may be a surprising observation for Westerners after 9/11 and the ensuing polarization of public opinion. But people who know the Islamic world more deeply tend to agree with those who see the attacks in Washington and New York equally as an assault on governments of Arab states and the image of Islam. It is, in fact, just this kind of excessive violence by al-Qaida terrorists and Muslim fanatics in Iraq and Afghanistan that could lead to an important differentiation in public opinion within Muslim societies. This would be a great opportunity for reducing fears and prejudices in western countries about Islam and the Arab world. Such indications can already be seen in Syria, where not only scholars but also popular public opinion rejects violence against civilians in the name of Allah.

Many of the old secularists have, for their part, shed ideological ballast after the collapse of communism and with the growing distance from colonial times. With new flexibility, these secularists are now concentrating on humanistic ideas and democratic goals. A symbolic incident was the renaming of Riad Turk's "Communist Party–Politburo" as the "Syrian Democratic Party." This happened at the first party conference held in twenty-five years in May 2005, when Turk finally gave up his post as general secretary. On this occasion, the members called for the abolishment of the death penalty for Muslim Brothers. (Already in November 2002, Bashar had released the seventy-one-year-old Turk after his arrest during the Damascus Spring because of poor health and his record of having spent almost twenty years in prison.)

Thus, the two sides, Islamists and secularists, may be able to find a common denominator despite their different origins and worldviews. It remains to be seen how effective this shared ground will be in turning the authoritarian regimes of the Middle East in a more liberal and pluralistic direction. The Islamic camp in particular continues to face an internal struggle amongst a wide range of conservative and radical forces. Neither should all Islamic welfare institutions as well as other activities based on religious identity and traditional ties be confused with civil society. The idea of a civil society is that all individuals can engage themselves in projects by their own motivations and out of their own free will. The playing fields must be open and transparent to all. Everybody should be able to freely enter activities or exit them at any time. This is part of the development from a parallel existence of closed communities to an open society. In turn, this is the best foundation for a democracy that does not divide populations into ascribed groups, but leads them to policy-oriented competition.

Unfortunately, despite the potential for a rapprochement between religious and secular intellectuals, the reality of everyday life in Syria leads to skepticism. During the past years, Syrian society has become visibly more conservative. Above all, social pressure on many women to obey ever stricter religiously interpreted norms has increased, whereas others have found new niches of freedom through mobile phones and the Internet. The rift in the population between supporters of secularism and conservative Islamic forces has grown. Whether moderate or radical Islamic tendencies prevail depends not least on the politics of external players. A violent upheaval in Syria would be neither in the interest of the West nor of the representatives of civil society in the entire Middle East.

The danger of the United States and its monolithic approach in the Middle East, focusing on military means rather than on diplomacy and political engineering, is that valuable potential is destroyed that could, in the medium term, bring about a positive change within the country through peaceful means. The alternatives presented by the United States in Iraq have not been convincing. Apart from the Americans' behavior, perceived by many as inconsiderate and culturally ignorant, their foreign policy contains conceptual errors that have impaired the chances of a hopeful new start in Iraq. The primordialization of politics next door has provided the Syrian regime—and large parts of the Syrian population—with good arguments for preserving the status quo.

The actions of US troops in Iraq have triggered defiant counter-reactions. It must be kept in mind that the consequences of political Islamization will last many times longer than a war. They will become part of the body of thought of generations to come through national education and the existing infrastructure, such as through Quranic schools and mosques. By contrast, a secular philosophy of moderate intellectuals or a liberal Islamic alternative à la Habash or Sanqer is harder to convey, particularly in a heated atmosphere like that of the Middle East. Such ideas require tenacious rational debate and a process of forming one's own opinions. They do not spread through easily recognizable symbols or the mobilization of masses with cheap slogans. The West can help to ensure that the loudest voices do not necessarily gain the most influence. But the problem is that most western countries, the Europeans included, have put the fight against radical Islamists on the top of their agenda without supporting moderate Muslims in return. Those Muslims are left alone, often jointly with secular civil society activists.

The West should be encouraged by the fact that the Syrian regime has not followed Saddam's example of Islamic populism, despite its entrenched situation. Instead, it tends to seek contact with moderate forces within the country. Neither should the West push the regime into the wrong direction and drive pan-Arabists into the Islamists' arms. Only in this way lies the hope that the imperfect secular heritage of the Baathists, distorted by tribal and confessional thinking, and corrupt politics, can be transformed into a moderate, pluralist state with a strong civil society. This would finally end the cooking of stones.

EPILOGUE

In May 2006, after the manuscript of this book had been typeset, the Baath regime launched the biggest crackdown on the Syrian opposition since the Damascus Spring. Several key intellectuals and activists, who feature prominently in the preceding chapters, have been arrested, among them Michel Kilo and Anwar al-Bounni. Kilo did not return home after he had been summoned to a questioning by the Mukhabarat on May 15. Two days later, Bounni was dragged away from his home under the eyes of his and his brother's family. While the lawyer was screaming and demanding to see an arrest warrant, he was forced into a car by two men and driven away. Only a few days before the incident, Bounni's license to practice law was revoked for up to four years, probably because he had become the director of the EU sponsored human rights training center in Damascus that the regime had closed down in March. Several other opposition figures were detained, too. Some charges that were raised against them might carry life sentences. At first glance, however, it was not clear if the regime fired a warning shot only, or if the crackdown was a more profound turn of policy, leaving Kilo, Bounni, and others behind bars for many years.

At a time when the eyes of the world are directed toward Iran and its nuclear ambitions, the situation in Syria has become increasingly tense. At the beginning of 2006, with the release of key protagonists of the Damascus Spring and the announcement of a new party law that was soon to be enacted, hope for peaceful change filled the tea houses of Damascus. But meanwhile the Syrian regime has further estranged moderate secular forces that are Syrian patriots. Kilo, for example, tried to push for a technocratic solution that would lead into a more pluralist political system. He, like many others, has repeatedly distanced himself from US attempts to establish democracy in the Middle East by forced and ill-considered regime change and refused any form of cooperation with US-supported opposition figures. Kilo is at least as pan-Arab as the Baathists.

Here comes to mind what I mentioned in the book earlier: In March 2003, the Syrian intelligence chief Bahjat Suleiman stated that the Syrian regime can be lucky that it "does not have enemies but 'opponents' whose demands do not go beyond certain political and economic reforms." Meanwhile, however, even well-meaning intellectuals have become increasingly skeptical about the regime's ability and willingness to reform.

The circle of power has narrowed considerably, and Bashar's regime is undergoing a period of contraction. Except for political veteran Farouq as-Shar'a, who is now Vice President, all key figures in politics, the intelligence, and the military have been replaced by Alawis. The circle of trust has narrowed to family bonds. Another indication is that Bashar has re-established contact with Rif'at, his once so hated uncle in exile in order to explore possibilities of reconciliation and save the family's heritage.

On the other side, more and more opposition members abroad seem to be crystallizing around ex-vice-president Khaddam in Paris and the Muslim Brotherhood leader Bayanouni in London. Both have become, most ironically, the champions of democracy, civil society, political and economic reform in Syria.

The outlook has become bleaker: The intelligent and moderate opposition forces inside Syria have been intimidated or imprisoned, and those outside Syria are compromising themselves by allying with the Khaddam-Bayanouni-tandem. If chaos takes hold in Syria, sound alternatives will be more difficult to establish themselves.

The final turning point was the disaster in Lebanon. If Bashar was involved in the killing of Hariri or not, he has by far underestimated the international reaction and the determination of Western countries, especially the United States, to pursue an uncompromising stance toward Syria. A sense of panic and helplessness seems to be in the air in Damascus. This explains many short-sighted decisions taken by the regime in recent months. Bashar has not only gambled away the goodwill of many opposition figures but he has also lost leeway in pursuing foreign policy strategies of his own. Moreover, the weakness of the regime contributes to the fact that it can less and less afford a powerful domestic front and thus provides less and less resistance to Islamists in everyday life.

When a leader and a regime become insecure, they commit mistakes.

Measures become defensive and short-sighted. Arrests become unsystematic. The original reform-mindedness of Bashar has given way to the priority of securing power.

Without the Second Palestinian Intifada, the undifferentiated US pressure on Syria since 2002 in the name of fighting global Islamist terrorism, and without the Iraq war, Syria would have surely had a greater chance to pursue a more relaxed and plucky path of reform and pluralization from within.

Having said this, the regime has committed numerous mistakes of its own that have maneuvered the country into this precarious situation. Among such missteps is the estrangement of moderate civil society forces, the reluctance to grant citizenship to (still moderate) Kurd compatriots, the bad management of the economic and political reform process, the weakness in the fight against corruption and nepotism, the alienation from European partners, particularly in the issue of human rights, and the handling of Lebanon.

After its withdrawal from Lebanon, Syria has not played a conciliatory and stabilizing role in the neighboring democracy. Like a snubbed child, Syria has been reluctant to recognize Lebanese sovereignty, to demarcate mutual borders, or to come to friendly terms with the government in Beirut. Whereas Syria's alliance with Hezbollah and increasingly Iran can be explained and also justified by a foreign policy rationale and raison d'état, more subversive activities like the killing of anti-Syrian voices in Lebanon and the arming of pro-Syrian Palestinian refugee militias is playing with fire. Syria brought stability to Lebanon, but Syria could also break it again.

It was the Lebanon issue that escalated into the major crackdown on the Syrian opposition. Michel Kilo, Anwar al-Bounni, and other intellectuals from Syria together with Lebanese figures had drafted and signed the Damascus-Beirut Declaration that called for mutual respect of interests and sovereignty of the two countries. It also urged the Syrian government not to interfere in Lebanese affairs. This was the red line. Aggravating the situation was the fact that the petition appeared on the eve of a UN Resolution draft put forward by the US, France, and Britain in the Security Council. Resolution 1680 stipulates the necessity to take measures to prevent the entry of Syrian arms into Lebanon, the demarcation of the border between Lebanon and Syria, and the exchange of ambassadors. Such a resolution is quite unusual and interferes heavily in the countries' domestic affairs.

It represents yet another attempt to clip Syria's wings. The regime may have inferred—or looked for a pretext to infer—that the signatories of the Damascus-Beirut Declaration have lined up with the foreign powers in this matter. But those who know Kilo and most of the other intellectuals will agree that this is a highly constructed nexus.

Lebanon has become a dangerous and emotional issue for the weakened Baath regime. The Damascus-Beirut Declaration was the first common petition of Syrian and Lebanese opposition figures and it added insult to injury. The Syrian government sent a clear signal that its patience had run out. Apart from this, however, no political strategy is discernible in Damascus. Bashar seems to have run out of steam. It is still time for him to use his various pillars of legitimacy within the population and the resources of his father's legacy to re-embark on a program of reconciliation and reform. Even now, the numerous moderate opposition figures would not slam the door at an honest common endeavor. The chances for Syria to return to a more hopeful and prosperous path without political upheaval or an Islamist intermezzo still exist. The obstacles and stakes, however, become higher every day.

Carsten Wieland
Washington DC, May 2006

NOTES

Chapter *1* Wrested from Slumber

[1] Syria's secret services consist of different organizations that independently operate prisons and interrogation centers. They are largely free of judicial control. Among them are Political Security ('amn as-siyasi); the Military Secret Service (al-mukhabarat al-'askariya), which is subdivided into the "Palestinian Branch," the "Investigative Branch," the "Regional Branch," and the "Air Force Branch," and the General Secret Service (al-mukhabarat al-'ama), with the subdivisions "Investigative Branch," "Domestic Politics Branch," and the "Foreign Politics Branch" (ICG II, S.2).

[2] On September 27, 2004, the leading member of Hamas, Izz ad-Deen as-Sheikhh Khalil, was killed by a car bomb in Damascus. On December 13, 2004, the Hamas official Misbah Abu Hueilah barely escaped a car bomb, also in Damascus.

[3] *Al-Hayat, al-Baath, al-Thawra* May 16, 2004; *AFP* December 30, 2004.

Chapter *2* Bashar and Breaches in the Leadership

[1] "Which Asad?" *Associated Press* March 18, 2005, quoting statements of Makhlouf from July 2000.

[2] Landis, in: *The Syria Review* (2004), pp.2-3.

[3] Ayman Abdul Nour in an interview with the author in Damascus on May 16, 2004.

[4] Ayman Abdul Nour in an interview with the author in Damascus on May 16, 2004.

[5] Interview with the author in Damascus on May 5, 2005.

[6] *Akhbar as-Sharq* April 12 and May 16, 2005.

[7] Hinnebusch (2001), p.165.

[8] Interview with the author in Damascus on September 30, 2003.

[9] Michel Kilo in an interview with the author in Damascus on November 2, 2004.

[10] Interview with the author in Damascus on March 11, 2004.

[11] Interviews by the author in Damascus. See also ICG Report I, p.4.

[12] Interview with the author on November 2, 2003, in Damascus.

[13] A concise overview of such key figures can be found in: Leverett (2005), p.71ff.

[14] As quoted by *Reuters* on Jan 6, 2006 ("Syria's Assad slams ex-deputy Khaddam-paper," taken from the Egyptian *Al-Usbu'a* newspaper), Bashar said: "I wish to say here that no one joined us in the last meeting between me and Hariri, so where did these allegations come from?"

[15] Interview with the author in Damascus on May 5, 2005.

[16] Interview with the author in Damascus on April 28, 2005.
[17] *Reuters* June 7, 2005.
[18] Interview with the author in Damascus on April 28, 2005.
[19] The opposition member Haitham al-Manna, quoted from ICG Report II, p.10.

Chapter 3 The Pillars of Regime Legitimacy

[1] ICG Report II, p.9.
[2] UNWRA statistic, June 30, 2003.
[3] Perthes (2002), p.212; Leverett (2005), p.124.
[4] Quoted from Leverett (2005), p.125.
[5] "Politik, Gewalt und Religion in Palestine [Politics, Violence, and Religion in Palestine]," Interview with Mash'al in: *Neue Züricher Zeitung*, May 8, 2004.
[6] Interview with the author in Damascus on November 2, 2003.
[7] Perthes, *Adelphi Paper* (2004), p.63.
[8] Interview with the author in Damascus on March 29, 2004.
[9] *Al-Hayat* July 28, 2003.
[10] Interview with the author in Damascus on April 28, 2003.
[11] Interview with the author in Damascus on April 4, 2003.
[12] Interview with a representative of the Jewish community in Damascus on September 17, 2003.
[13] Hinnebusch (2001), pp.19-20 from Quilliam (1999).
[14] *New York Times* August 5, 2004; *Counter Punch* August 10, 2004; *Washington Times* February 23, 2005.
[15] Interview with the author in Damascus on April 28, 2005.
[16] Interview with the author in Damascus on September 2003.
[17] A detailed reconstruction of the events and a discussion on the local power structures during the massacre can be found in: Fawaz (1994); Schatkowski Schilcher (1985), pp.87-106.
[18] Interview with the author in Damascus on October 9, 2003.
[19] Perthes (1990), p.230.
[20] Interview with the author in Damascus on September 15, 2003.
[21] Interview with the author in Damascus on March 25, 2004.
[22] *EFE*, February 8, 2005.
[23] George (2003), p.2. The data refers to the year 2001.
[24] George (2003), p.1.
[25] Quoted from the English translation of the Syrian news agency SANA.
[26] Interview with the author in Damascus on April 4, 2003.

Chapter 4 The Negative Balance

[1] Quoted from the English translation of the Syrian news agency SANA; see also: George (2003), p.32.
[2] Interview in *Syrian Times* May 25, 2003.

3 George (2003), p.170.
4 Interviews with the author in Damascus on April 4, 2003, and September 30, 2003.
5 Interview transcript published on March 30, 2006, by the Syrian Arab News Agency SANA.
6 Interview with the author in Damascus on May 16, 2004.
7 Interview with the author in Damascus on March 29, 2004.
8 More about the suppression of the Damascus Spring in: George (2003), p.47ff. Kilo and Seif are reported to have had different approaches for political change and had personal differences. However, opinions differ as to the extent of their disagreement, p.42. Seif had also criticized the corrupt practice in awarding the two state mobile phone licenses. This is what some people see as the actual reason for his arrest.
9 Perthes (2002), p.210.
10 Interview with the author in Beirut on February 17, 2004.
11 *As-Safir* March 15, 2003, quoted from ICG Report II, p.10; Sadiq al-Azm in an interview with the author in Damascus on May 22, 2003.
12 Perthes, *Adelphi Paper* (2004), p.27.
13 Presently, four private universities are operating. Among them are Qalamoun University in Deir Attyyeh, Mamoun University for Science and Technology in Qamishli, University for Science and Technology in Aleppo, and Union University in Raqqa. Four further universities are planning to open soon. Among them are Arabic-European University in Dar'a, Arabic-American University for Technology in Aleppo (Jebel Sam'an), Al-Andalus University for Medicine in Tartous, and International University for Science and Technology in Dar'a. Data according to *Cham Press* June 28, 2005.
14 *Al-Hayat*, November 21, 2004.
15 Interview with the author in Damascus on May 5, 2005.
16 Perthes, *Adelphi Paper* (2004), p.13.
17 Interview with the author in Damascus on May 5, 2005.
18 Quoted in: ICG Report II, p.12.
19 Report of the Syrian Committee for Human Rights (London), see: *Khaleej Times* June 28, 2004.
20 "Deputy Head of Syrian Journalists Union wonders at the term 'Syrian Kurdistan' launched by Mas'aud Barazani," in: *As-Sharq al-Awsat* March 21, 2004.
21 Interview with a Kurdish communist on March 28, 2004, in Damascus, and others who were involved in the developments.
22 Interview with Abdel Yusef, chairman of the Kurdish Yakiti Party (which split off from the Democratic Kurdish Party, the largest Kurdish party in Syria) in Damascus on October 26, 2003.
23 Interview with the author in Damascus on March 17, 2004.
24 *Al-Hayat* May 10, 2005.
25 Several conversations with Buthaina Shaaban in an interview with the author in Damascus on March 29, 2004.
26 Habermas, in: Balakrishnan (1996), p.290.
27 Interview with the author in Damascus on April 28, 2003.
28 Interview with the author in Damascus on May 7, 2004.
29 Hinnebusch, in: *DOI-Fokus* (2004), p.10; figures of the Delegation of the

European Commission to the Syrian Arab Republic.

[30] Hinnebusch (2001), p.2ff.

[31] Leverett (2005), p.84.

[32] *Cham Press*, quoting *The New York Times*, November 1, 2005.

[33] Perthes uses this term in spite of misgivings and integrates it into debates on theories of development. Perthes (1990), p.33, 209ff.

[34] Samir Altaqi in an interview with the author on May 7, 2004. See also ICG Report II, p.13; Perthes (1990), p.205ff makes a somewhat different classification.

[35] Interview in *Syria Times* May 25, 2003.

[36] Figures of the Syrian Ministry for Home Affairs, from *al-Bayan* July 12, 2004.

[37] European Commission figures of 2005. The Economist Country Risk Service 2003, p.15, still estimated only a 0.9 percent GDP increase for 2003, 2 percent for 2004, and 2.6 percent for 2005. The annual rate of growth of the population has been 2.4 percent since 2002.

[38] *ArabicNews.com*, December 28, 2005.

[39] *The Daily Star* September 14, 2004. The updated studies show that four million of those able to work in Syria do not participate in the productivity process or development. They constitute 45 percent of the Syrian manpower. Press reports indicated that the value of investments under law No. 10 since its issuance in 1991 amounted to just 30 percent of the $8 billion, which were supposed to be invested. This means Syria's plans need to be reviewed. It also needs an economic plan able to achieve an economic growth rate that exceeds 6 percent per year.

[40] European Commission figures of 2005.

[41] Perthes, in: *Survival* (2001), p.144; ICG Report II, p.13.

[42] Interviews by the author. ICG Report II, p.13 states 20 percent.

[43] Approximately one out of ten children has to work for money in Syria to support their family financially. Perthes, in: *Adelphi Paper* (2004), p.35.

[44] According to official estimates, quoted from: *Al-Hayat* July 17, 2005.

[45] Interview in: *Der Standard* April 1, 2003. Quotation from the interviewer's original text.

[46] In May 2004, workers with an income of up to 5,000 lira received a 15 percent raise, those earning between 5,000 and 10,000 a 10 percent raise, and for salaries over 10,000 there was a 5 percent raise. The last pay raise in the private sector (20 percent) was awarded in August 2002. *Khaleej Times* July 27, 2004.

[47] European Commission figures of 2005 and interview with a European diplomat in Damascus on May 1, 2005.

[48] Other reasons include a rise in the price of cement and other building materials, more restrictions on illegal constructions, and the fall in interest rates on deposit accounts by up to 3 percent, which has led private investors to enter the real estate market. Interview with a European diplomat in Damascus on May 1, 2005.

[49] First figure: George (2003), p.10. Second figure: Samir Altaqi in an interview with the author on May 7, 2004, in Damascus.

[50] The figures vary depending on the source. The UN Development Report 2003 gives an annual income of $1,175 for 2002. On the other hand, the government published an amount of only $1,038 for 2002 with a downward trend (in comparison to $1,115 for 1998; Statistical Abstract, Central Bureau of Statistics, Office of the

Prime Minister of Syria, 2003). According to UN figures, the average monthly wage in the public sector was $120 (8,200 Syrian lira) and $155 (6,200 Syrian lira) in the private sector. According to the Economist Country Risk Service 2003, the gross domestic product has stagnated at around $1,210 since 2002 (p.15).

51 *New York Times* May 13, 2004 (from interviews in *El País* and *La Repubblica*).

52 "Creating a Syrian dream, where none exists today," Joshua Landis, in: *The Daily Star* July 28, 2004. He cites IMF figures.

53 Perthes/Schwitzke, Paper (May 2003), p.7; Perthes, *Adelphi Paper* (2004), p.43; Neil MacFarquhar, "Syrian Party Watches Iraq With Unease and Ponders Its Own Fate," in: *New York Times* March 30, 2003, even states the amount of $4 billion worth of Syrian exports to Iraq. According to Perthes/Schwitzke the Syrian state budget amounted to some 420 billion lira (approx. $8.2 billion).

54 Ali Saleh in an interview with the author in Damascus on November 4, 2003.

55 George (2003), p.24.

56 "A travel consultant based in the United Kingdom," Basil Tallal Kudsi, in: www.all4syria.com, May 2, 2005.

57 Interview with a Western diplomat in Damascus on May 16, 2004.

58 *Akhbar As-Sharq*, July 5, 2005.

59 Interview with the author in Damascus on November 2, 2003.

60 The pressure came from neo-conservative, fundamental Christian members of the US Congress and supporters of the Maronite ex-general Michel Aoun, whom the Syrians neutralized in the Lebanese civil war. At the hearing in Congress at the end of 2003, nobody who rejected the Accountability Act was allowed to speak. The majority leader in the House of Representatives at the time, Tom DeLay, claimed that Syria was waging a war against the entire civilized world and was a threat to all free nations. Hinnebusch, in: *DOI-Fokus* (2004), p.9.

61 The United States exported goods worth $214 million to Syria in 2003. Syrian exports amounted to $259 million, mostly in the form of oil and similar products, which anyway are exempted from the embargo. *Associated Press* May 12, 2004. For the amount of Syrian exports to the USA: Economist Risk Service 2003, p.7.

62 *Al-Hayat* June 29, 2004.

63 In the first four months of 2005, Lebanese banks lost 3.2 percent of their deposits. *The Daily Star* 18 May, 2005.

64 See also: Perthes: "Der Mittlere Osten nach dem Iraq-Krieg – Neue geopolitische Grundlinien und Spielregeln [The Middle East after the Iraq war – New geopolitical baselines and rules]," in: *Neue Züricher Zeitung* April 24, 2004.

65 "Putin Confirms Sale of Short-Range Missiles to Syria," *AFP* April 22, 2005.

66 *Al-Hayat* December 21, 2005.

67 Figures from the Delegation of the European Commission to the Syrian Arab Republic; Gareth Smyth: "Conference highlights EU approach to handling Syria," in: *Financial Times* October 27, 2003; Sami Khiyami/Samir Seifan: "The Best Way Forward," in: *Syria Today*, No. 0, Winter 2004, p.17.

68 Interview with the author in Damascus on May 23, 2004.

69 *The Daily Telegraph* June 1, 2004; "Syrias geheimes Atomprogramm: Die Spur führt nach Hanau [Syria's secret nuclear program: the trail leads to Hanau]," in: *Spiegel online* February 28, 2004.

[70] Interview with the author in Damascus on April 28, 2005.
[71] Interview with the author in Damascus on April 28, 2005.
[72] Perthes (2002), p.192.
[73] Interview with the author in Damascus on October 15, 2003.
[74] *Cham Press* August 12, 2004.
[75] "Wir waren lebendig begraben [We were buried alive]," report in *Deutschlandfunk* "Eine Welt" by Kristin Helberg, March 6, 2004.
[76] Interview with the author in Damascus on February 28, 2004.
[77] Interview with the author in Damascus on October 15, 2003.
[78] Amnesty International and Syrian Committee for Human Rights (London). See: *The Region* June 19, 2004, *Khaleej Times* June 28, 2004, *Scoop* June 30, 2004.
[79] Statement by Amnesty International on April 24, 2004.
[80] Quilliam (1999), pp.45-46, 81-84.
[81] Interview with the author in Damascus on April 28, 2003.

Chapter 5 Che not Usama: Syrian Society and Western Ideals

[1] Interview with the author in Damascus on March 29, 2004.
[2] Lobmeyer (1995), p.351.
[3] Lobmeyer (1995), p.353, 355.
[4] Interview with the author in Damascus on July 5, 2004.
[5] Quoted from a radio report by Kristin Helberg, "Radikale Islamisten oder muslimische Demokraten? Chancen und Gefahren des politischen Islam in Syrien," in: *Deutschlandfunk* December 10, 2005.

Chapter 6 Excursus: Secularism in Syria

[1] The following account is based on a lecture given by the author at the Islamic Institute for Humanistic Knowledge (معهد الدراسات الإسلامي المعارف الحكمية) in Beirut. See: Wieland (2004), in: *al-Mahajjah*.
[2] Among others, Theodor Hanf made this distinction during the international conference, "God's Rule and Caesar's Rule: Exploring the Spaces between Theocracy and Secularism," in Byblos, Lebanon, September 9, 2003.
[3] Statistics from the Protestant Church of Germany (EKD) and the Catholic Bishops' Congress.
[4] Tibi (1971), p.64ff, 83.
[5] More on these different experiences with secularism in Europe and the Arab world, see: Esposito and Keane, in: Esposito/Tamimi (2000).
[6] Hinnebusch (2001), p.1, 70ff; Dawisha (2003), pp.295-296; Kedouri (1992), p.325ff; Mansfield (2003), p.323; Zeine (1966), p.150, pp.155-156.
[7] Lobmeyer (1995), p.115.
[8] More about Syria under French mandate, see: Khoury (1987); Mufti (1996), p.44ff.
[9] Lobmeyer (1995), p.193ff, Schweizer (1998), p.278.
[10] Seale (1988), p.173.

[11] van Dam (1981), p.110.

[12] Lobmeyer (1995), p.199.

[13] Lobmeyer (1995), p.211, 219ff; Batatu (1999), pp.227-229, p.327; Perthes (1990), p.16; Perthes, in: *Orient* (1990); van Dam (1981).

[14] Interview with the author in Damascus on February 2, 2004.

Chapter 7 Is Baathism Bankrupt?

[1] Among many others, particularly see the groundbreaking works by Deutsch (1966), Gellner (1983), and Anderson (1991).

[2] Lewis (1998), p.104.

[3] A good comparison of old and new historical writing is to be found in Jankowski/ Gershoni in: Jankowski/Gershoni (1997), p.3ff.

[4] Khoury, in: Jankowski/Gershoni (1997), p.286.

[5] Mufti (1996), p.187.

[6] Mufti (1996), p.256.

[7] The great Arab sociologist Ibn Khaldun (1332-1406) called this feeling of community or belonging together *assabiyya*. The term may derive from ties based on religion or common origin (tribe, clan) or both. In an ethno-national sense it is now also translated as "national feeling," to coin a modern phrase.

[8] Hinnebusch (2001), p.20.

[9] Muslih (1988), p.55.

[10] Bunzl (1983), pp.17-18.

[11] Khoury (1987), pp.535-562; Dawisha (2003), p.79.

[12] Jankowski/Gershoni in: Jankowski/Gershoni (1997), p.12; about Egypt, see Jankowski/Gershoni (1986); about the Palestinians, see Muslih (1988), p.131ff.

[13] For a detailed description of the concepts of the nation and the debate about the problematic term "ethnic group," see Wieland (2000), p.45ff. Specific to the Arab context, see, above all, Dawisha (2003), p.1ff, 52ff; Tibi (1971), p.80ff.

[14] Tibi (1971), p.103ff; Lobmeyer (1995), p.35ff; Kedouri (1992), p.282; Kienle (1990), p.18; Aoyama/ Khansa/al-Charif (2000); Arsuzi-Elamir (2003).

[15] Anderson (1991).

[16] Kaschuba (1997), in: *Ethnologie française*, p.502.

[17] Weber (1921), p.528; Khaldun (1377, English edition 1969), pp.102-103.

[18] Tibi (1971), p.73.

[19] Tibi (1971), p.87.

[20] Dawisha (2003), p.27ff; Muslih (1988), p.60, 67.

[21] Kedouri (1992), p.288.

[22] Muslih (1988), p.60.

[23] For a historiographical assessment of Hamid's rule between reform and reaction, see: Muslih (1988), p.47ff.

[24] Tibi (1971), p.94ff; Muslih (1988), p.60ff; Zeine (1966), p.92; Mansfield (2003), p.128ff; Kienle (1990), p.4ff.

[25] For the prehistory of the caliphate since Muhammad, see: Halm (1988), p.10ff, 17ff, 661. For political history, see Schulze (1990), p.446ff, (1994), p.88ff; Schimmel

(1983), p.119ff. Schimmel points out that the caliphate is not provided for in Islam but represents an ex-post facto.

[26] Mansfield (2003), p.228.

[27] Dawisha (2003), p.49.

[28] Tibi (1971), p.110. For Husri's ideology, see in detail Tibi from p.103ff; also Dawisha (2003), p.49ff.

[29] Kedouri (1992), p.295; Thomas von der Osten-Sacken/Thomas Uwer: "Die Araber-Macher," in: *Die Zeit* 14/2003; Tibi (1971), p.113ff; Aoyama/Khansa/al-Charif (2000).

[30] Schweizer (1998), p.261.

[31] Lobmeyer (1995), pp.35-36.

[32] Kienle (1990), p.8.

[33] Tibi (1971), p.104.

[34] Dawisha (2003), pp.298-302. Avineri argued in a similar manner in: Winkler (1985), p.240ff with a view to the components of social change and compares this with Jewish nationalism. Khoury also refers to this problem in: Jankowski/Gershoni (1997), p.286.

[35] Tibi (1971), p.190.

[36] For more about the life and work of al-Arsuzi, see Arsuzi-Elamir (2003); Aoyama/Khansa/al-Charif (2000).

[37] Concerning the details on the composition of the peasantry and their role in Syrian politics, see Batatu (1999).

[38] Perthes (1990), p.49; Petran (1972), p.107.

[39] Kelidar (1974), in: *Asian Affairs*, pp.16-22; quoted from Lobmeyer (1995), p.64.

[40] Initially, they were still supported by Nasserists and independent Unionists, whom they, however, discarded after the Nasserists' unsuccessful coup on July 18, 1963.

[41] Hinnebusch (2001), p.31.

[42] Hinnebusch (2001), p.3, 120.

[43] Hinnebusch (1989), p.99.

[44] Lobmeyer (1995), p.35, quoted from Abu Jaber (1966).

[45] Hinnebusch (2001), p.47ff; Lobmeyer (1995), p.101ff; Kienle (1990), p.10ff.

[46] Hinnebusch (2001), p.52ff.

[47] Literacy doubled between 1960 and 1989. In 1960 only 37 percent of the Syrians lived in towns; but in 1990 it increased to 50.5 percent. Hinnebusch (2001), p.104.

[48] Batatu (1999), p.177.

[49] Lobmeyer (1995), p.184.

[50] Hinnebusch (1990), p.145.

[51] More about the leader cult and its sometimes grotesque excesses, see Wedeen (1999).

[52] Seale (1998), p.440.

[53] Concerning the opening of Syria after 1991, see Kienle (1994).

[54] Concerning the failure of pan-Arab practice, see Mufti (1996) and Dawisha (2003).

[55] Interview with the author in Damascus on April 28, 2005.

[56] Interview with the author in Damascus on May 7, 2004.

[57] ICG Report II, p.i.

[58] Interview with the author in Damascus on May 5, 2005.

[59] Hinnebusch, in: *DOI-Fokus* (2004), p.12.

[60] Interview with the author in Damascus on March 29, 2004.

[61] Packer (2005).

[62] Janis (1982) gives an array of examples that ended in fiascoes because of groupthink. Packer (2005) mentions this dynamic in connection with the Iraq war, too.

Chapter 8 Opposition, Islam, and the Regime

[1] Perthes (1995), p.70.

[2] Lobmeyer (1995), p.399, 402.

[3] For more information see: Wild, in: *Der Islam* 48 (1972) 2, p.206ff; Schweizer (1998), p.336ff; Moubayed (2006), pp.428-430.

[4] These forces are united under the National Democratic Assembly, which is illegal but tolerated. It includes: the Arab Socialist Union (Nasserists) under Hassan Ismail Abdul Azim, who left the National Front a year after it was founded in 1973, the Syrian Communist Party Politbureau under Riad al-Turk (not to be confused with the legal Syrian Communist Party which belongs to the National Front), the Revolutionary Workers' Party, the Movement of Arab Socialists, and the Democratic Socialist Arab Baath Party.

[5] Petition of May 17, 2003, published in the newspaper *Akhbar as-Sharq*, quoted from MEMRI Newsletter of June 15, 2003.

[6] Interviews with the author in Damascus on February 11, 2004, and May 11, 2004.

[7] "Democratic Room in Syria," in: *Al-Nahar* April 21, 2004; Michel Kilo in an interview with the author in Damascus on May 11, 2004.

[8] *Akhbar as-Sharq*, August 12, 2004, and September 22, 2004.

[9] Signatories to the new alliance: National Democratic Assembly, Committee for Reviving Civil Society, Al-Atasi Forum, Human Rights Association in Syria, Committee for the Defense of Liberties and Human Rights, Arab Association for Human Rights - Syrian branch, Communist Workers' Party, Democratic Kurdish Alliance, Kurdish Democratic Front, Kurdish Yekiti Party, Kurdish People's Union, Committees for the Defense of Denationalized Syrians (*Sharq al-Awsat* January 21, 2005).

[10] *Gulf News* May 31, 2005.

[11] Interview with the author in Damascus on February 11, 2004.

[12] Interview with the author in Damascus on May 1, 2005.

[13] English translation taken from *Cham Press*, October 17, 2005.

[14] *An-Nahar* January 24, 2006.

[15] Ayman Abdul Nour in an interview with the author in Damascus on April 28, 2005; George (2003), p.93.

[16] In April in Damascus, Bashar met, among others, Sheikh Yusef al-Qaradawi, who is active in Qatar and heads the European Council for Fatwa and Research; Fathi Yakan, one of the founders of the Islamist Organization Al-Jamaa al-Islamiyya; the Lebanese representative of the Muslim Brotherhood; and Hamza Mansour, secretary general of the Islamic Action Front, the political arm of the Jordanian

Muslim Brotherhood. The spiritual leaders and activists came together for a conference over the interpretation of Islamic law in Damascus. See: "Damascus, Brotherhood set to reconcile?" in: *The Daily Star* May 26, 2004, also: "Would civilians succeed where security men failed?" in: *An-Nahar* June 1, 2004.

[17] Interview with the author in Damascus on June 6, 2004.

[18] George (2003), p.92.

[19] *Al-Madjalla* May 6, 2001, *al-Hayat* May 6, 2001.

[20] George (2003), pp.92-93.

[21] *Al-Hayat* November 27, 2005.

[22] Lobmeyer (1995), p.347ff.

[23] Interview with the author in Damascus on April 28, 2003.

[24] *An-Nahar* January 24, 2006.

[25] Interview with the author in Damascus on April 28, 2005.

[26] Interview with the author in Damascus on April 4, 2003.

[27] Interview with the author in Beirut on February 17, 2004.

[28] "Mixed signals from Washington leave Damascus confused," in: *The Daily Star* April 26, 2004.

[29] Lobmeyer (1995), p.364.

[30] Interview with the author in Damascus on November 15, 2003.

[31] Interview with the author in Damascus on June 30, 2004.

[32] Interview with the author in Damascus on February 9, 2004.

[33] Interview with the author in Beirut on February 17, 2004.

[34] Interview with the author in Damascus on November 12, 2003.

[35] Heck (manuscript 2004), p.6, 19, 26, pp.30-31.

[36] Singh (1996), p.69; Athar (1996), in: *Social Scientist*, p.83ff; Ruthven (2000), p.272ff.

[37] More on contemporary moderate Islamic figures worldwide in: Esposito/Voll, in: Petito/Hatzopoulos (2003), p.255ff.

[38] Concerning early Islamic pantheism and the rational approach of the Mutazilites, see: Tizini (1972), p.27.

[39] Interview with the author in Damascus on May 4, 2005.

[40] Hinnebusch, in: *DOI-Fokus* (2004), p.14, quoted from: Stalinsky/Carmeli, "The Syrian government," Oxford Business Group, "Online Briefing," March 31, 2005.

[41] Habash (2003), p.16, 35.

[42] Interview with the author in Damascus on May 11, 2004.

[43] Interview with the author in Damascus on March 16, 2004.

[44] Batatu (1999), p.261.

[45] Heck (2004 manuscript), p.23.

[46] *Akhbar as-Sharq* January 15, 2004; ICG report II, p.16.

[47] Interview with the author in Damascus on May 4, 2005.

Chapter 9 Syria the Rogue State?

[1] "Warum Hanadi zur lebenden Bombe wurde [Why Hanadi would become a living bomb]," in: *Die Welt* January 15, 2004.

[2] According to information from international journalists who visited the spot directly after the incident.

[3] Examples in: Wurmser (2000).

[4] www.all4syria.net, June 13, 2004, al-Hayat June 11, 2004.

[5] Frisch (2004), in: *Political Studies*, pp.401-403.

[6] National (pan-Arab) socialist education for the 12th grade (*tarbiyya al-qawmiyya al-ishtiraqiyya*), 2002/2003, pp.103-104, 242-243.

[7] See also: Leverett (2005), pp.10-12.

[8] A good manual on this is: Hoffmann (2001). The international law expert Shukri (1991) provides an early view that also includes state terrorism.

[9] Interview in the Egyptian newspaper *al-Ahram* April 24, 2004.

[10] *As-sharq al-Awsat* September 4, 2005; *Elaph* March 9, 2005.

[11] *Final Report of the Commission on Terrorist Attacks upon the United States* (2004), p.66.

[12] *Al-Hayat* December 21, 2003; *Spiegel online* November 21, 2005 ("A Tale of Extraordinary Renditions and Double-Standards").

[13] *Al-Hayat* March 30, 2005.

[14] *Akhbar as-Sharq* July, 12, 2004.

[15] *Reuters* April 29, 2004, taken from an interview with Asad by *Al-Jazeera*.

[16] "Mixed signals from Washington leave Damascus confused," in: *The Daily Star* April 26, 2004; figures in: *Akhbar as-Sharq* May 26, 2004.

[17] Both Iraqi diplomats in Syria and their colleagues in Libya are said to still support Saddam Hussein (*Washington Post* January 25, 2005).

[18] If Syria decides to go ahead with the plan to hand over the Sheb'a Farms to Lebanon, the pressure on Israel to withdraw from the land will rise. If it does not, as Bashar indicated at the end of 2005, Hezbollah would have justification to continue its operations in southern Lebanon against the "Israeli occupation", although legally it is not Lebanese territory. Sheb'a is recognized by the UN as part of the Israeli-occupied region of the Syrian Golan Heights since 1974, and not as Lebanese territory. Therefore, the UN announced in 2000 that the Israeli withdrawal from Lebanon was complete.

[19] Seale (1988), p.173.

[20] Danawi (2002), p.92.

[21] Interview with the author and other journalists and scientists in Beirut on February 19, 2004.

[22] Interview in *al-Ahram Weekly* June 9-15, 2005.

[23] *The Daily Star*, April 21, 2005, and *Le Monde Diplomatique* (German edition), June 2005.

[24] Nasrallah stresses, however, that these were Shiite fighters before the Hezbollah organization was founded.

[25] Interview with the author and other journalists and scientists in Beirut on February 19, 2004.

[26] Shlaim (2000), p.xiv.

[27] ICG Report I, pp.1-2, Enderlin (2002).

[28] This accusation is made in a twenty-four-page report by the Syrian Foreign Ministry to a UN fact-finding committee. *Al-Hayat* June 8, 2004.

[29] Hinnebusch, in: *DOI-Fokus* 2004, p.17.

[30] Interview with the author in Damascus on April 28, 2003; the communiqué was published in the Lebanese newspaper *An-Nahar* on February 23, 2005.

[31] *New York Times* March 29, 2005.

[32] *Sharq al-Awsat*, December 18, 2005.

[33] Seymour Hersh in a panel discussion at the Saban Center for Middle East Policy of the Brookings Institute on April 25, 2005. Quoted from: "Doomed but at What Cost?", Azmi Bishara, in: *al-Ahram Weekly* May 19-25, 2005.

[34] "Opposition blames Damascus," Mohelhel Fakih, in: *al-Ahram Weekly* February 17-23, 2005.

[35] *The Terra Net, Reuters*, December 22, 2005.

[36] Kassem (2004), p.156; *al-Ahram Weekly* March 3-9, 2005.

[37] "Is Syria Holding Fewer Political Prisoners than any other Major Middle Eastern Country?", Joshua Landis, in: www.syriacomment.com August 11, 2004.

[38] Telhami (2004), p.19.

Chapter 10 Contradictory US Policy

[1] About Shukri: "Mixed signals from Washington leave Damascus confused," in: *The Daily Star* April 26, 2004. About Shaaban: Interview with the author in Damascus on March 29, 2004.

[2] *Arab Times*, September 14, 2005; *Syria News*, November 21, 2005.

[3] Leverett (2005), p.147ff.

[4] More about the difficult—although not entirely hopeless—situation of women in Iraq, see: Coleman, Isobel: Women, Islam, and the New Iraq, in: *Foreign Affairs*, Jan.-Feb. 2006.

[5] One of the best accounts in this field is Ahmed Rashid's book about the Taliban (2001).

[6] Dreyfuss (2005).

[7] Augustus R. Norton (Boston University) in a lecture at the conference: "The Middle East After the Invasion of Iraq" on October 22-24, 2003, at the Danish Institute in Damascus. See also: Mansfield (2003), pp.398-399.

[8] James Zogby: "Attitudes of Arabs: An In-Depth Look at Social and Political Concerns of Arabs," Washington 2005, p.12.

[9] Amr (2004), p.iii, 1.

[10] Fukuyama, in: *The National Interest*, 2004.

[11] "Aboard Air CIA," in: *Newsweek* February 28, 2005. The Syrian cases involve the Canadian of Syrian descent, Maher Arar, who was intercepted by US authorities on a flight in New York and shipped to Syria where he was tortured. The same is true for Mohammed Haydar Zammar, a German citizen, who was brought to Syria at the end of 2001 and was interrogated there by German officials in summer 2002, which is against German law (*Spiegel online* November 21, 2005, "A Tale of Extraordinary Renditions and Double-Standards").

[12] Leverett in a statement to the US Senate, quoted from ICG Report II, p.21.

[13] *The Daily Star* January 18, 2005.

[14] Anonymous source and Samir Altaqi in an interview in Damascus with the author on May 7, 2004.

[15] Leverett (2005), pp.153-154.

[16] Interview with the author in Damascus on October 15, 2003.

[17] "Scowcroft zweifelt an Bushs Nahost-Plänen [Scowcroft questions Bush's Middle East plans]," in: *Die Welt* November 18, 2003, interview originally from the *Financial Times Germany*. Scowcroft and Kagan quotes from: "Breaking Ranks," by Jeffrey Goldberg, in: *The New Yorker*, Oct. 31, 2005.

[18] Raymond Hinnebusch (University of St. Andrews) in a lecture at the conference: "The Middle East After the Invasion of Iraq" at the Danish Institute in Damascus on October 25, 2003.

[19] Herfried Münkler: "Die Gunst der Stunde [A favorable opportunity]," in: *Frankfurter Rundschau* December 30, 2004.

[20] The International Institute for Strategic Studies (IISS), which is otherwise regarded as friendly to the USA and NATO, has published a study concerning this, see: "Wie der Iraq-Krieg die Qaida stärkt [How the Iraq war has strengthened al-Qaida]," in: *Spiegel online* May 25, 2004.

[21] *New York Times* May 13, 2004 (from interviews in *El Pais* and *La Repubblica*).

[22] Baradei in: *Al-Jazeera* July 22, 2004; Leverett (2005), p.13.

[23] George (2003), p.169.

[24] Interview with the author in Damascus on November 2, 2004.

[25] *New York Times* May 13, 2004 (from interviews in *El Pais* and *La Repubblica*).

[26] Interview with the author in Damascus on March 11, 2003.

[27] *New York Times* November 8, 2003.

Chapter 11 Political Options for the European Union

[1] Interview with the author in Damascus on April 26, 2005.

[2] "EU will der arabischen Welt bei Reformen zur Seite stehen [EU wants to assist reform in the Arab world]," *DPA* June 17, 2004.

[3] *Al-Hayat* April 11, 2005.

[4] Interview with the author in Damascus on May 1, 2005.

[5] Kitschelt in: *International Politics and Society* (2004).

[6] The debate about the specious reasons for a war with Iraq and a description of the developments in the lead-up to the war are well summarized in Packer (2005), pp.16-66 and Harrer (2003).

[7] ICG Report I, p.5.

Chapter 12 Conclusion

[1] Interview with the author in Damascus on March 28, 2004.

[2] JTA (Global Jewish News) June 29, 2004.

[3] Kitschelt, in: *International Politics and Society* (2004), pp.14-15.

INTERVIEWEES AND PARTNERS
IN CONVERSATIONS

Abdullah Hanna, historian
Abdel Yusef, chairman of the Kurdish Yakiti Party
Akram al-Bounni, journalist and human rights activist
Ali Saleh, economic historian
Anwar al-Bounni, attorney and human rights activist
Ayman Abdul Nour, engineer, member of the Baath Party, moderator of the Internet forum www.all4syria.com
Buthaina Sh'aban, Minister of Expatriates
Haitham Maleh, attorney and chairman of the Human Rights Association of Syria (HRAS)
Hakam al-Baba, journalist and ex-editor-in-chief of *Ad-Domari* (publisher, Ali Farzat)
Hassan Nasrallah, sheikh and leader of the Lebanese Hezbollah
Ihsan Sanqer, entrepreneur, former member of parliament
Kadri Jamil, Kurdish member of the Charter of Communist Unity
Leila Nahal, communist
Maya al-Rahabi, doctor
Michel Kilo, journalist and writer
Muhammad al-Habash, member of parliament, sheikh, and head of the Islamic Studies Center in Damascus
Nihad Nahas, communist
Jawdat Said, sheikh from Quneitra
Sadiq Jalal al-Azm, philosopher
Said al-Azm, journalist and ex-diplomat
Salam Kawakibi, political scientist and representative of the Center for French Culture (CCF) in Aleppo
Sami Khiyami, software engineer, consultant, economic advisor to the president in negotiations with the EU, recently appointed Syrian ambassador to London
Samir Altaqi, surgeon and analyst in the Center for Strategic Studies and Research (CSSR) at the University of Damascus
Selma Karkoutli, journalist
Tayyeb Tizini, philosopher and professor at the University of Damascus
. . . and many others who wish to remain anonymous.

BIBLIOGRAPHY

Monographs, collected works, and articles

Abdoh, Samir: ألطوائف ألمسيحية في سورية: نشأتها, تطورها, تعدادها *(Christian Denominations in Syria: Their Emergence, Development, and Enumeration)*, Damascus 2003

Abu Jaber, Kamel S.: *The Arab Ba'th Socialist Party: History, Ideology, and Organization*, Syracuse (NY) 1966

Anderson, Benedict R.: *Imagined Communities: Reflections on the Origin and Spread of Nationalism*, London/New York 1991

Aoyama, Hiroyuki/Khansa, Wafiq/al-Charif, Maher: "Spiritual Father of the Ba'th: The Ideological and Political Significance of Zaki al-Arsuzi in Arab Nationalist Movements," *Middle East Studies Series* No. 49, Tokyo March 2000

Arsuzi-Elamir, Dalal: *Arabischer Nationalismus in Syrien: Zaki al-Arsuzi und die arabisch-nationale Bewegung an der Peripherie Alexandretta/Antakya 1930-1938*, Münster 2003

Athar Ali, M.: "The Evolution of the Perception of India: Akbar and Abu'l Fazl," in: *Social Scientist*, 24 (1996) 1-3

Avineri, Shlomo: "Politische und soziale Aspekte des israelischen und arabischen Nationalismus," in: Winkler, Heinrich-August (ed.): *Nationalismus*, Königstein/Ts. 1985

al-Azm, Sadiq J.: *Critique of Religious Thought*, Beirut 1969, 8th edition 1997

Baroud, Ramzy: *Searching Jenin: Eyewitness Accounts of the Jenin Invasion 2002*, Seattle 2003.

Batatu, Hanna: *Syria's Peasantry: The Descendants of Its Lesser Rural Notables and Their Politics*, Princeton/Oxford 1999

Bunzl, John: *Israel und die Palästinenser: Die Entwicklung eines Gegensatzes*, Wien 1983

Choueiri, Youssef M. (ed.): *State and Society in Syria and Lebanon*, Exeter 1993

Cleveland, William L.: *The Making of an Arab Nationalist: Ottomanism and Arabism in the Life and Thought of Sati al-Husri*, Princeton/Oxford 1971

Dam, Nikolaos van: *The Struggle for Power in Syria*, London 1981

Danawi, Dima: *Hezbollah's Pulse: Into the Dilemma of al-Shaihid and Jihad al-Bina Foundations*, Beirut 2002

Davis, Scott C.: *The Road from Damascus: A Journey Through Syria*, Seattle, 2003

Dawisha, Adeed: *Arab Nationalism in the Twentieth Century: From Triumph to Despair*, Princeton/Oxford 2003

Deutsch, Karl W.: *Nationalism and Social Communication: An Inquiry into the Foundations of Nationality*, Cambridge (Mass.)/London 1966 (2nd edition)

Dreyfuss, Robert: *Devil's Game: How the United States Helped Unleash Fundamentalist Islam*, New York 2005

Emerson, Rupert: *From Empire to Nation: The Rise to Self-Assertion of Asian and African Peoples*, Cambridge (Mass.) 1960

Enderlin, Charles: *Le Rêve Brisé: Histoire de l'Échec du Processus de Paix au Proche-Orient 1995-2002*, Paris 2002

Esposito, John L./Voll, John O.: "Islam and the West: Muslim Voices of Dialogue," in: Petito, Fabio/Hatzopoulos, Pavlos: *Religion in International Relations: The Return from Exile*, New York/Houndmills 2003

ibid.: "Islam in the Twenty First Century," in: Esposito, J./Tamimi A. (eds): *Islam and Secularism in the Middle East*, London 2000

Farzat, Ali: *A Pen of Damascus Steel: Political Cartoons of an Arab Master*, Seattle, 2005

Fawaz, Leila Tarazi: *Occasion for War: Civil Conflict in Lebanon and Damascus in 1860*, Berkeley/Los Angeles 1994

Freitag, Ulrike: *Geschichtsschreibung in Syrien 1920 – 1990: Zwischen Wissenschaft und Ideologie*, Hamburg 1991

Frisch, Hillel: "Perceptions of Israel in the Armies of Syria, Egypt and Jordan," in: *Political Studies*, Vol. 52, No. 3, October 2004

Fukuyama, Francis: "The Neoconservative Moment," in: *The National Interest*, June 1, 2004Gellner, Ernest: *Nations and Nationalism*, Ithaca/New York 1983

Gelvin, James L.: *Divided Loyalties: Nationalism and Mass Politics in Syria at the Close of Empire*, Berkeley 1998

George, Alan: *Neither Bread Nor Freedom*, London 2003

Habash, Muhammad: *A Call to the West: Lectures on the Dialogue of Civilizations*, Damascus 2003

Habermas, Jürgen: "The European Nation-state: Its Achievements and Its Limits. On the Past and Future of Sovereignty and Citizenship," in: Balakrishnan, Gopal (ed.): *Mapping the Nation*, London/New York 1996

Halm, Heinz.: *Die Schia*, Darmstadt 1988

Harrer, Gudrun: *Kriegs-Gründe: Versuch über den Irak-Krieg*, Wien 2003

Heck, Paul L.: *Religious Renewal in Syria: The Case of Muhammad Al-Habash*, Damascus 2004

Heller, Erdmute: "Die arabisch-islamische Welt im Aufbruch," in: *Weltbild Weltgeschichte: Weltprobleme zwischen den Machtblöcken*, Augsburg 1998

Hinnebusch, Raymond A.: "Syria after the Iraq War: Between the Neo-con Offensive and Internal Reform," *DOI-Focus* No. 14, March 2004

ibid.: *Syria: Revolution from Above*, London/New York 2001

ibid./Drysdale, Alasdair: *Syria and the Middle East Peace Process*, New York 1991

ibid.: *Authoritarian Power and State Formation in Ba'thist Syria: Army, Party, and Peasant*, Boulder 1990

ibid.: *Peasant and Bureaucracy in Ba'thist Syria: The Political Economy of Rural Development*, London 1989

Hoffmann, Bruce: *Terrorismus – der unerklärte Krieg: Neue Gefahren politischer Gewalt*, Frankfurt/Main 2001

Janis, Irving: *Groupthink: Psychological Studies of Policy Decisions and Fiascoes*, Boston 1982

Jankowski, James/Gershoni, Israel (ed.): *Rethinking Nationalism in the Arab Middle East*, New York 1997

ibid.: *Egypt, Islam, and the Arabs: The Search for Egyptian Nationhood 1900-1930*, New York 1986

Kaschuba, Wolfgang: "Identité, altérité et mythe éthnique," in: *Ethnologie française*, 27 (1997) 4, p. 502

Kassem, Maye: *Egyptian Politics: The Dynamics of Authoritarian Rule*, London 2004

Keane, J.: "The Limits of Secularism," in: Esposito, J./Tamimi A. (eds): *Islam and Secularism in the Middle East*, London 2000

Kedouri, Elie: *Politics in the Middle East*, Oxford/New York 1992

Kelidar, A.R.: "Religion and State in Syria," in: *Asian Affairs*, 1/1974

Khaldun, Ibn: *The Muqaddimah*, Princeton 1969 [orig. 1377]

Khoury, Philip S.: "The Paradoxical in Arab Nationalism: Interwar Syria Revisited," in: Jankowski, James/Gershoni, Israel (ed.): *Rethinking Nationalism in the Arab Middle East*, New York 1997

ibid.: "The Syrian Independence Movement and the Development of Economic Nationalism in Damascus," in: *British Journal of Middle Eastern Studies*, 14/1988

ibid: *Syria and the French Mandate: The Politics of Arab Nationalism 1920-1945*, Princeton 1987

ibid.: "Divided Loyalties: Syria and the Question of Palestine 1919-1939," in: *Middle Eastern Studies*, 21/1985

Kienle, Eberhard: "Arab Unity Schemes Revisited: Interest, Identity, and

Policy in Syria and Egypt," in: *International Journal of Middle East Studies*, Vol. 27, February 1995

ibid.: (ed.): *Contemporary Syria: Liberalization between Cold War and Cold Peace*, London 1994

ibid.: *Entre jama'a et classe: Le pouvoir politique en Syrie*, Berlin 1991

ibid.: *Ba'th v. Ba'th: The Conflict between Syria and Iraq 1968-1989*, London/New York 1990

ibid.: *Ethnizität und Machtkonkurrenz in inter-arabischen Beziehungen: Der syrisch-irakische Konflikt unter den Ba'th-Regimen*, Berlin 1988

Kitschelt, Herbert: "Origins of International Terrorism in the Middle East," in: *International Politics and Society*, Vol. 1/2004

Landis, Joshua: www.syriacomment.com (blog with various articles and accounts on Syrian contemporary politics)

ibid.: "The United States and Reform in Syria," in: *The Syria Review*, June 2004

Laqueur, Walter Z.: *Communism and Nationalism in the Middle East*, 2nd edition, London 1957

Lesch, David W.: *The New Lion of Damascus: Bashar al-Asad and Modern Syria*, New Haven/London 2005

Leverett, Flynt: *Inheriting Syria: Bashar's Trial by Fire*, Washington, D.C. 2005

Lewis, Bernard: *The Multiple Identities of the Middle East*, London 1998

Lobmeyer, Hans Günter: *Opposition und Widerstand in Syrien*, Hamburg 1995

Mansfield, Peter: *A History of the Middle East*, 2nd edition, London 2003

ibid.: *The Arabs*, 3rd edition, London 1992

Moubayed, Sami: *Steel and Silk: Men and Women Who Shaped Syria 1900-2000*, Seattle 2006

Mufti, Malik: *Sovereign Creations: Pan-Arabism and Political Order in Syria and Iraq*, Ithaca/London 1996

Muslih, Muhammad Y.: *The Origins of Palestinian Nationalism*, New York 1988

Norton, Augustus R. (ed.): *Civil Society in the Middle East*, Vol. I, Leiden 1995

Packer, George: *The Assassin's Gate: America in Iraq*, New York 2005

The Permanent Constitution of the Syrian Arab Republic, Damascus, no date given (after 1973, published by: Office Arabe de Presse et de Documentation)

Perthes, Volker: *Syria under Bashar al-Asad: Modernization and the Limits of Change*, Adelphi-Paper 366, London 2004

ibid.: (ed.): *Arab Elites: Negotiating the Politics of Change*, Boulder/London 2004 ibid.: "Der Mittlere Osten nach dem Irak-Krieg – Neue geopolitische Grundlinien und Spielregeln," in: *Neue Züricher Zeitung*, 24.04.2004

ibid./Schwitzke, Anette: *After the Iraq War: Repercussions in the Levant*, paper presented at the GCSP/RAND workshop in Geneva, 4-6 May 2003

ibid.: Geheime Gärten: *Die neue arabische Welt*, Berlin 2002

ibid.: "The Political Economy of the Syrian Succession," in *Survival*, 43/1, Spring 2001

ibid.: *Vom Krieg zur Konkurrenz: Regionale Politik und die Suche nach einer neuen arabisch-nahöstlichen Ordnung*, Baden-Baden 2000

ibid. (ed.): *Scenarios for Syria: Socio-economic and Political Choices*, Baden-Baden 1998

ibid.: *The Political Economy of Syria under Asad*, London 1995

ibid.: *Staat und Gesellschaft in Syrien 1970-1989*, Hamburg 1990

ibid.: "Einige kritische Bemerkungen zum Minderheitenparadigma in der Syrienforschung," in: *Orient* 4/1990

Petran, Tabitha: *Syria*, London 1972

Quilliam, Neil: *Syria and the New World Order*, Reading 1999

Rabinovich, Itamar: "Arab Political Parties: Ideology and Ethnicity," in: Esman, Milton J./Rabinovich, Itamar (publisher): *Ethnicity, Pluralism, and the State in the Middle East*, Ithaca/London 1988

Rashid, Ahmed: *Taliban: Militant Islam, Oil and Fundamentalism in Central Asia*, London/New Haven 2001

Ruthven, Malise: *Islam in the World*, Oxford/New York 2000 (2nd edition)

Schatkowski Schilcher, Linda: *Families in Politics: Damascene Factions and Estates of the 18th and 19th Centuries*, Stuttgart 1985

Scheck, Frank Rainer/Odenthal, Johannes: *Syria: Hochkulturen zwischen Mittelmeer und Arabischer Wüste*, Cologne 1998

Schimmel, Annemarie: "Der Islam in unserer Zeit," in: Italiaander, Rolf (ed.): *Die Herausforderung des Islam: Ein ökumenisches Lesebuch*, Göttingen 1987

ibid.: *Der Islam im indischen Subkontinent*, Darmstadt 1983

Schulze, Reinhard: *Geschichte der Islamischen Welt im 20. Jahrhundert*, Munich 2003 (2nd edition)

ibid.: *Islamischer Internationalismus im 20. Jahrhundert: Untersuchungen zur Geschichte der Islamischen Weltliga*, Leiden 1990

Schumann, Christoph: *Radikalnationalismus in Syrien und Libanon: Politische Sozialisation und Elitebildung 1930-1958*, Hamburg 2001

Schweizer, Gerhard: *Syrien: Religion und Politik im Nahen Osten*, Stuttgart 1998

Seale, Patrick: *Asad: The Struggle for the Middle East*, London 1988

Shlaim, Avi: *The Iron Wall: Israel and the Arab World*, London 2000

Shukri, Muhammad Aziz: *International Terrorism: A Legal Critique*, Brattleboro 1991

Singh, Yogendra: *Modernization of Indian Tradition: A Systemic Study of Social Change*, Jaipur/New Delhi 1996

Stäheli, Martin: *Die syrische Außenpolitik unter Präsident Hafez Asad: Balanceakte im globalen Umbruch*, Stuttgart 2001

Stalinsky/Carmeli, "The Syrian Government," Oxford Business Group, "Online Briefing," March 31, 2003

Telhamy, Shibley: *The Stakes: America in the Middle East*, Boulder/Oxford 2004 (2nd ed)

Tibi, Bassam: *Arab Nationalism: A Critical Enquiry*, New York 1981

ibid.: *Nationalismus in der Dritten Welt am arabischen Beispiel*, Frankfurt/M. 1971

Tizini, Tayyeb: *Die Materieauffassung in der islamisch-arabischen Philosophie des Mittelalters*, Berlin (Ost) 1972

Weber, Max: *Wirtschaft und Gesellschaft*, Tübingen 1972[1921]

Wedeen, Lisa: *Ambiguities of Domination: Politics, Rhetoric, and Symbols in Contemporary Syria*, Chicago/London 1999

Wieland, Carsten: *Nation-state by Accident: The Politicization of Ethnic Groups and the Ethnicization of Politics, Bosnia, India, Pakistan*, New Delhi 2006

ibid.: "Thousands of Years of Nation-building? Ancient Arguments for Sovereignty in Bosnia and Israel/Palestine", in: Riegler, Henriette (ed.): *Nation-building Between National Sovereignty and International Intervention*, (Wiener Schriften zur Internationalen Politik, No. 10), Vienna 2005

ibid.: "The Bankruptcy of Humanism? Primordialism Dominates the Agenda of International Politics", in: *International Politics and Society*, 4/2005

ibid./Bieber, Florian (ed.): *Democracy and Human Rights in Multi-Ethnic Societies*, Ravenna 2005

ibid.: Zwischen Akbar und AKP: Moderate islamische Alternativen in Syrien (Between Akbar and the AKP: Moderate Islamic Alternatives in Syria), in: *inamo*, No. 40/2004

ibid. *Syrien nach dem Irak-Krieg: Bastion gegen Islamisten oder Staat vor dem Kollaps?* (Syria after the Iraq War: Bullwark against Islamists or State at the Brink of Collapse?), Berlin 2004

ibid.: "Domino auf der Achse des Bösen?" (Domino on the Axis of Evil?), in: *Die Politische Meinung*, No. 412, March 2004

ibid.: العلمانية والدين: الحدود من وجهة النظر الغربية ("Secularism and Religion: Demarcations From a Western Perspective"), in: *al-Mahajjah* 11/2004 ibid.: "Syrien nach dem Irak-Krieg—Stagnation oder Umbruch?" („Syria after the Iraq War—Stagnation or Upheaval?"), in *Orient* 1/2004

ibid.: "Domino auf der Achse des Bösen?" („Domino on the Axis of Evil"), in: *Die Politische Meinung*, No. 412, March 2004

ibid.: "'Ethnic Conflict' Undressed: Patterns of Contrast, Interests of Elites, and Clientelism of Foreign Powers in Comparative Perspective – Bosnia, India, Pakistan," in: *Nationalities Papers*, June 2001

ibid.: "Widersprüche auf dem Weg zum 'Nationalstaat': Dogmatische und politische Spaltungslinien unter den Muslimen in Indien und Bosnien" (Contradictions on the Way to the "Nation-state": Dogmatic and Political Cleavages Among the Muslims in India and Bosnia), in: *Afrika, Asien, Lateinamerika*, No. 3/2001, Berlin

ibid.: "Izetbegovic und Jinnah: Die selektive Vereinnahmung zweier 'Muslim-Führer'" (Izetbegovic and Jinnah: The Selective Appropriation of Two "Muslim-Leaders"), in: *Südosteuropa-Mitteilungen*, No. 2/2000, Munich

ibid.: *Nationalstaat wider Willen: Die Politisierung von Ethnien und die Ethnisierung der Politik – Bosnien, Indien, Pakistan*, Frankfurt/New York 2000

Wild, Stefan: "Gott und Mensch im Libanon: Die Affäre Sadiq al-Azm," in: *Der Islam*, vol. 48, issue 2, February 1972, p. 206-253

Wurmser, Meyrav: *The Schools of Baathism: A Study of Syrian Schoolbooks*, Washington, D.C. 2000, ed.: Middle East Media Research Institute (MEMRI)

Zeine, Zeine N.: *The Emergence of Arab Nationalism*, 2nd edition, Beirut 1966

Zisser, Eyal: *Asad's Legacy: Syria in Transition*, London 2001

Reports and Analyses

Amr, Hady: "The Need to Communicate: How to Improve US Public Diplomacy with the Islamic World," *Analysis Paper for the Brookings Institution*, Washington January 2004

The Economist Country Risk Service: Syria, London December 2003

Final Report of the Commission on Terrorist Attacks upon the United States (authorized version), Washington DC July 2004

International Crisis Group (ICG), Middle East Report No. 23/24: Syria under Bashar, Amman/Brussels, February 11, 2004, Vol. I: Foreign Policy Challenges, Vol. II: Domestic Policy Challenges

Statistical Abstract, Central Bureau of Statistics, Office of the Prime Minister of Syria, Damascus 2003

UN Development Report 2003
Zogby, James: "Attitudes of Arabs: An In-Depth Look at Social and Political
    Concerns of Arabs," Washington 2005

INDEX

191

About the Author

Dr. Carsten Wieland is a historian, political scientist, and journalist. He last worked and lived in Syria from 2003 to 2004 and speaks Arabic. Currently, he is a fellow at Georgetown University, Washington DC.

Before that, Wieland reported from the United States, the Middle East, and Latin America as a foreign correspondent for the German Press-Agency (DPA). In 1994, he worked as a freelance journalist in Sarajevo during the Bosnian War. Wieland studied at Duke University in North Carolina, Humboldt University in Berlin, and at Jawaharlal Nehru University in New Delhi.

After returning from Syria, Wieland worked as a senior executive at the Goethe Institute in Cairo and Munich, and subsequently as a political consultant with IFOK (Institute for Organizational Communication) in Berlin and Washington DC.